Boston:
Persons and Places

Mark N. Ozer

DEDICATED TO MY BROTHER HARVEY LEON OZER

The Esplanade

The basin, white with boats
The bandstand filled with white tiers of massed legionnaires
And Mayor Curley with a black silk hat
And his charming wife, tucked soft in grey fox furs

The colors are massed
And the breaths of the legionnaires in the audience
So bowled you over with their whiskey breaths.

And the speakers swayed, straining their veins
for the necessary word
That land far flung those freedoms,
and the fields of grain.

…A schoolgirl brought a posy up
And Mayor Curley removed his hat and waved.

~~~

Ruth Herschberger 1956

"In New York you are measured by how much you are worth, in Philadelphia by who was your grandfather, in Boston, by how much do you know?"

"Boston commands attention as the town which was appointed in the destiny of nations to lead the civilization of North America. As on the seal of the city of Boston, Sicut Patribus, Sic Deus Nobis! (So as for our Fathers, so God be for Us)."

Ralph Waldo Emerson

Table of Contents

ACKNOWLEDGEMENTS

I am particularly indebted to the staff of the Boston Public Library: to Linda McIver and especially John Devine of the Social Studies Reference section of the BPL, and to Evan Thornberry and Cathy Wood of the Leventhal Map Center of the BPL. Map reproduction is courtesy of the Norman B. Leventhal Map Center at the Boston Public Library.

Evan Thornberry has been particularly cooperative in providing our extensive use of maps to illustrate the development of Boston's physical character. John Devine contributed further by reviewing the manuscript in light of his familiarity with contemporary Boston as well as its history. Jim Campano of *The West Ender* and Duane Lucia of the West End Museum were particularly helpful in defining the issues surrounding that area as was Alan Gropman. Duane Lucia contributed further by offering a critical review of the early drafts and suggestions for improvement of the concluding chapter. Amy Schectman of the JCHE introduced me to issues of city planning. Jeannine Knox of the Emerald Necklace Conservatory, L'Mercie Frazier of the Boston Museum of African American History, Thomas Lester of the Massachusetts Historical Society, Elizabeth Roscio of the Bostonian Society and Carolle Moroni and Catharina Slautterback of the Boston Athenaeum all made their resources available. John Carroll of the MRWA and City Manager of the Town of Norwood provided his unique perspective. Tunney Lee both renewed old friendship and provided material on Chinatown. Frank Zitomersky provided his perspective on the Orange Line Extension while Fred Salvucci shared his personal experience in reference to the Big Dig. Joseph Zitomersky contributed his perceptions of the RDM in which we both grew up.

I wish to thank Lynn Kasdorf for his excellent work in book design and production.

INTRODUCTION

Boston was the first of the great ports on the eastern seaboard. Before New York, Philadelphia or Baltimore, it was a town perched on the edge of the continent. By 1700, it ranked third among British ports behind London and Bristol. It remained the largest town of British North America until 1760 when, limited by its site on a narrow peninsula, it was bypassed by Philadelphia and then New York. The poor glaciated acid soil filled with stones and the short growing season of its hinterland did not provide a fertile agriculture capable of supporting an export trade. It gained its sustenance from the sea; from the local fisheries and those at the Grand Banks and also the long distance carrying trade. During the 18th century, its triangular trade with the sugar islands distilled the rum from their sugar to buy slaves on the African coast to then feed the labor needs of the plantations as well as provide the fish and other food needed for their sustenance.

Bostonians acceded its primacy to the greater physical growth of their sister ports of New York, Philadelphia and Baltimore while retaining much longer primacy in cultural leadership. Uniquely settled by educated persons unlike the traders, adventurers and planters elsewhere, Boston was the source of much of the political thinking and actions that brought about the American Revolution. Its economy never fully recovered the depredations, which that war brought. Boston's opposition to the War of 1812 marked the eclipse of the Federalist Party and the political power of the New England states.

Despite being closest to Europe, Boston Harbor did not thrive on the direct trans-Atlantic trade from Liverpool. Regularly scheduled relatively frequent "packet line" service was established to New York as early as the 1820s A short period when it was the terminus of the Cunard Steamship Line at East Boston and the center for Irish immigration ended by 1848 in favor of more adequate transportation arrangements to the west offered by New York.

The German-based lines preferred Baltimore; the Belgian based Red Star Line favored New York and Philadelphia. Despite growth by Irish immigration during the first half of the 19th century, Boston entered fourth place behind Baltimore by 1860. Its expansion came by the laborious filling in of the adjoining waters, ultimately adding 2000 acres. It was from the start hemmed in by the adjoining independent towns. Boston however remained the "Sacred City" of the New England Yankees.

Industrialization came early to New England based on the waterpower of the rivers near Boston and the enterprise of its inhabitants. Cut off from a direct route to the growing west, its railroad was tardy in reaching Albany through the hilly Berkshires. There was not as short or direct a route west as provided by the New York Central for New York, the Pennsylvania Railroad for Philadelphia nor the B&O for Baltimore. Its conservatively invested wealth went elsewhere to build the railroads of the west, the textile industry of the south, and the shoe industry of St Louis.

Beyond its commercial development, its founders and their descendants never lost sight of its origins as a place coupled with Harvard College dedicated to the idea of "republican virtue," of godliness and community and the intellect. Its relatively close-knit elite, arising from a Calvinist source, remained confirmed in their rectitude even as their commitment to their religion declined. They initiated many of the reform movements of the ante-bellum era and the foundations of American culture. After the Civil War, literary trends began to arise in New York as did art and architecture while Boston itself had a short burst coincident with the filling in of the Back Bay and the Great Fire of 1872. The residues of that efflorescence has maintained the city's standing among the great cultural centers of the world.

By the 20th century, the large Irish immigration of the 1840s had inundated the elite's earlier political control of Boston itself. Old Boston acquired a reputation of stodginess and antiquarianism as the elite lived enclosed within their high social walls mainly outside the city limits. However, in the dark days of Second World War in the mid-20th century, an eminent foreign philosopher deemed it "in so far as the world of learning possesses a capital city...Boston approximates the position that Paris occupied in the middle ages." To an unusual degree, its hierarchical elite established a culture that took responsibility for the development and maintenance of the entire community.

Despite its relative insignificance in the greater economic and political life of the country, this city and its region's highly educated population in the 21st century continues to make an ongoing contribution to intellectual innovation extending into the age of the computer and biotechnology.

We explore the history of this relatively small yet significant world city from its founding in the 17th century through its contribution to American independence in the 18th century and then in the 19th century to its cultural flowering before the Civil War and its leadership in the Union cause during the war itself. It fell behind in the era of large scale industrialization both in wealth and influence. It leads once again in the late 20th century extending into the 21st when the Information Revolution has taken the place of the earlier one based on energy and machines.

In 2010, for the first time since the 1870s, the population rise in the core city has been greater than in the surrounding suburban belt. The words of the founder of the Lowell Institute at the time of its formation in 1836 still ring true that "the prosperity of New England, an otherwise barren and unproductive land, is based on the intelligence and information of its inhabitants," if perhaps no longer as clearly as he once had stated "on its moral qualities as heretofore." We explore the physical manifestations that remain of the history as well as the persons and their ideas in each era that created that history.

Chapter 1.
The City on the Hill 1630-1760

Introduction

The early settlers were fortunate that the coastal area was relatively empty of native inhabitants when they arrived. A serious epidemic attributed to yellow fever brought by some earlier contact with Europeans and carried by the ever present mosquitoes decimated the local native population. With the legitimacy of their political leadership seriously disrupted by the epidemic, the local natives enlisted the English settlers in their internecine wars before succumbing to the effects of their own interaction with the Europeans. The *Pawtuckeogs* are described as inhabiting the area north and east extending to the Merrimack River while the *Massachuseogs* were settled south of the Charles River, contributing their name to the Bay into which the Charles River empties and where the town arose. That name in the native language refers to "at the great hills" that surround the bay on the south.

Ground water was readily available; Shawmut, the Algonquin name for the peninsula, means "place for clear waters." These sources were tapped from early times for the benefit of the community by means of the "Conduit." In addition to those settling the port of Boston, a total of twenty thousand settlers came during the first decade of the Great Puritan Migration to farm and raise cattle. They settled from the start in towns on the north along the Mystic River in Medford and Chelsea; in the center along the Charles in Cambridge, Watertown and Waltham and in the south along the Neponset River in Dorchester and Milton. From the first, Boston was surrounded by a ring of independent towns, which to a great extent still remains so.

None of the rivers were long enough to enable access to a large hinterland; the rocky glaciated soil and short growing season limited further the produce that could be exported. Furs could be gathered; beaver remained important for but a short time in this limited watery riverine environment. Once the early heavy immigration ceased with the victory of their friends in the English Revolution, the forests surrounding the bay provided the lumber with which the ships were built to provide a livelihood.

The port was deep enough to accommodate ships yet the tidal flats and marsh lands were shallow enough to permit the building of wharves. The settlement grew from the start by extension of its limited land mass into the water. Ultimately, it quadrupled in size. In addition to shipbuilding; before long, the town was exporting fish to England as well as participating more directly in trade with the Catholic countries of Spain and Portugal. There the rules of abstinence made them ready customers. The trade in fish initiated by the 1640s led to an even larger and independent trade in lumber and provisions with the Cape Verde Islands and the Azores off the coast of Africa.

At the same time, the trade in slaves and the concomitant development of the plantations in the West Indies added that all important component to the trading network. Replacing the relatively poor soil and short growing season of its hinterland, the trading resourcefulness of the people of Boston established the pattern that was to sustain the city as the metropolis of New England. It also made their profitable additional carrying trade ultimately dependent in the next century upon the lax enforcement of the British Navigation Acts.

The names given to the settlements surrounding Massachusetts Bay reflect the origins of the settlers, some like Dorchester in the West country but mainly in Lincolnshire in East Anglia. Boston, the name of the town, is a corruption of St Botolph's Town from which John Cotton had come to preach the sermon to the first settlers departing from Portsmouth. The importance of their sources lies not so much in the sites from which they came but in their beliefs. Dissenting Protestant denominations appeared in England in the 17th century to contest the arrangements made by the religious settlement of 1559 after the accession of Queen Elizabeth I. That settlement established the Anglican Church independent of Rome but also equated loyalty to the English state to adherence to the national church. This requirement equated dissent from the national church to dissent from loyalty to the rulers, buttressed as they were in the 17th century by the Stuart claim of "divine right" derived from God.

There were, however, English Protestants who wished to go further in the implementation of the Reformation than carried out merely by separation from the rule of the Pope. Not calling themselves "separatists," they still sought "purification" of the rituals, of all ornamentation as sinful frivolity. Followers of the teaching of men such as John Calvin, they held themselves to be one of the elect by displaying the strictest standards of personal conduct, a commitment to a serious, sober and frugal way of life.

Discouraged by lack of religious purity evident in England and economic difficulties, John Winthrop from Groton Manor together with such as John Humphrey and Thomas Dudley, steward to the Earl of Lincoln, prepared to lead a group of their co-religionists to the New World. They bought the charter of the relatively unsuccessful "New England Company" that had been entitled to establish a colony on Massachusetts Bay. John Winthrop was appointed governor of what was to be a self-governing settlement by virtue of retaining physical possession of their enabling charter. They also required voting members of the Company to be actual members of their body of settlers. Moreover, it was clearly the *community* to which the members were to subordinate private interests to the public good. As though a "city on a hill," it was to be more than a mere trading company to be rather a model of a godly commonwealth, an inspiration for all humankind. The word "commonwealth," rather than "state" remains the title used to describe the nature of this community as the "Commonwealth of Massachusetts."

1.1 The Shawmut Peninsula

On their arrival in Massachusetts in 1630, the main settlement was eventually established on a small hilly peninsula. This area selected, known as Shawmut, less than two square miles in area, encompassed the boundaries of Boston for nearly the next two hundred years. The Trimountain on the peninsula consisted of three hills: Mount Vernon (a sanitized former Mount Whoredom), Pemberton and Beacon Hills with only the last still present today, and then only in part. The original settlement lay between the Trimountain and the Town Cove known still as the "North End."

In the estuary of the Charles River, the Shawmut peninsula was bound on the north by that river and connected on the south by a narrow neck of land to the mainland. This "Boston Neck," traversed easily only at low tide, could be easily protected against wolves and marauding natives. The extensive harbor could be easily protected from marauders since there was but one deep channel toward the south at Nantasket. The growth of the settlement occurred during this first interval by filling in marshland on the peninsula and extending wharves into the adjoining sea.

Figure 1 - Boston 1631

The adjoining map shows the town at its outset. Like an English mediaeval village, streets were laid out informally only as needed, to connect important areas as they developed. There was no preconceived plan or one that could be superimposed. Like that of London after the Great Fire, rebuilding after the recurrent fires maintained the existing property lines and did not provide an opportunity to realign the streets to a more rational or abstract order. As early as 1655, the streets were described as "crooked, with little decency and no uniformity." The Town Cove near a fresh water spring in the east facing the inner harbor became the Town Dock. Later it became Dock Square and held the public market within Faneuil Hall. Slightly south, was the Long Wharf that became King (later State) Street leading east from the Province House where the General Court met in session (today the Old State House). The major north south street had various names along its course including Cornhill, Marlborough, Newbury and Orange Streets (later united as Washington Street) that led by the Province House south to the "South

10

End" and the Boston Neck and thence to the mainland of Roxbury. The main intersection was thus the meeting of Cornhill and King Street at the Province House (rebuilt in its present form in 1747 after a fire). Going north from the Province House, one could enter the "North End" via Hanover Street and Salem Street to North Square and eventually to the ferry to Charlestown.

The South End and the North End were rivals that carried out their annual battle on Pope's Day (Guy Fawkes Day) on November 5th that commemorated the discovery of the Catholic-led Gunpowder Plot in Parliament. Taking over the town, their battle ended with the burning of the effigy carried by the other on the hill of the victor. Based on a spirit of mutual anti-Popery, the combination of the leaders of the two rival groups provided a ready-made organization to be called together in 1765-1766 to form the "Sons of Liberty" to oppose the Stamp Act.

1.2 John Winthrop and the Rule of the "Saints"

Crucial to the character and success of the Massachusetts Bay Colony was the involvement of John Winthrop as their leader. He was either governor or deputy-governor for twelve of the years from 1630 until his death in 1649.

Winthrop saw a departure to the New World as a way to escape the "corruption of religion and learning" and a great service "to carry the gospel abroad and raise a great bulwark against the Kingdom of the Anti-Christ." Moreover, he saw the move west to the New World as fulfilling the ancient prophecy of civilization renewed in the west. He thus initiated what became the mission of America to renew itself by the movement west.

Figure 2 - John Winthrop

John Winthrop came from a substantial family of cloth workers, the major industry of East Anglia. His grandfather Adam founded the family fortune by acquiring the manor of Groton during the Dissolution of the Monasteries initiated by Henry VIII. His father Adam had gone to Magdalene College at Cambridge and served as a lawyer but also had literary sensibilities. Through the influence of his wife's father who had been master of St Johns, Adam served as an auditor of the finances of Trinity and St John's College at Cambridge.

The only son John was born in 1587, the year before the victory over the Spanish Armada. After training at Trinity College Cambridge, young John Winthrop married Mary Forth, the heir to several estates. Like his father, he trained in law at Gray's Inn and grew in his role as lord of several manors. He became a dominant figure in his neighborhood and acquired the habit of command. He also came under the influence of a minister who had been suspended for non-conformity. Increasingly concerned with his own spiritual experience and intensely religious, Winthrop began a diary, which carried on for the next thirty years, served as a record not only of his personal spiritual journey but later his political life as the founder of the Massachusetts Bay Colony.

After the death of his second wife, John Winthrop married his third and last wife Margaret Tyndal, the daughter of a baronet. During the 1620s, an economic depression hit the cloth working industry and thus the raising of sheep upon which his prosperity depended. His financial status was threatened at a time when his sons were reaching majority and seeking opportunities. Now connected to the Puritan movement because of his own spiritual needs, he now entered a wider role. He sought redress from Parliament from the rule of James I with the claim that his behavior was leading to abuses of power and debasement of the religious and moral life of the country. The accession of Charles I in 1625 exacerbated the problem for Winthrop following the king's marriage to the Catholic Henrietta Maria and the further conflict with Parliament leading to its dissolution in 1629.

Recognized as a man of great ability, his personal influence was such that those from his own neighborhood formed one quarter of those leaving in the first fleet. On departure on Easter Monday 1630 on the *Arabella*, Winthrop began his *History*. He saw the passage across the ocean analogous to the crossing of the Red Sea by the Israelites. He saw further the new settlement a place where Justice and Mercy would reign, where Christians would share their bounty in holy covenant and to act as the prophet Micah had instructed "To do justly, to love mercy and walk humbly." Accordingly, in founding what was called a "commonwealth," he consistently opposed the grants of large amounts of land for fear that those raised higher would depress those who were lower far different from the pattern established in the other early colonies of Virginia and Maryland.

By 1631, the governmental structure he set up recognized that the project was not merely a commercial undertaking; it was a citadel of God's chosen people, "a government of Christ in-exile." "Freemen" from the entire colony would meet together four times a year in "general assembly;" and to meet once each year to elect a governor, deputy governor and court of fifteen assistants or "Executive Council." The term "freemen" no longer applied merely to those who held stock under the rules of the charter of the commercial company but applied to all those who may have contributed only their godliness. The original Company had indeed become a commonwealth; the government was analogous to a parliament.

By 1632, the selection of the governor would be by the freemen from those who were already assistants or magistrates. It may be noted that, although governors were elected annually, only six men filled this post during the first fifty years of the colony. A clearly hierarchical system was in place dominated by an upper class based on education, if not initially by property. However, a representative system was then devised when those elected would meet to deal with taxation in what came to be called a "General Court." The term, still in use today, was the one used for the meeting of the members of the original commercial Massachusetts Bay Company. By 1644, the original governance based on the charter given by the king to the Company was replaced by an elected bi-cameral assembly. The Executive Council representing the magistrates was restricted to certain areas like military affairs and customs duties while the General Assembly (or General Court) represented the freemen to deal with other matters.

The freemen of every "town" would also meet to deal with local matters in their own town meetings to make laws and to elect those "selectmen" who will govern the town between meetings. This was a form of government unique to New England. However, adult men who were not church members could not at this time vote, let alone hold office. The churches were organized on the "congregational" model, each congregation an independent unit, responsible for itself. Although all were required to attend, "membership," including participation in the Lords' Supper was not automatic or based on baptism but required election as one of the "saints." Covenanted membership was based upon a report of one's personal spiritual experiences, how one had reached the moment of conversion and subsequent behavior.

Education was fostered with free public schools established in each locale. It was necessary for children to read so that they could grow up able to read the Bible, to know what opportunities there were for salvation and what was sinful. The Boston Latin School was established in 1635 and Harvard College the year after where the name of its site was changed from Newtowne to reflect what had been their university town of Cambridge in East Anglia. That university had been near the former home of so many members of the community and where the Winthrop family had been closely connected. Having received a substantial bequest and half the library of a graduate of Emmanuel College living in Charlestown Massachusetts called John Harvard, the college was named for him in gratitude.

The library so started has been continuously the largest of its kind in the country if not the world. In 1641, Harvard College graduated its first class to fill the need for trained clergymen. Its curriculum that of the Divinity School of Emmanuel College at Cambridge, teachers were selected and retained primarily based on adherence to the Puritan concept of true religion.

The churches were not necessarily founded in a territorial parish model. The First Church in the center of the town of Boston soon added the Second Church in the North End (Old North) but other congregations proliferated regardless of possible geographical boundaries. For example, this Second Church arose in 1650 because a group of eight more radical Puritans were uncomfortable with the growing prosperity around them in the First Church. Attesting to its quarrelsome sectarian nature, within a hundred years, Boston held eleven Congregational churches, three of which resulted from schisms from existing churches.

There was division yet collaboration between the Church and State. As a religiously-based commonwealth, the State was responsible for protecting and supporting the Church; all laws must be in accord with the laws of God. The Puritan clergy representing the Divine Law worked in collaboration with the secular law represented by John Winthrop but were always separate from the civil authorities. For example, ministers could not be magistrates. Civil and political punishment for heresy might come from the state after a proper trial but not by the churches themselves. The Church had no authority in the government; actions of the Church per se did not affect civil or political rights.

Given the independent nature of Protestantism, dissidents soon arose within the colony who usually wished to separate further from the Anglican Church forms than the original Puritans might wish. John

Winthrop emphasized the need to maintain the structure and the limits to which the Massachusetts Bay Colony would adhere. He wanted to avoid the schisms to which independently minded congregations were prone. For example, Roger Williams claimed that ministers should not be paid by tax monies and questioned the nature of the relations with the aboriginal natives and the validity of the Church of England beyond that accepted by the Puritans. Banished, he eventually founded in 1635 a settlement at Providence Plantation. Anne Hutchinson was similarly banished for questioning some of the other tenets of the Puritan faith. She spoke in the name of unqualified personal connection with God while also representing dissenters from the economic policy.

With the rule of Parliament installed in England in the 1640s, the heavy emigration ceased from England to the Massachusetts Bay. The economy could no longer depend on the wealth of those immigrating to pay for the needed English imports. Ultimately unsuccessful were efforts to develop local manufacture of iron and cloth and to sell their fish to earn enough to buy their needs for manufactured goods. The triangular trade with the West Indies evolved to sustain the colony. The rule of the Puritan divines was eventually superseded by a more secular merchant class.

The restoration of the Stuart monarchy in 1660 led to an attempt to exert royal power over the independent Massachusetts Bay Colony. One issue was that voting had been restricted to members of the Congregational Church; still another was the attempt to control trade of the colony to the benefit of English ship owners and merchants. The two remained confounded to remain an issue that eventually underlay the fight for independence.

1.3 Increase Mather and the Congregational Church

Figure 3 - Increase Mather

Increase Mather was born in 1639 in Dorchester adjoining Boston, the son of the legendary Puritan minister Reverend Richard Mather. After training at Harvard College, he earned a M.A. at Trinity College in Dublin. He returned to Boston in 1661 after the end of the Cromwellian Commonwealth with which he had been connected. He married Maria Cotton, the daughter of John Cotton and his step-sister since the marriage of his father with John Cotton's widow. Their son born in 1663 was Cotton Mather who eventually succeeded his father as minister at the Second Church (Old North) in Boston's North End.

The minister of what was the then highly fashionable North End, Increase Mather was one of the leading Puritan ministers in Boston. Even in opposition to his own father, he stood for a more rigid application of the rule that baptism would not be available to children born of non-members, even if the latter had themselves been baptized. He took an active role in England working to reinstate the Charter of the Bay Colony after its revocation by James II in 1684. The close union between the church and state in the Massachusetts Bay since its start in 1630 had been severed by this revocation. The appointment of Sir Edmond Andros as royal governor of the projected Dominion of New England in 1686 significantly coincided with the establishment of the King's Chapel, opening in 1689 to be the first Anglican Church in Boston (only to become the first Unitarian Church in 1787).

Increase Mather led the fight against the introduction of the Anglican Church into Boston. He saw it accurately as an effort to erode the influence of the Congregational Church. For Mather, the Congregational Church was an instrument of those chosen by God; the "saints" who were to govern the state. As the spiritual vision of the Puritan church waned politically, its voice remained, rising all the more from orthodox pulpits. The purpose of the colony was to institute and maintain a holy community, not otherwise. Any loss of piety, changes in sacramental practices, and lowering of standards for church membership eroded the idea of a "true church" in New England.

In the mode of the prophet Jeremiah, Increase Mather saw any deviation from the way of God as responsible for the evils visited upon Massachusetts by King Philip's War when the Indians of western Massachusetts massacred many of the settlers. Drawing from his own extensive library, he wrote many pamphlets attacking the trends appearing in Boston during his lifetime that seemed to erode by individualism and materialism the commitment to the community.

Figure 4 - Cotton Mather

Cotton Mather was no less forceful than his father in maintaining the battle for piety into the next generation. Also pastor of the Old North Church, he excelled in his pastoral duties while writing some four hundred published works of all kinds. His library, probably the largest in colonial America, exceeded seven thousand volumes. Amassed over several generations, the circulating library in the Mather family home in the North End was the capital of the "Republic of Letters" in North America. A member of the Royal Society, his interests extended to the protection against smallpox in the epidemic of 1721. He learned of the practice of inoculation in Africa. Mather recommended it but was opposed by the physicians of the town who warned against the dangers of contagion.

John Calvin, along with many other different reformers, was read as a champion of the godly cause. They shared the belief that Roman Catholicism had been a millennium-long captivity during which the true faith had been hidden, but that true believers like themselves, the saving remnant of the saints, had always managed to preserve that faith. One of Mather's writings was *Theopolis Americana: An Essay on the Golden Street of the Holy City* in which he predicted, in line with ancient writings, the existence of such a place in America. There was the intimation that such a place might exist, with Boston the luminous place predicted. Such was the religious background for Boston's social and political reform movements of the next generation.

In line with his historical-religious thinking, like his father in the time of the King Philip War, Cotton compared the present problem facing Boston to the unfolding of the Hebrew Scriptures. The restoration of the charter sought by his father in England was compared to the restoration of the Jews to Jerusalem after the Babylonian Captivity. Finally, with the accession of the Protestant monarchs William and Mary in 1688, the charter was reinstated in 1691 but religious uniformity was dead. A royal governor would be appointed and voting would be based on property, not on church membership.

The once dominant Puritan oligarchy was forced to permit the entry of parsons reciting the hated Anglican *Book of Common Prayer*, which Mather equated to Romanism. This in turn he connected with the civil and ecclesiastical policies of the London-based "Council of Trade and Plantations" to implement a greater degree of imperial control over trade policies. The Anglican Church was an instrument of imperial policy and the presence of King's Chapel at Tremont and School Streets its outpost in Boston. After 1702, the well-funded "Society for the Propagation of the Gospel in Foreign Parts" (SPG) became active in increasing the presence of the Anglican Church. Christ Church on Salem Street in the North End was established in 1723; Trinity Church in the South End at then more fashionable Summer Street in 1733 (later after the fire of 1872 in Copley Square).

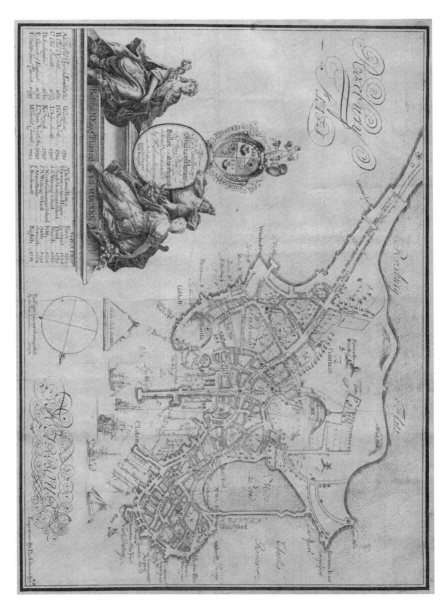

Figure 5 - Boston 1728

Boston was the largest town in British North America with a population of 12,000 by 1720. It was also the most sophisticated by virtue of its more frequent interaction with Europe's intellectual currents. The first American newspaper appeared in 1704 followed by the two others in the next decade. However, the adjoining map shows the town remaining within the original Shawmut peninsula. The Boston Common on the west remained as joint pasture land fronting onto the Back Bay with grazing limited so as to "protect the commons." Immediately to the north of the Common was the undeveloped high hill of Trimountain with three hillocks; the highest was called Beacon Hill after its usage. Going farther north, one reaches eventually to the Charles River with Cambridge Street ending in a marsh going to that town where Harvard College had been founded.

The town of Boston had begun to take on a sense of permanence and prosperity as the influence waned of the Puritan clergy to be replaced by an oligarchy of the wealthy merchants. Mansions arose of the men made wealthy by the carrying trade. Streets previously unpaved and nameless like country roads, after 1700 had names affixed that remain like Milk, School, Summer and Winter. The ongoing tension was the tendency to forget that "New England was a plantation of religion, not a plantation of trade." Trade was valuable but it served the community best when subordinated to the demands of religion, and of the community as a whole. However, the desire to succeed in trade and live the full life of English gentlemen was stronger than any counterforce the clergy were able to offer.

Epitomizing the rise of the new oligarchy was Thomas Hancock, one of the richest, whose mansion rose on Beacon Street adjoining the Boston Common.

1.4 Thomas Hancock and the Merchant Elite

Nathaniel Hancock was the founder of the family in the New World. Arriving in 1634, he settled in Cambridge. His son, also Nathaniel, a shoemaker, fathered thirteen children including John who studied at Harvard College. He became a minister in nearby Lexington and had in turn a son Thomas born in 1703. With the elder brother placed in the ministry, the second son Thomas was sent to Boston to become a bookseller and opened up his own shop in 1724.

After marrying the daughter of a fellow bookseller, Thomas began to stock a larger variety of stock although Bibles remained his main stock-in-trade. Driven out of the book business by competition, he entered into triangular trading and shipping ventures. In accordance with the mercantilist system of the Navigation Acts, the major trade of Boston was to supply the food, particularly fish, and timber needs of the sugar islands in order to pay for the costs of English manufactures. A large part of the Hancock trade was also in whale oil (used for lighting) and whale fins (bones for corsets) or seal skins bought from Nantucket whalers in exchange for rum or victuals; later to be sold in England to be traded for manufactured items. Less legally and less frequently, fish might also be bought from the fishing ports of Marblehead and Salem that would be sold to the Mediterranean Catholic countries. Lemon fruits and other tropical goods would be exchanged for wine from the Portuguese island of Madeira or even traded in Dutch Surinam.

In the 1730s, Thomas Hancock built his mansion on Beacon Street on a lot with a 135 foot frontage on the Boston Common and an average depth of 300 feet. Adding over his lifetime, the country-born non-conformist Hancock reached the heights of Boston society. He eventually owned all of Beacon Hill including the land between Joy, Bowdoin, Mt Vernon and Beacon Streets. From 1739 to 1744, the War of Jenkins's Ear with Spain provided opportunities for privateering and increased trade via the Dutch island of St Eustatius.

War with both the French and Spanish during King George's War between 1744 and 1748 made trading more difficult. However, aided by his relationship with Governor William Shirley, Hancock profited by a contract to supply the British forces manning the forts in Newfoundland and then at Louisburg. Aided by his connection with a politically well-placed London agent, the French and Indian War from 1755 to 1763 was again particularly profitable. For example, Hancock was involved in the forced transport of the French-speaking Acadians from Nova Scotia after its return to English control and supplying Wolfe's Campaign to Quebec in 1760.

The Hancock involvement in manufacturing was far less significant than the general merchandising and shipping. However, one major interest, suggestive of the future, was paper making from rags using the tides on the Neponset River in what is now Milton where also the earliest chocolate factory was founded. Childless, Hancock adopted his sister's son John. Born in 1737, John Hancock was removed from his humble home in Braintree and installed in the Hancock mansion in Boston. He trained at Boston Latin School and Harvard College and became known for his luxurious tastes. Upon the death of his uncle, the estate was assessed as the largest in Boston with a valuation of nearly 20,000 pounds with the next largest that of James Otis only one-tenth as large.

The rich colonial merchant class of 18th century Boston had its golden age commemorated in the work of John Singleton Copley. Born to uncultured parents probably in 1738 on Boston's Long Wharf, he was likely taught by his émigré British step-father Peter Pelham. The latter was married to his widowed mother sometime around 1748 when the boy was aged ten. Before age twenty, young Copley was executing drawings with excellent anatomical precision indicating some training and exposure to artistic prints.

Copley's great commercial as well as artistic success was based on his ability to compose his pictures and to convey his figures' status in a flattering fashion comparable to the British aristocratic portraits of the time. He showed mastery of textures, whether of skin or velvet and lace. He provided his subjects with dazzling personae that they wanted to project, enhancing with their portraits their social status that one could display along with Chippendale furniture and rococo silver teapots. Although his education was deficient in spelling, he also spoke and acted as a gentleman.

Married to the daughter of the Anglophile agent of the East India Company, it was his wife's family tea that was dumped in Boston Harbor in December 1773. A member of the class he not only painted but with which he identified, he left his native country to go to Europe in 1774 with his Tory relatives. Finally settled in London, he became a painter of the fashionable history scenes that brought him even further recognition.

Figure 6 - Boston 1769

As the population of Boston rose by 1760 to 17,000, the land in the South End was converted from farmland to house lots; the North End was even more densely populated. The adjoining map shows Boston on the eve of the American Revolution. The stratification of society had increased; the number of the property-less had quadrupled while the overall population had doubled. The New England colonies were heavily involved in the victory in the Seven Years War (French and Indian War) with one out of three men of military age involved in the fighting. The conquest of French Canada in 1760 and the end of the war in 1763 was celebrated in Boston. Basking in the success of the British Empire and the glorification of the new King George III, there was little to suggest that the period to follow would mark a new republican era in Boston history.

Chapter 2
The Center of Revolution 1760-1814

Introduction

The street names of Boston still reflect the impact of the Revolution with the imprint of names such as Federal and Franklin, James Warren and James Bowdoin. King Street became State, Queen became Court and the main north-south street incorporated its previous several segments into a Washington Street. During these years and particularly after 1774 during its blockade, the business of Boston stopped; its population fell precipitously. During the British occupation of the winter of 1775-1776, all the trees were cut down for fire wood; the population decimated by smallpox. The action during the War for Independence shifted to the Middle Colonies and eventually to the South before the defeat of Cornwallis at Yorktown in 1781. However, Boston did not recover its prosperity during the rest of the Revolutionary War. Independence also destroyed Boston's share in the direct trade between England and North America, now shifted to British bottoms.

During this post-Revolutionary War era, the first of Boston's several bridges was the Charles River Bridge that replaced in 1786 the former ferry run for the benefit of the Harvard Corporation from the North End to Charles Town. Then in 1793 a West Boston (a later version was named after Longfellow) Bridge from Cambridge Street led to central Cambridge. The later Craigie Bridge carrying the Middlesex Canal and the Newburyport Turnpike went to Lechmere Point in East Cambridge. The populated area began to expand beyond the boundaries of the Shawmut Peninsula, particularly to the north. Streets were also laid out in the formerly relatively unpopulated western quarter "West End" to connect to the bridges.

Boston began to recover from the effects of the Revolutionary War with a population rising to 30,000 by 1810. Like the other eastern ports, it benefited from the opportunities for the carrying trade by the Napoleonic Wars, but to a lesser degree than Baltimore that now outranked Boston as the third largest city. By virtue of its access to nearby wheat farms, Baltimore took a preeminent role in the West Indian trade upon which Boston had previously depended. Boston's trade expanded to the fur trade of the Columbia River thence to the Hawaiian Islands and the Orient.

2.1 Boston and the American Revolution

The death of Thomas Hancock in 1764 made his heir probably the richest man in America. Now twenty-seven, he continued to live at the Hancock mansion under the watchful eye of his doting Aunt Lydia. However, the opportunities that had been offered to Thomas Hancock were not as available to his heir. Business, buoyed by wartime military expenditures, had dried up. What was true for the large firms like that of Hancock was even more true for the others. The revolutionary activity starting in the 1760s and the support for non-importation occurred against the backdrop of the depression that took place in the colonies during those years, nowhere worse than in Boston. There was a drying up of the West Indies trade as well as the shortage of money to repay the debts incurred for British manufactures that bankrupted several Boston firms.

The British Empire, achieved over the previous one hundred and fifty years almost in a fit of absent-mindedness, needed policing. It was now thought by Parliament to provide opportunities to recoup the costs incurred in its growth as well as the costs of a standing army. The Proclamation Act of 1763 established the boundaries of the newly acquired possessions in the Ohio Valley precluding the expansion of the seaboard settlements into the trans-Appalachian area. A standing army was needed to police this boundary to protect the fur trade and the Indians. The Sugar Act of 1764 cut out the lucrative triangular trade where molasses from sugar had been directly imported from the French West Indies to be converted to rum. The impositions of the Stamp Act in 1765 would fall heavily on trading since stamps would be used on all commercial and legal documents. In response, men as important as Hancock joined the other merchants in opposition to importation of British manufactures.

In addition, there were riots, orchestrated by Samuel Adams and others of the merchant and higher "mechanicks" class by the "Sons of Liberty" obstructing the sale of stamps in Boston. Made up of the artisans of the lower trades and apprentices, day laborers and seamen, they acted nevertheless under the auspices of the more prosperous artisans of the higher trades called the "Loyal Nine." Controlled by the latter, the Sons of Liberty were useful as an outlet for the violence that the economic resentments might otherwise have created.

The protests of the London agents of the colonists seemed effective and the Stamp Act, never having gone into effect, was repealed. Hancock had identified himself and his fortune with the popular cause and was elected to the General Court for the first time in 1766. The celebration of the repeal of the Stamp Act was marked by a large reception at Hancock's house. In turn, the Townsend Acts issued by Parliament in 1767 taxed the imports of luxury items bought by the influential rich such as tea and glass. The Acts also strengthened the customs service in the collection of duties, also of great concern to the merchants. It was significant that the funds so generated would pay the royal customs officials, removing them from the influence of the colonial assemblies that had been their previous source of pay.

The Boston merchants that supported the patriot cause tended to be those to lose the most by enhanced enforcement of the British mercantilist system. They tended to be those who both imported from Holland and exported to Southern Europe. The limitations incurred by the restrictive British mercantilist system were clearly detrimental to their interests. They allied themselves with the popular party led by Samuel Adams in support of a non-importation agreement. It came into effect against the Townsend Acts once again in 1769 but based more on economic issues than constitutional ones.

Samuel Adams again took an active role in making the opposition to taxation more widespread within Boston by enlisting his elite allies. The town was now the storm center of a much larger movement within the other colonies.

2.2 Samuel Adams and the American Revolution

Figure 7 - Samuel Adams

His great-grandfather Henry Adams left Somersetshire with his nine children to settle in Braintree just south of Boston in 1638. His grandfather John was a sea captain who settled in Boston. His father Samuel was born in Boston in 1689 and opened a malt shop; prospering, he married Mary Fifield, the daughter of a leading businessman. Samuel, the namesake of his father, was born in 1722 and was the elder son of those surviving. Educated at the Boston Latin School and then Harvard College, in 1740 he defended his thesis for a master's degree to the effect that "it is lawful to resist the Supreme Magistrate, if the Commonwealth cannot otherwise be preserved," the position that he developed during the years following 1765.

While still at Harvard, Adams became involved, along with his father, in the organization of the "Land Bank" a vehicle for the issuance of paper money to alleviate the problems of debtors and the shortage of specie in the colony. The bank was strongly opposed by many of the elite but was a tenet of the "popular party" in the Boston town meeting. The family fortune disappeared when the Land Bank was closed by British government fiat in 1753. That action had been encouraged by the elite party in Massachusetts and Governor Shirley. The popular party that he represented had one of its ongoing tenets inflation by issuance of paper money. Based on his own personal difficulties with an oppressive government and with the aid of those merchants whose interests were affected, he remained persistent in leading the popular party toward independence.

Young Samuel took over the family brewing business and married Elizabeth Checkley, the daughter of the minister of the important Old South Church. Beset with liens based on the Land Bank case, the threat to seize his property was met with successful civil disobedience. His brewing business dwindled and his efforts became entirely devoted to civil disobedience and political action. Based on the Massachusetts Charter and the British Constitution, his stance also led a group of Boston merchants to see their prosperity incompatible with membership within the British mercantilist system.

The passage of the Sugar Act in 1764 was the first of a series of efforts by Parliament to tax the trade of the colonies. While remaining conservative in his religious convictions, Samuel Adams laid out the principles that would be the foundation for the revolutionary political program that he will follow to success. First, he appealed to self-interest of the English traders in that duties would stifle trade that was to the ultimate benefit of the British economy. Secondly, he appealed to the colonists to agree to non-importation of English goods to which the large merchants, heavily indebted to their British suppliers, agreed in their own interests. He also claimed in his widely distributed writings that economic and political freedoms were intertwined. If the government can tax trade, why not then land and other possessions so destroying the right to tax by the colonial assemblies and thus the ability for self-government?

A "non-importation" of British goods could be successful only if all the colonies were united. Massachusetts could no go alone. Virginia was to be key. His strategy therefore was to create a united response. His manifesto for a united non-importation agreement against the Sugar Act also encouraged Patrick Henry to run for the Virginia House of Burgesses. He in turn will give his famous speech to ignite that important colony toward the passage of the Virginia Resolutions of 1765 opposing the subsequent Stamp Act.

The protests against the Sugar Act in 1764 did not take fire; however, the following year the Stamp Act took effect. This time, there was wide spread opposition to its far reaching effects, particularly on merchants, newspapers and lawyers who were the most articulate members of the community. Before being prorogued by the royal governor, the Massachusetts legislature uniting the popular party and an allied group of the elite issued a call to the other colonial legislatures to come to a Stamp Act Congress. Once South Carolina agreed, eight other colonies followed. In the meantime, the Sons of Liberty (under the control of the higher ranking merchants in Boston) in an act of civil disobedience frightened the Stamp Act sales agents into resignation.

Give the degree to which the economy was in depression from the effects of British trade restrictions, the Boston tradition of mob violence associated with the Pope's Day ignited the riots against the Stamp Act in the summer of 1765. Several weeks later in August 1765, another less controlled mob destroyed the home of Lieutenant Governor Hutchinson in the North End. Adams opposed such vandalism as detrimental to his cause but nevertheless used the threat of such violence as a goad. The Stamp Act Congress in New York in October 1765 reaffirmed the rights of colonial legislatures alone to levy taxes and presented the first-ever united petition to Parliament and the king, both steps toward eventual independence.

With Samuel Adams now elected in May 1766 to his own seat on the General Court, he had an official position from which he could carry out his agenda. The repeal of the Stamp Act was a credit to his strategy of using the London merchants dependent on the American trade to exert their influence on Parliament while organizing a united American front in opposition. In May 1766, Samuel Adams was now the Clerk of the Massachusetts House as the patriot coalition captured the lower house in May 1766.

The Townsend Acts went into effect in November 1767. There was to be more direct royal control over the salaries of colonial officials with more stringent reinforcement of import duties by customs agents. Samuel Adams contended that government without consent was again being imposed and taxation without representation. Coupled with this was the potent rumor that there was an intention to establish the Anglican Church and an episcopacy, always a sore point in Massachusetts since the time of Increase Mather.

Once again, Samuel Adams caused a circular letter to be issued by the Massachusetts General Court to the other colonies to develop a united front. The organization of boycotts of British manufactures also helped alleviate the distress experienced by local artisans whose goods need no longer compete. In response, the British sent to Boston a man-of-war to enforce the revenue laws. The fuse leading to violence had been lit.

Hancock was a major trader accustomed to the evasion of customs duties. The customs agents in Boston were driven off his ship *Lydia* in April 1768. *The Liberty,* another of Hancock's ships then arrived, this time likely to be carrying dutiable Madeira wine on board. The illicit wine cargo was removed while the customs agent was forcibly detained. Fighting erupted against the seizure of the ship while it was being confiscated by marines from a British man-of-war then in port. The first major popular outburst since the Stamp Act riots in August 1765, Hancock and his ships had become the focus of the opposition to the Crown. The royal governor asked for a greater military presence in Boston and additional troops arrived in October 1768. Boston had become an armed camp. Acting on exaggerated reports from persons such as Lieutenant-Governor Hutchinson, King George III, in his opening speech to Parliament in December 1768, claimed that Boston was "in a state of disobedience...likely to throw off dependence."

Samuel Adams used the press, particularly the *Boston Gazette*, to spread the word for non-importation by the other colonies. The royal governor dissolved the Virginia House of Burgesses for its support of non-importation; the delegates met on their own at the Raleigh Tavern in Williamsburg in May 1769. Once again, in response to the organized boycott, the decision was made in London to repeal all the duties, only excepting that on tea.

The troops quartered in Boston remained. On 5th March 1770, the soldiers, taunted by a crowd of boys, fired into the crowd in front of the Province House. The "Boston Massacre" had occurred. A meeting at the Old South Church addressed by Samuel Adams demanded the removal of the troops. The stunning political victory that led to the removal of the troops is the moment commemorated in the portrait of the now formidable Samuel Adams.

The duty on tea remained. The effect of the arrangement with the East India Company made tea smuggling no longer profitable, undercutting some of the large Boston merchants. Bypassing the large merchant importers, the East India Company was dealing outside the established channels by selling directly to the smaller merchants. Samuel Adams wrote a series of newspaper articles invoking John Locke and Montesquieu and the theory of "natural rights." Thus laying out his case for independence, he reflected the long term interest by the colonial merchant elite in establishing economic sovereignty. In addition, the physician and activist patriot Joseph Warren listed the grievances to form the basis for the "conversations" to be carried out. Entitled *The Votes and Proceedings of the Freeholders of the Town of Boston*, it served to develop discussions in each locality identifying their response to the issues outlined. To maintain the unity of the colonies, Samuel Adams organized in 1772 "Committees of Correspondence" to review this document.

Once the Boston town meeting unanimously approved the document, a request went out to others for a "free communication of sentiments." Starting with Cambridge in Massachusetts, towns everywhere used the existing town meeting structure that bypassed the need for the assemblies subject to control and dismissal by the royal governors. These standing committees would discuss the report of the Boston town meeting and express their sentiments in response. Other colonies including Virginia joined in this extraordinary network. The committee structure of secret meetings in which all could be heard was effective in creating consensus that could lead to a "declaration." Indeed, Benjamin Franklin called it the "Boston Declaration."

Its revolutionary aspect was that the list of rights and grievances was not a petition addressed to a king or other authority for redress but to the people for action in response to the cry of distress from Boston. This was a republican alternative to a hierarchical one but also an emotional one. By December 1773 at the time of the destruction of the tea in the famous "Tea Party," 140 towns had already participated in this exercise that encouraged unity but also political action. It was a prototype for the later "Declaration of Independence."

In the meantime, tea was consigned to be landed with the duty attached. Prevented from being landed, the tea was dumped into Boston Harbor in December 1773. In response, the Port of Boston was closed to take effect on 1st June 1774; more troops arrived to be quartered on the Commons. With the groundwork laid by the "committees," in September 1773, Samuel Adams called for the first time for a "Congress of American States." The call was answered with a "Continental Congress" to meet in Philadelphia in September 1774 to respond to the attack on Boston. Many moderates in the Middle Atlantic states agreed to the meeting since they saw the calling of a congress as a tactic to preclude action that would be more precipitous.

John Adams was careful at the Congress to have representatives from Virginia take the lead rather than those from Massachusetts to insure united support. Following the lead of the so-called "Suffolk Resolves" created in the Boston area, in each colony local governments took over as the royal government disintegrated because of the non-payment of taxes. However, reflecting the influence of upper class patriots, these resolves were moderate in nature, advising against any riotous acts. Militias were formed with Massachusetts again in the lead.

In April 1775, the local militia was alerted that British troops were on their way from Boston to Lexington to capture Samuel Adams and John Hancock preparatory to their imprisonment and trial in London for treason. A battle took place first on the Lexington Green and then at Concord Bridge. By the end of the day, one hundred American militia men and several hundred British soldiers had been killed. The Second Continental Congress, already meeting at the time of Lexington and Concord, on the suggestion of John Adams, appointed the Virginian George Washington as army commander to take effect in July 1775. In the Battle of Bunker (Breed's) Hill in Charlestown in June, the British drove the militia off the hill only after two unsuccessful charges and the loss of a thousand men. War had begun.

In January 1776, Thomas Paine's widely read *Common Sense* made a cogent case for independence. At the same time, George III had initiated a major expedition to invade the colonies to end the insurrection. The colonists were under attack and parleys to end the dispute peacefully failed. In March 1776, the British were forced to evacuate Boston in the first great victory of the war. Richard Henry Lee of Virginia made the resolution for independence in the Continental Congress. On the initiative of John Adams, a committee was appointed to draft a "Declaration of Independence" with Thomas Jefferson of Virginia to do the actual writing.

Samuel Adams had succeeded in creating the wide spread support necessary for a war generated by the imposition of the Navigation Acts on the commerce of Boston. That war would lead eventually to independence of a united country. The road was yet a long one that would be led by others. He was later out of place among the Founding Fathers who deplored the concept of the overthrow of authority for which he had been the exemplar.

The coloration over the years of the role of Samuel Adams leading to independence reflects the efforts during the 1830s by conservatives to downplay the model offered by the heroes of the Revolutionary era. They portrayed him as an early proponent who was a radical troublemaker, a mere "propagandist" who stirred up the passions of the mob. His actual correspondence belies these characteristics. He did not advocate violence and held as late as 1774 a hope that American liberties might be achieved within the British Empire. Moreover, his personal religious commitment to an ascetic life, to public life as a leader of the popular party placed him outside the culture of the settled class that ruled after the disruption of the revolutionary era. Samuel Adams was perhaps more in the line of the Great Religious Awakening earlier in the 18th century as well as 17th century English Puritans that were his ancestors.

Shays Rebellion in 1786 in western Massachusetts reflected the deflation that made it difficult for the smallholders to repay their wartime debts. It also frightened the propertied class. By pointing out the weakness of the Confederation, it became one of the several factors leading to the meeting of the Constitutional Convention in 1787 to form a more powerful central government. Another was the need to create a unified response to British trade restrictions that singularly affected the state of Massachusetts. The remedies provided by the Constitution made Massachusetts a bastion of the Federalist Party in the early days of the republic.

The "mixed government" advocated by John Adams became the accepted model for the U.S. Constitution with a strong executive analogous to a king; an indirectly elected Senate analogous to an aristocracy and a popularly elected assembly. In the absence of the exiled old Tory elite, men such as John Hancock rose to political prominence as Massachusetts governor from 1780-1793, Samuel Adams as lieutenant governor from 1789 to 1793; and then governor from 1794 to 1797. Josiah Quincy was elected to Congress and, most prominently, John Adams became vice-president and then the last president who was a member of the Federalist Party and the founder of an American dynasty.

2.3 John Adams and the Federalist Party

During 1774, in his first visit to another American town, Adams found Philadelphia wanting in comparison to Boston in every way aside from their more agreeable manner, their markets and their charitable foundations. Prefiguring the generations of New Englanders that followed, he particularly found Boston superior in morals, religion and education. He lost no time, however, in replicating Philadelphia's Philosophical Society which, to his chagrin, Boston lacked.

Figure 8 - John Adams

Descended from the branch of his family that remained as farmers in Braintree, John Adams was born in 1735 to a family that was neither powerful nor famous. He retained the morality of his Puritan background in his inner being while becoming more liberal in his religious practice. He was the first of his branch to train at Harvard College. He attended on the insistence of his father with a view to the ministry but then read law in Worcester in his own pursuit of greatness. Like any other devout Puritan, he was always earnestly concerned in his diary about his virtuousness. His marriage to Abigail Smith, the daughter of a neighboring clergyman, united him with an extraordinarily astute life partner.

John Adams participated first at a local level in the opposition to the Stamp Act led by his distant elder cousin Samuel. He came to notice when, emulating James Otis, Jr his mentor in the Boston bar, he successfully defended the British soldiers after the Boston Massacre. He returned to political notice, again in assistance to his more prominent cousin, when he replaced Otis in the General Court in 1770. He was active in the activities leading to the calling of the First Continental Congress to draw up a "Declaration of Rights and Grievances." With little faith in compromise, he was particularly active during the intervening winter and spring of 1775 after Lexington, Concord and Bunker Hill in moving the Second Continental Congress toward the "Declaration of Independence."

Based on his basic belief in hierarchical government, his "Thoughts on Government" written in the spring of 1776 advocated the principles of three branches of government with the checks and balances that eventually appeared in the U.S. Constitution. He opposed Thomas Paine's formulation of a single legislative chamber in the Pennsylvania 1776 state constitution as potentially too radical. His more conservative suggestions for a bi-cameral legislature and independent judiciary first took effect when the Massachusetts Constitution he helped write was adopted.

During the Revolutionary War, John Adams served on ninety committees of the Congress and as chair on twenty five; was chair for a time of the important Board of War and Ordnance of the Continental

Congress that oversaw and supplied the army. He was then part of the team negotiating the implementation of the 1778 Treaty of Alliance with France, succeeded in receiving financial assistance from the Dutch and finally achieved the 1783 Treaty of Peace with Great Britain. During the last, he was particularly insistent, in the interests of New England, in the inclusion of a proviso recognizing the American rights to access to the fisheries off the Canadian coast. The Cod remained the Holy Grail of Massachusetts.

During the Confederation, Adams was the less effective envoy to Great Britain while Thomas Jefferson was minister to France. He unsuccessfully sought the empowerment of the weak central government of the Confederation to counteract the British actions in cutting off the American carrying trade from the West Indies, a major source of concern to New England.

While living in Britain, Adams underwent a further transition in his political thinking based on his reading of the character of the British Constitution. He was much taken with writings of Henry St John, Viscount Bolingbroke. Bolingbroke argued for the efficacy of "mixed government" and the unifying role of the "patriot king." Rather than his earlier emphasis on the balance between the executive, legislature and judiciary, Adams became even more focused on the importance of maintaining a balance among the political classes in what he considered the all-important legislative branch.

Adams placed particular importance on limiting the power of the branch of the legislature representing the common people. In his response to Turgot, the French physiocrat who advocated a unicameral legislature, Adams saw the role of the relatively disinterested executive to mediate between the tendency of the rich to create an oligarchy and the poor to create a "democracy" that would in his opinion lead to anarchy. The experience of the trajectory taken by the French Revolution further strengthened his view.

His *Defense of the Constitutions of Government of the United States of America* in 1786 strengthened the hand of the conservatives for the bi-cameral legislature. He also feared that the executive would not be independent enough, subject as it was to Senate approval of appointments. He wished to invest the executive with an irrevocable veto. Privately, he did not even rule out the eventual need for a hereditary aristocracy or executive to protect against the anarchy he feared above all else. This opened him up to charges of monarchism that pursued him throughout his political career.

It also opened him up to the critique by the liberal tradition that his mode of analysis based on classical history constrained him. He was accused of being antiquated by focusing on fixed classes and choosing to ignore the result of the equality of opportunity that characterized post-revolutionary America. He countered from his own soul and his own experience that each sought to raise oneself above the other and equality cannot exist although it may be the role of government to constrain the excesses of inequality of opportunity.

Despite the enmity of the group around Alexander Hamilton, having received the second largest number of votes in the fledgling Electoral College, John Adams was selected to be vice-president to balance the ticket of the southern George Washington for the latter's two terms. Although not completely allied with the economic interests of the Hamiltonian Federalists, Adams was strongly in favor of the ratification of the Jay Treaty establishing commercial relations with Great Britain. As political parties began to form, he then was selected in the presidential election in 1796 as the Federalist candidate against Democrat-Republican Thomas Jefferson. Adams and his New England Federalists, looking always to London, saw England as the bulwark against Jacobinism.

His preferred role was that of virtuous statesman in the role of the "patriot king," above all party. His isolation during his presidency arose not only from his own personal flaw to act defiantly on principle. Above all, he had the ill-fortune of having succeeded George Washington. Problems deferred by his predecessor's impeccable credentials and bottomless reputation now surfaced. In his characteristic way, Adams regarded any concern for his own political self-interest as a violation of virtue. Alexander Hamilton spread innuendo of Adam's vanity and deprecated his ability in advance of any action taken as president. Adams also inherited the problem of an impending war with France. Ignoring in an excess of virtue any concern for re-election, he held to a neutral role for the United States in the world torn between Britain and France as he held to the neutral role of the executive in the country.

To his ultimate credit, he disentangled American foreign relations from French influence without actually going to war. He carried on in

1797-98 a "quasi" naval war with France following the practice of attacking American shipping in the West Indies. The U. S. Navy was activated and the Department of the Navy established to support it with Benjamin Stoddert its first secretary.

The U. S. Congress had authorized in 1794 the building of six frigates that were the foundation of the U.S. Navy. One of these was the *USS Constitution*, associated with Boston to the present day, built there in 1797. These heavier than usual American frigates were a hybrid between the larger "ship-of-the-line" and an ordinary frigate. Throughout the 1790s, this building program moved forward fitfully in response to the threats offered by the Algerian barbary pirates; then after peace with them in 1796, with the threat by the French in the "Quasi-War" in 1798. Each of the ships was built in a different port in private shipyards.

The wooden-hulled ship built in Boston received the sobriquet of "Old Ironsides" for its resistance to bombardment in its victory under Captain Isaac Hull vs *HMS Guerriere* in August 1812 after having also defeated the French *L'Insurgente* during the Quasi-War in 1798. Charles Francis Adams, writing in 1913, considered the day of victory in August 1812 to be the day in which the United States entered history as a "world power." Secretary of the Navy Benjamin Stoddert also established a Navy Yard in the Charlestown section of Boston where was assigned responsibility for refitting ships after the War of 1812. Remaining active until the 1970s, it still is where the *USS Constitution* lies.

Figure 9 - USS Constitution

Prickly and disdainful of political dealings, Adams initiated the "Alien and Sedition Acts" to suppress criticism and the threat he felt emanating from the democracy. However, in the first turnover of political control, he led the Federalist Party to give way to their rival Democratic-Republican Thomas Jefferson for president in the election of 1800. He retired to his Braintree farm where during the rest of his long life he defended his reputation against any and all enemies. His son John Quincy, his grandson Charles Francis and great-grandson Henry Adams for the entire 19th century claimed the right based on their name to affect American politics.

The transfer of power in 1800 marked the beginning of the diminution of the role of New England and Boston in national affairs. More than just a political party, Federalism encompassed a world view. They believed in a government that entrusted power to a natural aristocracy claiming dedication to the common interest of the people as a whole rather than the narrow interests of factions. They defined "democracy" as the unbridled pursuit of self-interest at the expense of the common good by factions that could easily lead to anarchy. The health of the new republic would be maintained by those who, by ownership of property, would be beyond corruption or the blandishments of demagogues and maintain order and stability. No longer was it merely the fact of having migrated to the New World that made Boston "the city upon the hill." The free republican government they claimed to have been the mainstay was now their model for the world.

The Federalist Party never again regained the presidency as the country expanded and suffrage was extended beyond the propertied. Its adamant opposition to the war in 1812 against England was manifested in a refusal to finance the war and to mobilize the Massachusetts militia. Ultimately, a convention was called at Hartford in 1814 to consider secession. The Federalist Party never recovered from its talk of disunion despite its apparent vindication in opposition to a war ill-conceived and poorly run. The news of the treaty of peace and, moreover, the victory at the Battle of New Orleans overtook the petitions the delegates were carrying from Hartford to Washington. Their grievances had become moot. In a surge of nationalism, the memory was of the victory on Lake Erie, the glories of "Old Ironsides" in its battles on the high seas and above all the Battle of New Orleans.

With garden plots still attached to many houses, the greater wealth enabled expansion into the farther reaches of the South End and the now even more fashionable West End on its way to Cambridge and Harvard College. The West End also incorporated Beacon Hill into the city with its buildings by Charles Bulfinch.

2.4 Charles Bulfinch and Boston Architecture

Figure 10 - Charles Bulfinch

The son of a prominent physician who had, like his own father the first Dr Bulfinch, trained as a physician in Europe. Young Bullfinch had graduated from the Boston Latin School and Harvard, the latter in 1781. He married Harriet Apthorp, a first cousin, the daughter of one of the richest families in Boston. In 1787, Charles Bulfinch returned from his Grand European Tour that included study of the architecture of Christopher Wren in London and the Adam brothers in Bath. He also visited Paris and Nimes under the tutelage of Thomas Jefferson.

While his training and early work was in the tradition of the "gentleman architect," after the loss of his fortune in real estate ventures, he became the first American-born professional architect. His career in Boson during the next thirty years changed the face of Boston into a Federalist city of brick and granite not only as its most important architect but also

Working for the Federalist elite, the first of a series of houses is the three-story Harrison Gray Otis House of 1796 that still remains at Cambridge and Lynde Streets; as does the enlarged Faneuil Hall Market. The former pasture of the Hancock House on Beacon Street became the site of the new State House with its golden dome in 1798, reminiscent of London's Somerset House.

Once the State House was completed, the hilly land behind it was bought from the John Singleton Copley family by a syndicate called the Mount Vernon Proprietors headed by Harrison Gray Otis. The area was developed as Mount Vernon Street with buildings by Bulfinch including Louisburg Square; the latter eventually laid out in the Greek revival style with the statue of Aristides the Just. The homes built for Otis were somewhat grand in their width; the houses of his neighbors occupied lesser ground; leas ostentatious, they had a taut brick surface and strictly rationed detail.

Harrison Gray Otis soon abandoned his new house on Cambridge Street to build 85 Mt Vernon Street on his way to his final house at 45 Beacon Street, all by Bulfinch. The leveling of the top fifty feet .of the Mt Vernon Street hill began the filling in of the Back Bay, the first of many such ventures that created the enlarged city. The extension of Charles Street to the West Boston Bridge led to the transformation of Southac Street (now Phillips Street) from the less pleasing name of Mount Whoredom.

University Hall at Harvard College by Bulfinch still remains as does his last work in Boston, the central building of the Massachusetts General Hospital. North of the West Boston Bridge, it is made of granite brought from Chelmsford by the Middlesex Canal. The design built around the dome that surmounted the clinical amphitheater is said to derive from that of the Pennsylvania Hospital in Philadelphia, the nation's first. Having impressed President James Monroe on the latter's visit to Boston in 1817, Bulfinch was invited to come to

Washington DC where his great work included the completion of the U.S. Capitol with the dome covering the central Rotunda.

Figure 11 - The Massachusetts State House

Figure 12 - The Massachusetts General Hospital

2.5 The Harvard Medical School and the Massachusetts General Hospital

Figure 13 - Dr Benjamin Waterhouse

Benjamin Waterhouse, was born in 1754 in Newport Rhode Island to a Quaker family. After apprenticeship to a local physician, he trained in London and Edinburgh before graduating from the University of Leiden in 1780. Although a mild Federalist and a friend of John Adams, Waterhouse became associated with the Jeffersonians in conjunction with his advocacy of vaccination with cowpox originated by Jenner. He was forced to leave the faculty of the Harvard Medical School when it moved to Boston in conjunction with the founding of the Massachusetts General Hospital.

Founded in 1782, the first classes of the Harvard Medical School were in Holden Chapel in the Harvard Yard in Cambridge. Ezekiel Hersey (H'1728) had bequeathed money for a professorship of anatomy and one of physic some years before. The first appointments were those of John Warren and Benjamin Waterhouse to their respective chairs.

The Waterhouse dismissal from the Harvard Medical School was only partially connected with the move itself but with his being excluded from participation in clinical teaching that would go on at the Boston almshouse. James Jackson, a close friend of John Warren, the Hersey Professor of Anatomy and Surgery, was appointed adjunct clinical professor attending at the almshouse instead of Waterhouse. The latter was opposed by the Harvard Corporation and its ultra-Federalists. Caught between Federalists and Jeffersonians in the state legislature, the Boston medical establishment led by the Warrens carried the day.

The Massachusetts General Hospital (MGH) when founded in 1811 was the third such, following the Pennsylvania Hospital in 1751 and the New York Hospital in 1771. The Boston Almshouse on Leverett Street provided only eight beds for paupers; the new hospital was designed to contain at least thirty such beds for teaching purposes. Although delayed by the War of 1812, funds were available by 1817 to purchase land on North Allen Street near the Leverett Street site of the almshouse and an estate in Charlestown for the asylum. The present day central Bulfinch building was designed to accommodate one hundred and fifty patients with all the required amenities.

Another example of the hegemony of the original elite was the continuity of their role in medicine exemplified in the MGH through the generations. John Warren (1753-1815), the brother of famous Joseph Warren killed at the Battle of Bunker Hill, was Hersey Professor of Anatomy and Surgery at the medical school. He was the father in turn of John Collins Warren (1778-1856). The latter graduated from Harvard College in 1797 and then trained in Paris and Edinburgh and with Sir Astley Cooper at Guy's Hospital in London in anatomy and surgery. One of the founders of the MGH, both Warrens led in the move of the medical school to Boston and the dismissal of Waterhouse. However, the latter was the one that prevailed that the McLean Asylum be situated in a separate place outside of Boston, first in Charlestown and then after 1895 in Belmont.

The relationship of the MGH to the elite was not purely philanthropic. Chartered in 1818, the Massachusetts Hospital Life Insurance Company was awarded the plum of a monopoly of the life insurance business in Massachusetts with the provision that one-third of its profits go to the support of the Massachusetts General Hospital. Actually primarily a trust management company rather than a life insurance company, the key finance committee became a preserve of the elite. The mercantile fortunes founded in shipping and trade were now invested in textile factories in Boston and vicinity. The Life Insurance Company proved a ready source of loans to finance these mills on very flexible terms as needed. Considered as the "savings bank of the wealthy," their family fortunes also become trusts lasting as long as three generations to be managed by the company ("The Boston Trust") with investment "always in view of safety of capital." The selective character of their loans, almost entirely limited to the support of their textile investments, restricted opportunities to the detriment of future growth in New England as the economy expanded.

After the death of his father, John Collins Warren became Hersey Professor of Anatomy and Surgery at the medical school and longtime surgeon to the hospital. He epitomized the surgeon of the pre-anesthesia era, renowned for his speed and his unbending nature in face of the outcries of the patient. The founder of the Warren Anatomical Museum as well as the *New England Journal of Medicine*, he is particularly noteworthy for permitting in October 1846 the dentist Dr William T.G. Morton to administer ether to a patient undergoing surgery in what now recognized as the famed "Ether Dome." His statement "This is no humbug" is credited with encouraging the relatively rapid acceptance of this procedure, revolutionizing the practice of surgery. It was around that same time that the medical school moved from its original site in Boston to a site on North Grove street adjacent to the MGH and Dr. Oliver Wendell Holmes Sr became its dean. The Warren dynasty continued with his son Jonathan Mason Warren (1811-1867) a surgeon at the MGH who carried out the first skin grafts and rhinoplasties. The son John Collins Warren II (1842-1927) was in turn surgeon at the MGH where he did work on bacterial infection.

Richard Clarke Cabot (1868-1939) exemplifies the continuity of this tradition of service by the elite families even further into the 20th century. Born in Brookline, he was the grandson of the sailor Samuel Cabot who had the good fortune to marry Elizabeth Perkins, of the family wealthy from the China trade. His father James Cabot studied philosophy in Europe and taught at Harvard along with practicing law and writing biography. After finishing his training in bacteriology in 1892, Richard Cabot chose the relatively less prestigious job of directing the out-patient department of the MGH that served as a dispensary for the poor. There he was innovative in the use of social workers, incorporating treatment for the social and psychological as well as more purely physical needs of his poor patients in the West End surrounding the hospital. Characteristically, in the spirit of *noblesse oblige*, he paid the social workers their salaries until finally accepted as necessary by the MGH.

One result of the Revolutionary fervor was the rise of at least a few former mechanics such as Paul Revere to positions of prominence in post-Revolutionary Boston. His new-found status as a manufacturer expressed itself in some of the early industrial activities of the Federalist period that included the fitting-up of the frigate *USS Constitution*.

2.6 Paul Revere and Early American Industrialization

Revere was not only a silversmith. He made copperplate engravings including the famous one depicting the "Boson Massacre" and wired in false teeth. The latter was most notably the means by which he was able to identify the body of Dr Joseph Warren after the Battle of Bunker Hill, his friend, fellow St Andrew's Masonic Lodge brother and fellow patriot. During the successful agitation over the Stamp Act, Revere was closely allied to the "Loyal Nine" that controlled the larger mass of seamen and wharf workers that provided the rioters. He also was a leader of the artisans who provided the support crucial for the success of the non-importation agreements that underlay the success of the patriot cause. It was at this time in 1768 that John Singleton Copley painted his portrait as an artisan in the prime of life.

Figure 14 - Paul Revere

Apollos Rivoire was a Huguenot immigrant from the Bordeaux region who had learned the high trade of goldsmith from Boston's leading silversmith John Coney. Married to Deborah Hitchhborn, daughter of a local artisan, their son born in 1735 carried on both his father's anglicized name and trade after his death in 1754. With an education limited to the North Writing School, Paul Revere was Boston's leading silversmith for the next fifty years. Elite among his fellow artisans, he was not a gentleman like his cousin who became a lawyer after graduating from Harvard. His life as a craftsman and then industrialist extends far beyond his fabled role in the early days of the American Revolution. Nonetheless, it was his role as a Son of Liberty and early messenger in the patriot cause that ultimately provided the opportunity for the rise of "mechanicks" like Revere to positions of wealth and respectability.

During the 1770s, Revere was employed, often to the detriment of his silversmith business, under the auspices of his friend and fellow Mason Dr Joseph Warren, as a courier by the Massachusetts

Committees of Correspondence ranging as far as New York and Philadelphia. This activity included the ride alarming the countryside in April 1775 for which he has become most famous. After the withdrawal of the British forces from Boston in March 1776, he continued as an officer in the Massachusetts militia in several rather unsuccessful campaigns before retiring finally in 1779. He was never able to achieve an appointment as an officer in the Continental Army, presumably at least in part due to his lack of educated class status.

In 1770, Revere moved his home and business to the house on North Square that still remains. During the post-Revolutionary War era, his business increased and he was able to manufacture on a larger scale by using silverplate by fusing silver onto copper. The profits generated by his silver shop enabled him to branch out into other businesses and rise to the level of gentleman identified by the change in his title to "esquire." By the 1790s, his goldsmith business was run by his son Joseph Warren Revere while, still in the quest of wealth and social standing, he became involved in the larger business of running an iron and brass foundry in Boston. He supplied many churches with their bells and the North End shipyards with nuts and bolts including the brass fittings of the *USS Constitution*.

After 1800, he transferred most of his business activities to Canton Massachusetts where he bought an old ironworks to develop the first American mill for rolling sheet copper. The needs for sheathing the hulls of ships for the growing U.S. Navy provided the support for this budding domestic industry. An interest-free loan by the Federal Government enabled Revere to build the mill on his property in Canton. Responsible for sheathing the dome of the new State House and re-sheathing the hull of the *USS Constitution*, the rolling mill became the foundation of the long lasting firm of Revere Copper & Brass whose copper bottomed cookware still serve in thousands of American kitchens.

One of the recognized leaders of the artisan class of shop owners and businessmen, Revere helped organize support in 1788 for the ratification of the Constitution. He did not, however, receive a federal appointment such as Director of the U.S. Mint to which he aspired perhaps because he remained a Federalist in opposition to the policies of Presidents Jefferson and Madison. Particularly active in Freemasonry from 1760 onward, by the time he retired from business in 1811, he had become wealthy and immortalized along with his wife Rachel by portraits by the fashionable portraitest Gilbert Stuart, That pair reside at the Museum of Fine Arts alongside the earlier one by John Singleton Copley of young Paul Revere the "mechanick."

In the 1790s, in the absence of the former triangular trade with the sugar islands of the West Indies, the China trade offered an alternative triangular trade. Otter furs bought in Vancouver Sound found a ready market in Canton China with chinaware and textiles on the return voyage. As early as 1787, the *Columbia*, setting out from Boston was the first ship flying the American flag to circumnavigate the globe. Boston merchants led by Francis Cabot Lowell built the India Wharf as the center for the trade with the Orient.

There were few other opportunities for investment. Unlike other port cities with which it competed, its river system did not lead to the creation of many canals. The sole hand dug Middlesex Canal fed by the Concord River opened in 1802 from the Merrimack River at Lowell to Charlestown. Among a spate of turnpikes, one extended Washington Street south via Dedham to Attleboro and Providence; another extended Boylston Street in Brookline west via Framingham to Worcester; and still another northeasterly from across the Mystic River at Broadway in Chelsea to Topsfield and Newburyport.

During the War of 1812, Boston shipping interests benefited from freedom from the British blockade of the American ports to its south on the Delaware and the Chesapeake dating from early 1813. Boston profited particularly from the export of the lumber from Canada that served British naval supremacy and the "licensing" of grain to feed British troops in Portugal. However, starting in late 1813 under Admiral Cochrane, the British blockade began to include New England more actively; the British occupied an area around Penobscot Bay in Maine, still then part of Massachusetts. Once again, there was destruction of the shipping upon which Boston's prosperity had been based.

However, along with some "new men" from more northerly Essex County, the previous mercantile elite invested their wealth to become the industrialists of the new era. The impetus toward replacing the import of manufactures from Britain had first arisen during the period of the Confederation. Immediately after the Revolution, British manufactures flooded the American market. It had been one of the factors leading to the Constitutional Convention in Philadelphia in 1787 and need for a stronger central government to redress the unfavorable trade balance with England. Economic self-sufficiency was one of the tenets of Hamiltonian Federalism with the development of manufacturing at Paterson New Jersey on the falls of the Passaic River to be one of his early projects.

When British manufactures flooded the market after the end of the War of 1812, industrialization had already occurred to a greater extent in the United States. Boston merchants took the lead. With cotton textiles the most prominent, Boston reinvented itself by creating an industrial hinterland and a role as a banking center. The form that industrialization took in New England reflected its origins within the mercantile ownership class rather than its origins in the artisan class. The latter characterized the Philadelphia textile industry that focused on a wider and more costly range of products such as carpeting.

2.7 Francis Cabot Lowell and American Industrialization

Boston merchants, their shipping interests curtailed by the war, were anxious to find domestic investment opportunities. Land speculation and Boston real estate offered only limited opportunities. Manufacturing, particularly of basic cotton cloth, seemed to offer opportunities for continued dividends. Boston entrepreneurs connected by family ties and led by Francis Cabot Lowell founded in 1813 in a former paper mill America's first completely integrated textile factory in Waltham on the Charles River.

Figure 15 - Francis Cabot Lowell

The first Lowell arrived in Newbury Massachusetts in 1639. John Lowell (1704-67) was the first to go to Harvard College. His son (1743-1802), in turn his namesake, known as the "Old Judge" was the true family founder. A member of the Continental Congress and of the Harvard Corporation, he represented the transfer of power in that ruling body from the faculty to the substantial Boston merchants. His first son and namesake, a child by Sarah Higginson, walked in his father's footsteps as a lawyer and member also of the Harvard Corporation. The son of his second wife Susan Cabot was born in 1775 in Newburyport Massachusetts, his mother of a ship holding family also from the North Shore of Massachusetts Bay. Educated at Phillips' Academy Andover and Harvard College, he married Hannah Jackson of a similar background whose family became closely associated with him in his business dealings. Prosperous from trade with the Orient, Lowell was also active in real estate ventures in Boston such as the development of commercial property on Broad Street connected to the India Wharf. To complete his generation, his other half-brother Reverend Charles Lowell, minister of the West Church, was the son of the third wife and the father of James Russell Lowell, the poet.

During a visit to England and Scotland starting in 1810, Lowell had memorized the technology for weaving that he then re-created in his highly profitable "Boston Manufacturing Company". The first American mill established by Samuel Slater at Pawtucket Rhode Island in 1790 had initiated the industrial revolution in America by using imported methods for mechanized carding, drawing and spinning cotton but not the power loom for weaving. The last was still done by hand by local weavers mainly in their homes. Now for the first time, under Lowell's direction, a machine shop built the needed machinery to make the well-capitalized Waltham mill unique with its improved power loom. Lowell and his mechanic Moody made several other improvements in the machinery that further reduced costs and led to extraordinary profitability. Moreover, Lowell set up a joint-stock company with preferred stockholders at the then astounding level of $400,000 drawn very much from "friends and family." His vision was to control the entire process, to simplify it and to seek economies of scale, the "American" system of manufacture.

After Lowell's death in 1817, the other stockholders chose to increase their profits by selling their patented machinery and issuing additional stock. Having exhausted the water power capacity of the Charles River, development occurred farther north with a thirty-foot fall on the faster flowing Merrimack River. The city named after Lowell (formerly East Chelmsford) was one of its byproducts along with the Middlesex Canal. A far more highly capitalized "Merrimack Manufacturing Company" secured the land and water rights to create at Lowell a replica of Manchester England. Machine shops built the textile manufacturing machinery for mills elsewhere; water power and then steam driven mills arose throughout New England that provided the hinterland for investment by Boston and its financiers. The area manufactured both textile machinery and cloth.

Initially, they drew from a labor supply of poor hill farmers and of young women whose potential male partners had migrated to more fertile land to the west. The mill owners were careful to maintain in their employee boarding houses the moral standards of the locale. New England provided an ideal environment with its available water power, humidity to aid in spinning, and pure water for bleaching. Large scale cotton manufacture in New England was the beginning of American industry.

Figure 16 - Daniel Webster

Born in 1782 to a farmer who was a strong Federalist in Salisbury New Hampshire (later Franklin), Daniel Webster trained at Phillips' Exeter Academy and then Dartmouth College. His career was strongly influenced by his reading law at the office of Christopher Gore in Boston. A leading Federalist, Gore was wealthy by buying undervalued Revolutionary War government debt, redeemed at par. Gore was also a partner in the Boston and Lowell Manufacturing Companies and a major stockholder in the privately-funded West Boston Bridge.

Webster, first a Federalist Congressman from New Hampshire and then from Massachusetts, became a highly paid proponent of the Boston Associates in their varied interests. He was closely associated with Lowell in persuading the U.S. Congress to pass in 1816 a tariff protecting the domestic textile industry and in other later activities to the benefit of the Boston manufacturers. For example, he fought in Congress on their behalf when they were, in favor of tariffs on woolen goods in 1828. They and he fought far less actively for tariff on cotton goods in 1824. In the latter, their competitive advantage favored them over other cotton manufacturers.

Once again, in the 1830s, Webster led in the passage of a law protecting patent rights, another major source of income of the Boston Associates. His close connection with the Boston "cotton Whigs," dependent as they were on the use of Southern cotton in their mills and the market for their cheap cotton cloth for slave garments, may have also contributed to his highly controversial advocacy for the Fugitive Slave Law as part of the Compromise of 1850.

Chapter 3
Boston the Hub of the Universe 1815-1865

Introduction

The loss of Federalist political hegemony furthered the complaint of the Boston elite that the promise of American culture had not borne adequate fruit. The Federalist criticism of the degradation of American politics with the rise of the manufacturers was accompanied with the familiar litany of lack of literary accomplishment. They looked back nostalgically to the times when stability was more valued than growth; self-denial was preferable to individual freedom and deference rather than social equality was the ideal. In 1831-32, the aristocratic DeTocqueville found American culture superficial and shallow subject as it was to the values of the marketplace and popular sovereignty that imposed the ordinary preferences of the average person on everyone else. However, rather than antithetical to high culture, Emerson saw the new economy as liberating and creative if committed to "private obedience to [the] mind," the undeveloped human potential of each. Laissez-faire would extend from the material to the spiritual; no longer, would there need be concern with the social dimension of human existence such as the commitment to "virtue," the concern of the revolutionary generation.

By 1840, the population of Boston approached 100,000, equal to that of Philadelphia and just below then second ranked Baltimore. Still primarily mercantile, nevertheless the port fell far behind New York in carrying only about 8% of the exports and 12% of the imports of the entire country. The capital invested in manufacturing was similar to that of Baltimore but only half of that of Philadelphia. Even the textiles produced in the New England mills found their way via New York and Philadelphia to serve the west.

The business of Boston itself became mainly finance, insurance and banking. The likelihood of future growth of the city was less than the others as reflected in the lesser number employed in construction. The rise of immigration in the next decade changed it all. The formerly one-dimensional city of English origin and Protestant religion was confronted by what seemed to them to be an invasion that threatened their very existence. The process by which the immigrants were incorporated into the life of the city affected the history of the city henceforth.

3.1 Making the City of Boston

In 1822, almost two hundred years after its founding, the city of Boston was incorporated. The long held vision of a small town governed by the old forms of government no longer sufficed. The seven thousand qualified voters of a population of nearly 45,000 could no longer fit into a town meeting in Faneuil Hall in the localized Puritan republic. One mark was the need to pass laws to enforce Sabbath observance previously enforced by community consensus. Another was the need to maintain clean streets and build more adequate markets.

Figure 17 - Mayor Josiah Quincy

Josiah Quincy was mayor of Boston from 1823 to 1829 and president of Harvard College from 1829 to 1845. Born in Boston in 1772, he trained at Phillips' Andover Academy and graduated from Harvard College in 1790. A lawyer, he was active in Massachusetts state politics and

Federalist member of Congress from 1805 to 1813. One of the lasting fruits of his tenure is the "Public Garden" on land reclaimed from the Back Bay; still another is the granite Greek revival Quincy Market House dating from 1825 facing the harbor directly behind Faneuil Hall Market. The land reclaimed from the harbor of the former Town Dock became Dock Square that extended to the present limit of Atlantic Avenue.

Quincy Market still stands recently renewed with its surrounding warehouses on North and South Market Streets. Its architecture is reminiscent of the ancient Greek democracy and of the contemporary Greeks fighting for independence against the Ottoman Turks. This same style is also exemplified in the granite monoliths of the still-extant Boston Custom House by Ammi Burnham Young at India and State Streets. The local granite whether in use of Egyptian, Greek or Gothic style characterized Boston in the early 19th century.

Figure 18 - Boston Quincy Market

The North End never recovered its fashionable standing from the exodus of the Loyalists during the Revolution. Salem and Hanover Streets became sites for small tradesmen. Fashion moved west and south. Growth occurred first on Dorchester Heights (South Boston) annexed to Boston in 1804. In order to expand beyond its original limited boundaries, Boston began to fill in the surrounding bays. The Boston Neck leading south to the mainland became widened. Front Street (named Harrison Avenue in 1844 after the newly deceased president) ran parallel to Washington Street on newly reclaimed land of the South Cove. Mill Pond to the north dating from 1643 was filled in under the direction of Charles Bulfinch with land fill from the former Beacon Hill to form the "Bulfinch Triangle." Causeway Street followed the former line of the dam and Canal Street runs along the canalized Mill Creek.

The main improvement was the beginning of enclosure of the Back Bay by a dam running along what became Beacon Street from Charles Street to what was then Sewell's Point in Brookline; the east and west basins were divided by what became Massachusetts Avenue. Water would enter the upper basin from the Charles River at high tide and drain from the lower basin at low tide. The height differential between the two was designed to provide power. This scheme became less successful with the advent of steam power in the 1830s and the intrusion of the railroads whose embankments made the Back Bay into a sewer. An area west of Charles Street was retained to become the Public Gardens adjoining the Boston Commons. The last remaining portion of Beacon Hill called Cotton Hill after its 18th century occupant Cotton Mather was cut down to form Pemberton Square to the east of the State Capitol in the 1830s.

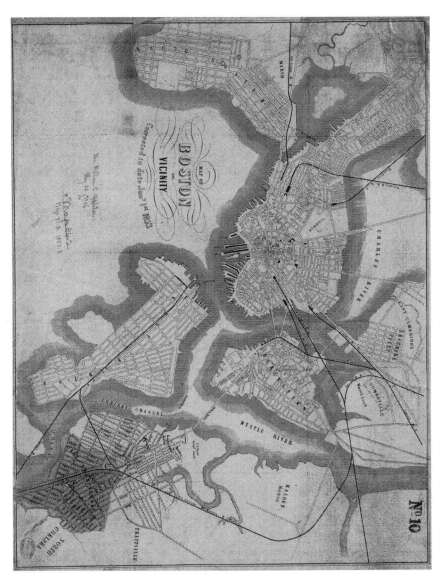

Figure 19 - Boston 1850

The adjoining map shows the development of the railways entering Boston from all directions that necessitated the filling in of land to accommodate them. The population of Boston tripled during the years 1830 to 1860, reaching nearly 180,000. The large number of new immigrants provided a labor pool willing to work for low wages that generated an industrial boom. By the end of this period, horse cars ran from Scollay Square near the Town Dock extending the walking city's two mile radius from City Hall an additional half-mile to the new areas in the South End along the Boston Neck, thus creating the first residential suburbs.

The factory system helped create a new aristocracy of wealth and power as members of the old mercantile elite merged with those who made their profits in the cotton mills. A group of about forty families made up the interlocking group united by blood and intermarriage that not only owned mills but real estate, banking, insurance and the railroads that radiated from the city. They also wielded political power not only in the city and state but in the Congress via the Whig Party Senators Edward Everett and Daniel Webster.

Their multi-dimensional hegemony made the so-called "Boston Brahmins" a true upper class that distinguished Boston from the more fragmented elites of other cities. Moreover, to an extent unique to Boston among the other port cities, the Boston elite was not only clearly defined but of a similar nature in British origin and Protestant religion.

Alexis DeTocqueville, when visiting in 1831, found Boston, unlike so many other cities in the United States, "a pretty town in a picturesque site on several hills in the middle of the waters." Then already clearly the cultural center, the young French aristocrat appreciated Boston society comparable to that of upper class Europeans and so different from the money-conscious spirit "which makes New York society so vulgar."

In the next generation, Paris became the standard by which Boston measured itself as a world city. The Second Empire style of architecture with its mansard roofs appeared in the Hotel Vendome along Commonwealth Avenue on the new streets of the Back Bay but also in the Boston City Hall on School Street. Analogous in expansiveness to the contemporary Parisian boulevards, the name given to the grand boulevard of Commonwealth Avenue in the Back Bay district reflects the fact that the entire area was developed under the aegis of the state government. Holding ownership of the land in consideration of its original origin as a tidal flat, the entire area was laid out as a whole. The adjoining map shows the streets of the Back Bay already platted)

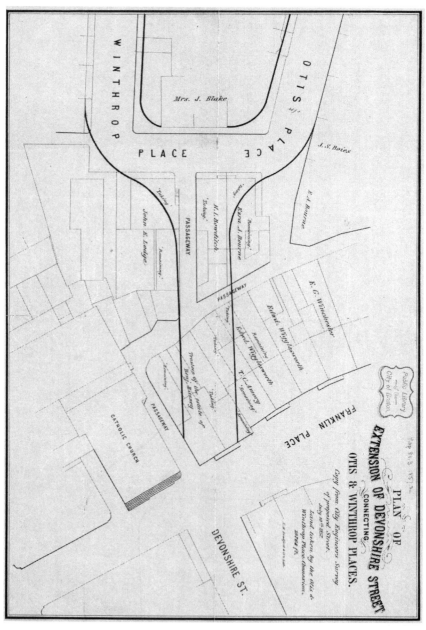

Figure 20 - Boston late 1850s, Back Bay Streets platted

Boston English High School was established in the 1820s as the first "high school," designed to train students in the practical courses necessary for business and science. Boston Latin School continued to be the conduit for training for the professions. Harvard College remained the educational bastion. Even for outsiders, it became an entry into the elite. Edward Everett, the son of a poor but highly respectable clergyman in Dorchester, became after graduation from Harvard and its Divinity School minister of the upper class Brattle Street Church. Suspect for such failings as choosing to live in Boston rather than Cambridge, he was redeemed by his marriage to the daughter of Peter Chardon Brooks, Boston's richest man. He held a series of important offices such as Massachusetts governor, secretary of state and membership in the U.S. Senate but the culmination for most Bostonians was his presidency of his alma mater.

The horse-drawn railroad appeared for the first time in 1826 to bring granite from the quarry in Quincy to where it could be carried by water to commemorate the 50th anniversary of the Battle of Bunker Hill in Charlestown. Just five years after the Baltimore & Ohio opened as the first common carrier, by 1835 the Boston & Lowell (B&L) to the north, the Boston & Providence (B&P) following the old turnpike to the south and the Boston & Worcester (B&W) the one to the west all opened. The burst of railroading appeared to meet the needs of Boston to overcome its deficiencies based on the absence of water borne transport to tap its hinterland.

Reflecting the excellent passenger patronage, double tracking of the B&W started in the early 1840s and the Western Railroad extended from Worcester to the New York State Line in 1841. However, the two did not amalgamate to form the Boston & Albany until the 1860s. By then Cornelius Vanderbilt had created the connection for the New York Central (NYC) to Lake Erie and Boston lost out to New York to have its own trunk line to the west. The NYC took control of the B&A in 1900. The Hartford and New Haven Railroad (H&NH) started in the 1830s, merged in 1872 with the New York and New Haven (NY&NH) to form the NYNH&H Railroad. The NY&NH had connected as early as 1848 with the New York & Harlem Railroad to reach New York City. This "Consolidated" Railroad became the heart of the NYNH&H that had acquired the Shore Line Route from Boston through Providence to New Haven, thus creating an all-rail route that put out of business the old Fall River Line to New York by overnight steamboat. The railroads serving southeastern Massachusetts since 1835 consisted of the Boston & Providence that joined in 1888 with the Old Colony from Boston to Plymouth and Fall River. These and still other rail lines became amalgamated in the 1890s into the NYNH&H under the aegis of J.P. Morgan. In his quest to control all transportation in New England, Morgan amassed so much debt that the railroad could never again become viable.

The need over the next two decades from the 1830s to the 1850s to accommodate the railroads in close proximity to other earlier commercial development could not be easily met within the narrow confines of the Shawmut peninsula. The filling in of portions of the adjoining harbor occurred as well as the building of further bridges. In the 1830s, the Boston & Lowell Railroad was the first to enter on the north via a new Lowell Street; the Eastern Railroad from Salem came to Noodle's Island (East Boston) from which a ferry brought passengers to Commercial Street in the North End before later coming to a station on Causeway Street in the 1850s. The Boston & Maine station was also eventually in the 1840s on Causeway Street, creating the still extant North Station complex on the land reclaimed from Mill Pond. The Boston & Worcester followed the existing Boston & Albany tracks across the Back Bay; the Boston & Providence also crossing the former near present day Back Bay Station (Park Square) obstructed the water flow in the reclaimed area eventually leading to the filling in of the entire Back Bay.

Much of the reminder of the South Cove was filled in to form Albany Street to provide a terminus at Kneeland Street for the Boston & Worcester (eventually the Boston & Albany in 1867) that also became Beach and Lincoln Streets and eventually in 1899 the South Station complex at Dewey Square. To be the first section of a direct railway route to St Louis, the Western Railroad in 1842 completed its track from Worcester to the Hudson River near Albany.

The reformist impulse expressed in the enlargement of the city also included better provision for the "deserving poor" as well as temperance and prison reform. An adequate municipally owned water supply was part of this reform movement. The need went far beyond the problem of fighting fires to provide for all domestic needs. Clean water was seen not only to improve health but improve morals and encourage temperance. By 1848, the privately owned Boston Aqueduct that brought water from Jamaica Pond was replaced by a municipally owned aqueduct from Long Pond and Lake Cochituate in Middlesex County. The water first filled the Frog Pond in the Boston Common in a great fete with a reservoir at Boylston Street in Brookline. Impounding the Sudbury River seventeen miles west in the 1870s, the holding reservoir was at Chestnut Hill (later to be the site of Boston College). In the 20th century, that system was replaced by the Quabbin Reservoir under the auspices of the Metropolitan Water Board impounding the Swift River farther west while the Chestnut Hill reservoir remains a recreational area lined by paths.

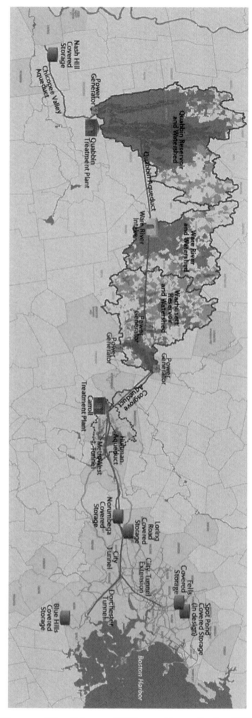

Figure 21 - Map of Water Supply in 1918

3.2 The Athens of America

The loss of Federalist political hegemony furthered the complaint of the Boston elite that the promise of American culture had not borne adequate fruit. The Federalist criticism of the degradation of American politics with the rise of the manufacturers was accompanied with the familiar litany of lack of literary accomplishment. They looked back nostalgically to the times when stability was more valued than growth; self-denial was preferable to individual freedom and deference rather than social equality was the ideal. However, rather than anti-thetical to high culture, Emerson saw the new economy as liberating and creative if committed to "private obedience to [the] mind," the undeveloped human potential of each. Laissez-faire would extend from the material to the spiritual; no longer, would there need be concern with the social dimension of human existence such as the commitment to "virtue," the concern of the revolutionary generation.

Despite its decried pervasiveness, the men of business in Boston still tried to preserve suspicion toward the values of the marketplace. The elite of Boston endorsed the development of the fine arts particularly literature; high culture was a cure for the ills of the marketplace rather than one of its products. They saw their own city as already the leader in American intellectual circles, to make it further the "Athens of America," to make up for the loss of political influence and the possible future economic stagnation by the influence of its cultural institutions and the high-minded virtue of its citizens.

In its character of the most "civilized" and "educated" region in the new republic, New England could unite the old European and the new American values. Drawing upon the ongoing tension between its original role as a community to meet religious goals rather than merely materialistic ones, the ideal ethos of the merchant elite was that of a morally responsible person answerable to family and friends in what was still a close-knit society. The ideal businessman would risk his property for his honor and the good of others. For example, following the Panic of 1857, Nathan Appleton, one of the major owners of cotton mills, offered to sustain some of his colleagues threatened with ruin. The trader must be truthful, fair and honest, not taking excessive profit.

The gentleman's pursuit of balance together with a sense of social responsibility also shaped the Boston's elite's relationship to culture. A particular commitment to the love of learning and bibliophilia marked the Boston elite. As early as 1779, John Adams having observed the operation of a Philosophical Society in Philadelphia, encouraged the charter in Boston of what became the "American Academy of Arts and Sciences," accomplished the next year. After sharing space in a variety of buildings owned by others, the Academy in the early 1900s settled on Newbury Street, then adjacent to the Massachusetts Institute of Technology. Following the 1950s, it was housed in an Italianate Beaux-Arts mansion in Brookline before moving to Irving Street in Cambridge. With up to two thousand fellows and the widely distributed journal *Daedulus,* it strives to maintain a conversation amongst the different strands of the arts and sciences.

In 1791, the Reverend Jeremy Belknap of the Federal Street Church organized the "antiquarian" society known as the Massachusetts Historical Society (MHS), the first such in the United States to be concerned with American history. The Academy of Arts and Sciences and the MHS organizations met on consecutive days and has had members in common. The organizations maintained a tradition of non-academic scholarship in which professionals and amateurs mingle together in mixture of both learned societies and clubs.

Still closely associated with the two previous organizations is the third. "The Boston Athenaeum" was known first in 1804 as the "Anthology Society". One of the typical Boston mixtures of clergymen, merchants, physicians and lawyers, it published the *Monthly Anthology and Boston Review.* Francis Lowell and his brother-in-law Dr James Jackson were among the incorporators of the "Boston Athenaeum" in 1807. There was a reading room (newsroom) open long hours and a non-circulating book depository library. Patterned as a "public-private" library after the Athenaeum established in 1798 in Liverpool, the name was in the spirit of the ancient Greek temple dedicated to the goddess of wisdom. It was a place where scholars taught their students; orators and poets might rehearse their works. At its initial price of $300 a share, it was clearly designed to be an exclusive refuge for the rich. Its first librarian was William Smith Shaw, the nephew of Abigail Adams and her husband's private secretary when president.

Figure 22 - The Boston Athenaeum

These same men, all related by ties of class and family, established in 1815 the quarterly *North American Review* (NAR) in the model of the *Edinburgh Review*. It became the prime expression of the goal of Massachusetts conservative elite to foster a genuine American culture while enhancing the role of New England as the nation's intellectual center. Until the founding of the *Atlantic Monthly* in 1857, the NAR was edited in Boston as the foremost publication in the United States for "elevating culture," while disparaging southern culture and distrusting egalitarianism. Constrained by its unbridled sectionalism and fear of democracy, it was unsuccessful in its Whig political goals for the National Bank while somewhat more effective in its intellectual ones.

By 1830, the Athenaeum library contained 27,000 volumes and was housed in the elegant mansion donated by the China merchant James Perkins in then fashionable Pearl Street (present day Post Office Square). By 1858, the library contained 70,000 volumes and had moved to its permanent abode at ten and one half Beacon Street, an Italianate palazzo patterned after the Pall Mall clubs of the period. Membership not only provided access to what was the finest private library in the country but also what amounted to a patent of nobility. Libraries were an important way to demonstrate both cultural attainment and family stability in the model offered by the then current affluent British Victorian aristocracy.

Culture also afforded the opportunity to serve the community. The Athenaeum was a way of lifting the reputation of Boston over New York or Philadelphia. It exemplified Boston's reputation for fostering intellectual pursuit instead of a "pernicious pursuit of luxury." Boston was to be a city of taste in which intellectual pleasures led to a virtuous reign of truth. The role of the wealthy as patrons of culture was compared to Renaissance Florence. For example, the largess of the Perkins family to the Athenaeum was compared by Mayor Josiah Quincy to the Medici's. Contributions were a way to be "noble" in the restrained display of one's wealth. The Lowell family established the Lowell Institute that endowed a series of lectures with the munificent sum of $250,000 (to be governed by the trustees of the Athenaeum). In doing so, John Lowell Jr defined "the prosperity of New England, an otherwise barren and unproductive land, to be based on the intelligence and information of its inhabitants but also as heretofore on its moral qualities."

The religious impulse was always strong in New England. How to reconcile the traditional Calvinism with the increased individualism and sense of accomplishment derived from the existence of the new republic? In the traditional New England culture, the primary responsibility of the individual had been to the community as a whole, defined as church, town, kin or all three. Puritan forbearers had looked to the community of the saints; republican descendants could now find definition as members of a virtuous community of the civic-minded.

Unitarianism became the religion of the Boston elite. It placed greater emphasis on the beneficence of God, the innate goodness of man and the availability of salvation to all. James Freeman began preaching a "Unitarian" rather than a "Trinitarian" faith in 1784 at the King's Chapel in Boston. By the early 1800s, nearly all Congregational pulpits in and around Boston had been taken over by Unitarian preachers. Recognition came in 1804 when the "Unitarian" Henry Ware, the preacher at the Second Church, was appointed Hollis Professor of Divinity at Harvard College. Highly prestigious, this oldest endowed chair was the one that set the standards for the Massachusetts ministry. William Ellery Channing H'1798 was the contemporary eloquent preacher at Boston's Federal Street Church who brought Unitarianism as an entity into the wider social setting.

3.3 William Ellery Channing and the Boston Religion

Figure 23 - William Ellery Channing

William Ellery Channing, born in Newport Rhode Island in 1780, was the grandson of William Ellery, a signer of the Declaration of Independence. He trained in the ministry at Harvard College during the tumultuous time of the French Revolution but deviated from his New England Calvinist Congregational background in becoming one of the leading proponents of Unitarianism. Deviating from the orthodox Trinitarian doctrine, he was the representative for the liberal tendencies that pervaded Boston.

"Unitarian Christianity", his widely reprinted landmark sermon in 1819 at the dedication of the First Unitarian Church of Baltimore, was the key text that defined the new group. Its belief was in the unity of God reflecting also the unity of society; that the Bible was a book written by men, to be understood by men; and that predestination makes machines of men. Unitarianism also denied the doctrine of "original sin" and the godhead of Jesus and his substitutionary atonement. The purpose of Jesus as a prophet is merely to "lift forth piety in the human breast."

Although actually a moderate in many ways, Channing as pastor of the Federal Street Church deviated from his orthodox predecessors by emphasizing that "God had made human nature capable of moral choice and capable of ever increasing understanding, akin to the divine." He called "a mind free which jealously guards its intellectual rights and powers, which calls no man master and does not content itself with any passive or hereditary faith." His synthesis of piety and human rights is based on the supreme worth of the human person but yet took the middle ground of reconciling religion with the Enlightenment, only later leading in the following generation to the eventual development of a Protestant humanism.

The new Boston religion of Unitarianism provided a way for the elite to reject the "fire and brimstone" of the old Calvinist religion and the "excesses of enthusiasm" produced by orthodox revivalists while still retaining their commitment to moral and ethical standards. Channing had influence on an entire generation of reformers that followed in his footsteps in advocating educational and prison reform as well as opposition to slavery. For example, Charles Sumner was one who considered Channing's faith in the perfectibility of man him to be his own.

The American Unitarian Association was founded in Boston in 1825 where it still resides. Harvard's Department of Moral Philosophy was the stronghold from 1805 to the dawn of the Civil War of the specific brand of Unitarianism of northeastern Massachusetts, with its preoccupation with right conduct. The elite of the urban-commercial city, unlike even the less prosperous rural population of western Massachusetts, could readily accept their status of human dignity as a just reward for a life of human virtue. Certain other factors peculiar to

Boston permitted its rapid spread including the town's relative sophistication and foreign connections as well as the dominant role held by the wealthier pew holders in the selection of ministers within the formerly Congregationalist churches.

Unitarianism was attacked by the orthodox Calvinists such as Reverend Jedediah Morse of Charlestown's First Church as being merely half-way to "unbelief." In 1809, John Codman of Dorchester's Second Church refused to exchange pulpits with the Unitarian ministry leading eventually to the formation of a separate Unitarian church in Dorchester. The orthodox members of the Old South Church banded together to form a separate association with their own Park Street Church at the corner of Tremont Street ("Brimstone Corner"). It was the haven for those who now called themselves "evangelical" with the Andover Theological Seminary their new cradle. In addition to the charges of religious laxity, the Unitarians were accused of being the church of the rich, well born and the learned but not appropriate to the ordinary people, as indeed it was.

Already closely indentified with members of the Transcendalist movement, the assertions by Ralph Waldo Emerson in his 1838 address to the graduates of the Harvard Divinity School seemed to provide support for these attacks by the orthodox. Having been invited by the students and not the faculty, he urged an open rejection of the supernatural origin of the Bible by Unitarians. He had in fact resigned his Unitarian ministry before making his statement. It was therefore possible and deemed essential to many of the members of the Unitarian Association and the faculty to distance themselves from Emerson's heretical views and also from Transcendentalism.

Figure 24 - Ralph Waldo Emerson

Born in Boston in 1803, Ralph Waldo Emerson was the second son of William Emerson, the liberal preacher at the important Old South, the First Church. Known as Waldo, young Emerson started at age nine at the Boston Latin School where emphasis on declamation and oratory was preparation for a public life. Although descended from a family that would be recognized as one of the elite, the early death of the father left them in genteel poverty. He entered Harvard College in 1817, a place already considered excessively liberal by the more orthodox members of his family. In accordance with his family tradition, he later went to the Harvard Divinity School where he studied under William Ellery Channing. In 1829, Emerson became a pastor of Old North; Boston's Second Church, once the home of Increase and Cotton Mather but now a Unitarian Church.

Emerson left the Unitarian ministry in 1832 based on his distaste for the sectarianism into which all religions had fallen, including Unitarianism. He opposed participation in the Lord's Supper as an example of the formalism that now seemed intrinsic to all religion rather than true devotion to one's own internal sentiment. He continued to preach the rest of his life but a more secular philosophy. It was expressed in his famous Harvard Divinity School lecture in 1838 that questioned the divinity of Christ and the veracity of the Biblical miracles. He remained preoccupied as to how to maintain a concern for the common good when the economic and political system increasingly assured the right to pursue one's own individual private interests?

The election of Andrew Jackson in 1828 indicated the final breakup of the old Federalist political order. Further, no longer was there to be an established church in Massachusetts. All the churches competed with each other; each defined themselves by exclusive sacred forms and doctrines. Emerson's own personal evolution reflected a response to the growth of his native city and the break-up of the tight community of which he and his family had been an integral part. The role of articulating the common good was now the role of the intellectual. Under the influence of the Unitarian philosophers at Harvard, rather than despair in the evil in man, there was faith in his possibilities by accepting man's nature as inherently good. The spiritual self (mind) is not merely equal to the material self but the more significant since it was the part of what might be considered as the divine within oneself.

Emerson spent the winter of 1834-1835 considering his future. He concluded that his calling was to be a "scholar." In his "American Scholar" address at Harvard in 1837, he called for the need to rely on one's own internal promptings as to what to do rather than social custom. The true scholar is not merely defined by traditional standards of learning but by a readiness to heed the voice of nature. In the midst of the breakdown in the unity of society, one can seek to find that unity in nature. Since one's own nature will mirror the laws of the universe, the goal of life is to learn what it means for each individual by "self-improvement" to be a virtuous man and to act on that knowledge. How might he live such a life and influence the lives of others?

The Lyceum movement exemplified by the "Boston Society for the Diffusion of Useful Knowledge" provided a vehicle by which Emerson could create a public role for himself outside the ministry. Living in Concord, Emerson joined in 1836 the Transcendental Club that became the nucleus of his philosophical circle of mainly fellow liberal Unitarians. Claiming derivation from Emmanuel Kant, they believed in a romantic idealism and a belief in "transcendental," eternal ideas, finding truth in the unity of nature. In literature, the transcendentalists championed the work of Thomas Carlyle and Samuel Coleridge. In religion, they found man able to attain religion without the need for belief in miracles. The group included his closest friend Bronson Alcott and Margaret Fuller who shared with Emerson the editorship of *The Dial*, their literary magazine from 1840 to 1844. He befriended Henry Thoreau and Nathaniel Hawthorne; and, much later, Walt Whitman.

Emerson is most influential for his *Essays* that were published starting in the 1840s. Most notable were "Self-Reliance" and "Conduct of Life." Widely recognized, he lectured extensively throughout his life and was considered America's leading intellectual figure. The wide scope of Emersonian interests reflected the ferment of New England life in his generation from the 1820s to the 1840s. Moreover, a child of the Christian religion and the American idea of republicanism, he also represented his New England origins as he led to an individualism beyond religion and the state. He advocated the filling of one's head and not only his pocket, particularly now that one's fortune had been amassed by one's forbearers.

Emerson's address on the "American Scholar" took place as the high point of the Harvard commencement in August 1837. The large number that filled the First Parish Meetinghouse included such Harvard luminaries as Edward Everett, Joseph Story and William Ellery Channing as well as Harvard President Josiah Quincy. Although not his major theme, the American dependence on British literature was a recurrent one; Emerson issued the call for an American national literature wherein popular culture would be the seedbed of the uniquely American genius. The "American scholar" was to be a student of life and a liver of life, not merely of books. Yet Emerson's other more personal theme was the need for the scholar to lead a life that was solitary and removed from the commonplace.

3.5 Nathaniel Hawthorne and the "New England" Romance

One of Emerson's protégés was the younger Nathaniel Hawthorne whose work was considered even in his own time as the mark of the flowering of American literature. A renaissance in literary life was part of the reformation of religion led by Emerson and his fellow Transcendentalists. Although he tempered his Calvinism with "heart," Hawthorne in turn was a child of Puritans. He found his subjects there and the preoccupation with the salvation of the individual soul. On firm Calvinist ground, he believed in the total depravity of man; but nevertheless felt it tempered in the individual by its universality. Even his belief in universal depravity was colored by an un-Puritan sympathy for the sinner; and for his detestation for sins of the intellect above the sins of the flesh held so uniquely important by the 17th century Puritans.

The anatomy of sin was the core of Hawthorne's thinking and the main theme of several of his novels that dealt with alienation from the oppressive community as the topic of the genre in this era of "New England romances." They were characterized with a concern with 17th century history while allowing for a literary approach. However, his exploration of the Calvinist theology, its way of life and even its role as the bulwark of American liberties in the 17th century is but his vehicle. His approach is not that of a moralist or an analyst, he dealt with moods and inner struggles, a poet of human hearts and souls.

Figure 25 - Nathaniel Hawthorne

Nathaniel Hawthorne was born in 1804 in his ancestral Salem Massachusetts where his family had lived since their arrival in the early days of the Massachusetts Bay Colony. His ancestor had been a judge in the Salem witch trials. His grandfather David Hathorne was a ship captain who profited as a privateer during the Revolutionary War. His father Nathaniel Hathorne was also a ship captain, active in the China trade who died in the West Indies in 1808 of yellow fever. Because of his father's early death, the family lived in poverty dependent on the meager support of his mother's prosperous family. He added the letter 'w" to his surname by 1830; it served distinguish himself from his Puritan forbearers, including the judge noted for the persecution of non-Calvinists and unrepentant for his role in the Salem witch trials.

Following an accident, he became invalided as a boy for a time that led to his becoming devoted to books and petted by his sisters. A writer since childhood, he went to Bowdoin College from 1821 to 1825. There he met Franklin Pierce as well as Henry Wadsworth Longfellow, both remained lifelong friends. He temporarily entered the utopian Brook Farm settlement in West Roxbury along with his future wife Sophia Peabody. Her sister Elizabeth Peabody ran a bookstore that published several of her brother-in-laws books as well as *The Dial*. He was a colleague and neighbor in Concord Massachusetts of Ralph Waldo Emerson. The community of writers living in Concord was highly inbred with jealous passions among the members. One such triangle involved both the Hawthorne's with Margaret Fuller, also at that time involved with Emerson.

Living then in the Berkshires, Hawthorne later became a close friend of Herman Melville. Always solitary and shy, he remained highly dependent on others, particularly his wife. Hawthorne's greatest success was *The Scarlet Letter* written in 1850, followed immediately by *The House of the Seven Gables* in 1851. Their great success did not bring him wealth because of the prevalence of pirated copies. Interspersed with his literary career were therefore his appointments to various governmental posts necessary to supplement his income. His friend President Franklin Pierce appointed him to the plum position of Consul in Liverpool from 1853 to 1857. Like so many of his fellow Bostonian "intelligentsia," the moral issue of the 1850s for him was the abolition of slavery coupled with women's rights, concerned with the rights of the individual as opposed to an oppressive community.

3.6 The Boston Abolitionists

As late as 1850 and the passage of the Fugitive Slave Law, support for abolition of slavery was not widespread beyond the small number of the New England intelligentsia. Frequently strongly based like Garrison upon religious conviction, they were also committed to a broader sense of reform that increasingly found its focus in anti-slavery. In the 1840s, Wendell Phillips and Charles Sumner joined Lloyd Garrison who had been laboring since the 1830s in that cause by the publication of *The Liberator* newspaper. They were known as "abolitionists" for their commitment to immediate rather than gradual emancipation, for their concern for the rights of those freed and for opposition to the principle of colonization of those freed to places like Liberia. There had also been support from respected figures like James Russell Lowell, James Greenleaf Whittier and Ralph Waldo Emerson as well as within Boston's freed black community who provided much of the subscription list of Garrison's newspaper.

Ancient republicanism in Rome and Greece had been based on slavery; slaves freed their masters from drudgery and gave them the opportunity to consider the public good. John Calhoun supported Southern slavery as assuring equality among all who were white; rather John Quincy Adams saw instead the domineering quality of the slave owner. "The National Republicans" under Adams found their ideology in opposition to Jackson but claimed they also represented the national interest across class lines. Evolving into the Whig Party, their name claimed the mantle of those who opposed the Stuarts and George III. Starting in 1831, John Quincy Adams as a Whig represented Massachusetts in the House of Representatives.

The annexation of Texas could symbolize the victory of the "slave power" that pervaded American political life following the Missouri Compromise. Rather than the claim of freedom for the American settlers, it appeared to be a response by slave owners to the emancipation of slaves by Mexico in 1829. Postponed from 1836 to 1845, Adams opposed annexation, rightfully claiming that war with Mexico would follow.

Petitions to Congress had been an accepted practice based on the Declaration of Independence and the First Amendment. Petitions to abolish slavery had been recurrent. From the start of his Congressional career, Adams had presented such petitions to abolish slavery and the slave trade in the District of Columbia. In 1836, the House passed a resolution forbidding the large increase in anti-slavery petitions from being considered. At the beginning of each new Congress, despite being reviled, Adams invoking his personal familial connection with the Declaration of Independence, fought against the re-institution of this "gag rule." In 1842, he offered a petition from Haverhill Massachusetts that seemed to evade the rule. It sought dissolution of the Union on the grounds that "one section of the country was being drained to sustain the views and course of another."

This echoed in some way the stance of the abolitionists under William Lloyd Garrison. They had avoided political participation on the grounds that the U.S. Constitution was an evil compact that institutionalized the slave power by incorporating the "three-fifths rule" recognizing slavery. Adams became a popular figure when an attempt by the House to censure him was unsuccessful. The suppression of these petitions being conflated with the larger issue of the suppression of liberty, it brought the issue to the forefront in Washington and the gag rule was finally overthrown in 1844. Adams recognized as an heroic "man of principle," the mantle of Boston reformism was passed to a new generation while also shared with a wider circle than the Adams family.

In 1845, Lewis Hayden, an escaped slave from Kentucky, first appeared in Boston to raise money for the building of an African Methodist Episcopal (AME) church in Detroit. Living in New Bedford, he was accepted in 1847 as an "agent" in the anti-slavery crusade by the American Anti-Slavery Society as a speaker similar to the role of Frederick Douglass. He then moved in 1849 to Boston where he opened a clothing store and a boarding house on South Street that became a station on the Underground Railroad. He was thus in a position to participate in the response in Boston to the Fugitive Slave Law following the Compromise of 1850. Breaking with the non-violence espoused by Lloyd Garrison, Hayden was elected president of the black community and member of the bi-racial "Committee on Vigilance and Safety". Their goal was to act in defiance of the Fugitive Slave Act, to protect actively the 2000 black citizens of Boston, many of whom were fugitives.

The implementation of the Fugitive Slave Law of 1793 had long come into conflict with personal liberty laws in the northern states. As early as 1836, the Massachusetts Judiciary had been receptive to freedom of slaves taken to a free state. The "Latimer Case" in 1842 in Boston once again showed opposition to slave catching. Excitement in the North was fed by *The North Star* edited by Frederick Douglass and by *Latimer's Journal* edited by the renowned mathematician and abolitionist Dr Henry I. Bowditch. It was the passage of the Fugitive Slave Act and its aggressive implementation under Federal law in the

1850s that jeopardized those living under the protection of Massachusetts law. Moreover, it required prosecution of those who participated in helping fugitives. The apparent impingement on the liberty of whites as well as blacks brought to a larger public in Boston the issues so long avoided.

Headed by the Unitarian minister Theodore Parker, Bostonians of substance such as Richard Henry Dana, Jr, Dr Samuel Gridley Howe (founder of the Perkins Institution for the Blind) and John Albion Andrew (later Republican Civil War governor) were among those who volunteered their services to the Boston Committee of Vigilance and Safety to protect fugitives. Dana's support for anti-slavery arose out of his own experience of the brutality with which seamen were treated documented in his book *Two Years before the Mast*. However, in 1851, in an early test case of the recently passed Fugitive Slave Law, Charles Lowell, the minister of the West Church, was the only one of the well-known ministers to participate at a meeting in Faneuil Hall designed to unite in protection of fugitive slaves living in Boston. A large show of police force in this 1851 case supported the judicial decision to return to slavery the fugitive whose name was Sims.

However, subsequent community efforts were successful to remove threatened fugitives to safety in Canada and elsewhere along the Underground Railway. By the time of the case of Anthony Burns, a member of the Twelfth Baptist Church of Leonard Grimes, the passage of the Kansas-Nebraska Bill in 1854 had made support for fugitives widespread, even in the business community. Boston now mourned his capture as though for a popular hero. Thousands lined the route in witness to their support of the fugitive when a large military force escorted Burns to the ship returning him to slavery. No further slaves were sent back. The Fugitive Slave Law had now been nullified in Boston and the South looked upon Boston as its bitterest enemy. Despite the economic interests of the Boston cotton mill owners ("Cotton Whigs"), the moral issue so long espoused by the handful of abolitionists appeared to triumph.

The "Boston Hymn" composed by Ralph Waldo Emerson and read at the celebration of the issuance of the Emancipation Proclamation on January 1st 1863 recognized the close connection of the people of this city and the cause of the abolition of slavery. Even more moving and far more popular was the "Battle Hymn of the Republic" by Julia

Ward Howe, the wife of the abolitionist Samuel Gridley Howe. She wrote it from the earlier tune created at Fort Warren in Boston Harbor called "John Brown's Body." Boston seemed to epitomize the Union cause in the Civil War, devoted as it now was to the abolition of slavery.

William Lloyd Garrison chose Boston as his home in light of its history as the "Cradle of Liberty" but found little support there. The degree to which he could arouse anger is illustrated by a mob that dragged him through the streets after attacking him in his printing offices in Boston in 1835. It was then a city then hardly more sympathetic to his cause than places in the South. However, by the end of the decade hundreds of Garrisonian anti-slavery societies had appeared throughout New England. During the 1840s and 1850s, the anti-slavery elite found no support among the recent Irish immigrants competing with Boston's small free black population for unskilled jobs.

Uncompromising in his opinions but also politically astute about the fate of third parties, Garrison refused to endorse the commitment to political action that during the 1840s and 1850s created the Liberty Party. Later the anti-slavery forces eventually entered via the Free Soil Party into the coalition that elected Abraham Lincoln in 1860. Garrison claimed the Constitution to be tainted by its support for the maintenance of slavery, to be a "covenant with death and an agreement with hell." He bitterly broke with Frederick Douglass and others when advocating break-up of the Union to separate from the slave holding states. Despite his long standing pacifism, Garrison was supportive of Lincoln during the Civil War. Confident that the war would lead to emancipation, he was circumspect in seeking the Proclamation. He supported conscription against a Boston mob and broke his long standing refusal to vote by doing so for Lincoln in 1864 based on the Republican Party commitment to the passage of a constitutional amendment regarding slavery. He felt that his life work reached its final achievement in 1865 with the passage of the 13th Amendment.

Figure 26 - William Lloyd Garrison

William Lloyd Garrison, born in 1805 in Newburyport Massachusetts, grew up fatherless and poor. Addressed as Lloyd, he was apprenticed to a printer and became a newspaper editor. Sober and industrious and a deeply religious Baptist, he was converted to a lifelong commitment to anti-slavery views in 1828. Self-educated, he became in 1831 editor of *The Liberator*, the leading anti-slavery newspaper committed to "Emancipation Now." Unlike the American Colonization Society founded in 1816 that expressed contempt and favored deportation to Africa of those freed, Garrison was an abolitionist who also supported equality for the 400,000 already free in the United States but living under onerous Black codes. He founded what was at first a tiny New England and American Anti-Slavery Society with a largely free black membership. He also advocated women's suffrage and temperance.

Figure 27 - Wendell Phillips

Among Garrison's most influential adherents was Wendell Phillips. Born in Boston in 1811 into a prominent family, he went to Boston Latin School, Harvard College and Harvard Law School. He committed himself to the cause of anti-slavery at a meeting in Faneuil Hall in 1837 sponsored by Garrison. He spoke eloquently in commemoration of the memory of Elijah Lovejoy killed while defending his press from an anti-slavery mob in Alton Illinois. Continuing to speak on the Lyceum circuit. he joined Garrison in the 1840s in his drive toward repeal of the Constitution and the dissolution of the Union.

During 1854 while opposing the implementation of the Fugitive Slave Law, Phillips was indicted for his participation in the attempted rescue from jail of Anthony Burns. However, impatient with Lincoln's conciliatory policy toward amnesty for former Confederates, Phillips broke with Garrison in 1864 and considered supporting Salmon P. Chase for president before the latter's withdrawal; and then John C Fremont.

Figure 28 - Charles Sumner

Charles Sumner was born in Boston in 1811, the eldest of nine children, to a father who had attended Harvard but earned little as a lawyer until appointed Sheriff of Suffolk County. Young Sumner, born on the wrong side of Beacon Hill, went to Boston Latin School on his own initiative despite his father's initial objection and then to Harvard College. Although an uninspired student, he was an assiduous reader and became an accomplished speaker. A protégé of Associate Supreme Court Justice Joseph Story at Harvard Law School, he studied constantly. Entering law practice, he preferred being an editor of his mentor's papers and on the editorial board of *The American Jurist* and an instructor at the Law School.

Under the influence of William Ellery Channing, Sumner became concerned with prison and educational reform and with slavery Encouraged by his friend Samuel Gridley Howe, Sumner supported the efforts of Horace Mann to establish normal schools for teacher education. He first received public notice for his 4th of July 1845 oration in which, along with the Peace Society founded by Channing, Sumner went beyond the cautious stand of his elders to argue forcefully in the presence of a largely military audience against the glorification of war and its utter uselessness.

Not yet identifying with the Garrisonian abolitionists; nevertheless, he now joined with the group of younger "Conscience Whigs" in opposing the annexation of Texas as a slave state in 1845. Opposed to the subsequent Mexican War and the spread of slavery into the conquered territories, he intemperately attacked the conservative Boston Whig establishment for their willingness to compromise with what he considered an unmitigated evil. He broke from the Whig Party in the election of 1848 to join the newly formed Free Soil Party. As a result of engineering the temporary alliance of the Free Soil and Democratic Party, he was eventually elected by a very narrow margin to be United States senator from Massachusetts in 1851, to remain until 1874.

In the spirit of equality abroad in that year of revolution throughout Europe, in 1849 he took the case of a black child denied entrance to a school near her home in favor of the single segregated black public school. He criticized racial inequality in terms of its human and social costs as "cramping liberty" to those on both sides of the color line rather than merely its legal or moral incongruity. Eventually in 1855, Massachusetts was the pioneer in outlawing segregated public schools. Along with others such as Salmon P. Chase, Sumner in Congress spoke in opposition to the Fugitive Slave Law incorporated in the Compromise of 1850.

His speech on the "The Crime against Kansas" given on May 20-21 1856 opposed the violent implementation by Southerners of the Kansas-Nebraska Act of 1854. That speech personally impugning South Carolina's Senator Butler led the latter's distant relative Congressman Preston Brooks to attack Sumner on the Senate floor. Badly injured, Sumner became a martyr to the abolitionist cause. Now a member of the newly formed Republican Party, he was seen as having joined the long series of New England's martyrs struggling to uphold liberty.

Sumner's commitment to racial equality continued throughout his career. From his position as long time chair of the Senate Foreign

Relations Committee, he exerted his power to support domestic initiatives for racial equality. These included emancipation in the District of Columbia in 1862 and the thorough implementation of reconstruction after the end of the war in that jurisdiction under the direct control of the Congress. At a national level, he supported the impeachment of President Andrew Johnson in 1867. Particularly during the session of 1869-1870, he was the leader in requiring equal rights as a condition for readmission of former states of the Confederacy, leading to the eventual passage of the 15th Voting Rights Amendment in 1870.

Deprived of his committee position because of his opposition to the annexation of Santo Domingo, he nevertheless supported his enemy President Grant in the passage of the Enforcement Act of 1871 against the Ku-Klux Klan. Faithful to the end, even as a "Liberal Republican" opposing President Grant's re-election in 1872, he futilely still tried to attach a more sweeping guarantee of black civil rights to the bill granting final amnesty to former Confederate officials.

1848 had marked the beginning of the break-up of the Whig Party that had safeguarded the interests of the Massachusetts Brahmins. Split on the issue of slavery, the so-called "Conscience Whigs" entered the Free-Soil Party. With Martin Van Buren the candidate for president and Charles Francis Adams for vice-resident, the Free Soilers ran better in Massachusetts than anywhere else, eventually achieving a large representation in the legislature. Sumner, head of the Free Soil state committee, welcomed a Democratic liaison by injecting a "class bias" as well as anti-slavery into his party platform. In 1848, he had opposed equally "the lords of the lash and of the loom."

Closely following on the introduction of the bills relating to the Compromise of 1850 such as the Fugitive Slave Act, the election of Charles Sumner to the U.S. Senate as a Democrat in succession to the late Daniel Webster marked the overthrow of the long standing Whig Party supremacy in Massachusetts.

Former Whig leaders like the wealthy Amos A. Lawrence eventually organized the conservative business elements to form the Constitution Union Party in the election of 1860. The candidacy of the long standing Whig politician and Harvard president Edward Everett for vice-president in 1860 election reflected the party's strong Boston origins. In a final blow, with the ascendency of the Republican Party and

Lincoln taking 63% of the Massachusetts vote in the election of 1860, Amos A. Lawrence received only 7% of the vote for his gubernatorial candidacy among the voters of Groton Massachusetts, the home of the Lawrence family.

3.7 Boston and the Civil War

The Civil War closed off supplies to the New England cotton mills; by the summer of 1862, two-thirds of all spindles had been idled and production was one-quarter of normal. However, woolen mills proliferated and the making of uniforms was highly profitable with the use of what was called "shoddy." Ready-made clothing also became popular. Large scale manufacture of shoes for equipping soldiers became a New England industry based on the invention of special machinery modifying the standard sewing machine. The Springfield Massachusetts Armory produced 350,000 rifles annually using interchangeable parts. The Alger Iron Works in South Boston, manned largely by Irish workmen, produced many of the "Rodman" cannons used in coast defense. Ironclads rolled off the shipyards at City Point, also in South Boston. The industrial revolution that had started in New England a generation earlier now accelerated fed as it was by government contracts.

John Albion Andrew had been elected governor as a Republican in 1860. An anti-slavery lawyer, he had been a "Conscience Whig," and a member of the Free Soil Party. He was energetic in organizing and equipping the Massachusetts militia even before the attack on Fort Sumter. Four Massachusetts regiments were among the first to be activated with a total of twenty-three regiments formed during the first year of war. The 800 men strong 6th Massachusetts entrained on April 17th to Washington; on the 19th, they arrived at Baltimore's President Street station to be transported by horse car to the Camden Street station of the Baltimore & Ohio (B&O) to reach besieged Washington. After seven of the ten companies had crossed, violence broke out with casualties to both the troops and the crowd. The 6th Massachusetts was among the first of the volunteer regiments to arrive in Washington; they formed the garrison that helped lift the siege of the city. Those wounded in the riot in Baltimore were hospitalized in the Washington Infirmary, the first casualties of the war.

Figure 29 - Benjamin Butler

Placed in command of the Massachusetts militia regiments as brigadier general through his political connections in Washington, the unlikely figure of Benjamin Butler cut a wide swath during the war. A Lowell mill-owner noted for his support of such radical innovations as the ten-hour day, he was without significant military experience. Although a Democrat and originally pro-slavery, he retained his appointment by Lincoln as major-general of volunteers throughout the war. Although incompetent militarily, he represented support by both important constituencies of "Radical" Republicans and War Democrats.

In direct command of the 8th Massachusetts designated to follow the 6th Massachusetts, he arrived in Philadelphia on April 20th to find the railroad line to Baltimore and beyond to Washington disrupted. The Maryland authorities had destroyed the bridges from the north along the Northern Central Railroad from Harrisburg while a mob destroyed the bridge carrying the Philadelphia, Wilmington and Baltimore Railroad (PW&B) to its President Street station near Fells Point. Also destroyed were the telegraphic connections from the north to Washington. The capital was besieged, cut off from reinforcements and from any connection with the north.

Using the still intact PW&B line from Philadelphia to Perryville on the Susquehanna River, subsequent troop movements under Butler were able to bypass Baltimore. They used a ferry from Perryville to join the Annapolis line of the B&O and then enter Washington. There was particular care that the ferry boat landing in Annapolis was on the federally-owned soil of the U.S. Naval Academy to allay Maryland's Southern sensibilities. Finally, on April 25th, the 7th New York and the 8th Massachusetts marched down Pennsylvania Avenue to relieve the isolated capital city.

In early May 1861, Butler also on his own initiative occupied the crucial Relay House immediately outside Baltimore where the B&O Washington Branch ran to the national capital; he then occupied Baltimore itself a week later in mid-May. Relieved of his command in Baltimore by General Winfield Scott for far exceeding his orders, Butler was commander of Fortress Monroe, garrisoned by several other New England regiments. There again, he had a fundamental influence on the course of the war by confiscating the slaves working for the Confederacy and declaring them "contraband." Within two months, about nine hundred escaped slaves had gathered near the fort. This initiated the process by which the Fugitive Slave Law came to be abrogated in practice, the passage of the Congressional Confiscation Acts and the eventual issuance of the Emancipation Proclamation.

Once transferred to Louisiana after the capture of New Orleans, Butler again operated freely outside of regulations. He enlisted in the spring of 1862 several regiments of New Orleans free blacks enrolled in the "Louisiana Native Guards" who had once been part of the Confederate Army. Not only were they the first regiments with blacks as fighting soldiers, they were unique by having their primarily black officers remain in place. The issuance of the Emancipation Proclamation on January 1863 finally included the provision for the active recruitment of blacks, previously used only as auxiliaries, into the Union army.

Figure 30 - Oliver Wendell Holmes, Jr

Another military engagement with implications for Massachusetts troops occurred in October 1861 at Ball's Bluff near Leesburg Virginia. In a poorly organized assault and even more poorly managed retreat across the Potomac River, many casualties occurred. These included many of the Harvard men who were officers in the 20th Massachusetts Regiment including 2nd Lieutenant Oliver Wendell Holmes Jr. Mustered in late August 1861, this regiment fought throughout the war in every subsequent engagement of the Army of the Potomac. Holmes, promoted to captain, was also seriously wounded at Antietam in September 1862 and once more before the end of the war.

The casualties of the 20th Massachusetts were the greatest of any of the Massachusetts regiments. For example, on July 2nd 1863 at Gettysburg, while being held in reserve, the regiment was nevertheless in the line of fire of Confederate artillery that led to the death of their commander Paul Revere Jr. On the next day after the sustained Confederate barrage, they met Pickett's Charge and managed in hand-to-hand combat to help close a crucial break in the line near the copse of trees on Cemetery Ridge. Considered by many the "High Water Mark" of the Confederacy, the memorial stone for the 20th Massachusetts at the site is of Roxbury pudding stone, the material that underlies much of the southern basin of Massachusetts Bay.

The 1st South Carolina Colored Regiment was one of the first recruited starting in mid-November 1862 from the Sea Island area on the Carolina Coast already occupied by Union forces. Its colonel was Thomas Wentworth Higginson, a Boston abolitionist and Harvard College graduate who had been a supporter of John Brown and the Emigrant Aid Society supporting anti-slavery settlers in Kansas. Formerly a captain in 51st Massachusetts stationed at Beaufort South Carolina, the other members of the new regiment's officer corps were also mainly from New England abolitionist families. Similarly, commanding the fellow 2nd South Carolina Regiment was another abolitionist who had also fought in "Bleeding Kansas." Together, they participated in the capture of Jacksonville Florida.

In addition to being an important source of long staple high quality cotton to New England mills, the Sea Island area was also home to a large scale New England-based and staffed educational program for the freed slaves. Sponsored by the "Boston Education Commission," it was funded by prominent Boston Republican businessmen like the railroad investor John Murray Forbes and was led by the assistant pastor of the Old South Meeting House.

Figure 31 - Robert Gould Shaw and the 54th Massachusetts

In an action long sought by free blacks like Lewis Hayden and Leonard Grimes in Massachusetts and other northern states, the colored regiment first raised in the north to be "ever sent to war," was activated by Governor John A Andrew in January 1863. Recruitment was encouraged by black leaders including Frederick Douglass whose own son Lewis was one who enlisted. The 54th Massachusetts Colored Regiment was led by Robert Gould Shaw, the scion of a leading New England abolitionist family with inherited wealth. He attended Harvard during 1856-1859 but did not graduate and travelled widely in Europe.

Shaw took command of the 54th on the request of Governor Andrew, anxious for its success by having a man associated with such impeccable upper class credentials. Arriving in Boston from their nearby training camp, Shaw led his men in late May 1863 past thousands of spectators up Boylston Street around the Boston Common and eventually along Beacon Street by the State House and the reviewing stand with Governor Andrew. This was the review later commemorated in the monument on the Boston Common opposite the State House by Augustus Saint-Gaudens that celebrates Shaw in his nobility above his troops.

The 54th joined the 2nd South Carolina in early June 1863 in its first expedition near St Simon's Island; and then later in the summer in the much larger attack on Charleston Harbor. On 16th July, three companies of the 54th manned the right of the Union line on James Island. In this its first major engagement, it fought well alongside the white 10th Connecticut Regiment even without food or potable water. On the 18th July, they took part in another attack on Morris Island. Unknown to the commanders, Battery Wagner in Charleston Harbor needed to be attacked from a very narrow beach that made the attack by the tired and hungry 54th much more difficult with deadly consequences including that of their commander. Acclaimed as heroes, the 54th and Robert Gould Shaw were the subject of poems and the iconic statue by Augustus Saint-Gaudens on the route of march they had taken past the State House. Their bravery against great odds paved the way for the greater acceptance and equality of pay for all the subsequent approximately 200,000 members of the U.S. Colored Troops.

In addition to emancipation and greater acceptance of blacks as potential free citizens was the concomitant more independent role of women during the Civil War. Again part of the reformist agenda heavily peopled by Bostonians, women's rights including suffrage were frequently coupled with involvement in the anti-slavery crusade. Since they were abolitionists before becoming suffragists, the "Women's Loyal National League" in Boston under Elizabeth Cady Stanton, Susan B Anthony and Lucy Stone propagandized for loyalty to the Union, for emancipation and for a constitutional amendment confirming abolition of slavery.

The key differences appeared when the word "male" was inserted into the body of the 15th Amendment that caused a split not only between the abolitionist and the feminist movements but a split in 1869 within the women's rights movement itself. The "American Women's Suffrage Association" under the Bostonian Lucy Stone accepted the 15th Amendment giving suffrage to black males while the "National Women's Suffrage Association" under the New Yorkers Elizabeth Cady Stanton and Susan B Anthony did not. This breach was not to be healed until the 1890s.

Even without the long deferral in the success of the feminist movement focused as it was on women's suffrage, women did begin to act independently albeit within their own still traditional nurturing role during the war. Such independent activity carried over into the post-Civil War era.

3.8 Clara Barton and the Civil War

Figure 32 - Clara Barton

Immediately after the blooding of the 6th Massachusetts on Baltimore streets, Clara Barton walked over from her job at the Patent Office to their bivouac in the Rotunda of the U.S. Capitol. She discovered that many of men were from near her home near Worcester Massachusetts and nursed them to health. Born in Oxford Massachusetts in 1821, she discovered her life role to be a nurse when, merely eleven years old, she nursed her brother to health after a severe injury. A school teacher, she was denied because of her gender the executive position in a school she had founded. She moved to Washington in 1854 in response to the opportunity offered to women for jobs in the Patent Office at pay equivalent to men only to lose her job under the next presidential administration. She returned to Washington for a job at the Patent Office in 1860 in time for her new expanded role in the Civil War.

She next found her role to bring supplies to help the wounded directly on the battlefields starting at the Second Battle of Bull Run in the summer of 1862 and particularly at the Battle of Antietam in September 1862. Once the army ambulance service improved on the battlefield, she later founded the "Office of Missing Soldiers" to record all those hospitalized or wounded to identify those eligible for pensions. After the war, she became active with Susan B. Anthony in the women's suffrage movement, an ongoing commitment for the rest of her life. During the Franco-Prussian War in 1871, she once again brought help to soldiers and refugees. She founded in 1881 the American Red Cross that she led until the turn of the 20th century.

It is significant that the institutionalization of help on the battlefield occurred via the "United States Sanitary Commission" (USSC). Rather than Boston, it originated and was sustained by persons from New York. By its superior resources and initiative, New York now began to take leadership from Boston in this field as it had in others. The genesis of the USSC was a group of upper class women in New York City who met at the Cooper Union on April 30, 1861 to form the "Women's Central Association for Relief" (WCAR). Hannibal Hamlin, Lincoln's Vice-President, chaired the meeting. Dr Valentine Mott, the leading medical figure of the city, accepted the presidency. The well-born Miss Louise Lee Schuyler (a descendent of the family of the wife of Alexander Hamilton) was executive secretary.

Its president was Henry Whitney Bellows. Born in Boston, he graduated from Harvard College in 1832 and the Harvard Divinity School in 1837. In 1839, he became minister of the First Congregational (Unitarian) Church in New York City (later called All Souls). During his lifelong ministry, he became the leading representative for his church throughout the country. The treasurer of the USSC was the New Yorker George Templeton Strong. Born in

New Jersey in 1820, he was a graduate of Columbia University in 1838 and the Columbia Law School. A law partner in what became New York City's oldest lasting law firm, he was also a vestryman of the Episcopal Trinity Church in lower Manhattan.

Chapter 4
The Proper Bostonians 1865-1914

THE GREAT FIRE AT BOSTON,
NOVEMBER 9th & 10th 1872.

The Fire began on Saturday evening, and raged for 15 hours, destroying over Sixty Acres of Buildings, among which were whole blocks of the finest Granite Stores on the continent, and property estimated at nearly $ 100,000,000.

Figure 33 - The Great Fire of 1872

Introduction

At the start of the 19th century, the business district was limited to the export trade and centered on the waterfront and the market halls augmented by the Quincy Market built in the 1820s. After the Civil War, the central business district of warehouses that existed south of the Long Wharf (now State Street) became the site of manufacturing. It increased in size to affect the residential area of inner South End. The old tenement area of Fort Hill was gradually removed to form what is now Post Office Square; the hill itself was taken down to provide the fill on which Atlantic Avenue was built. The Great Fire of 1872 cleared the area to the west sparing only the Old South Church. The area became further committed to warehousing to hold the wholesale trade in wool and leather goods that moved down from the North End in the last quarter of the century.

The wholesale food markets remained to the north of State Street and impinged on the residential area of the North End. That area's Italian immigrant inhabitants were required to live near these premises to appear early for their work in the produce markets. The long existent financial area of banks and insurance also lay to the north of State Street; as it increased, it impinged on the elite residential area of Beacon Hill but did not extinguish it. As dry goods fell in price due to improvements in manufacturing and mass consumption increased, it became worthwhile for manufacturers to begin to display goods in showrooms for direct sale to the consumer. This brought about the retail area on Washington and Tremont Streets between the wholesale area and the Common. The streetcar lines running on those streets supported the transport of the shoppers causing the streets to become so congested to be supplemented after the turn of the century by subways. The first line ran along the Common between Park and Boylston Streets, the other on Washington Street.

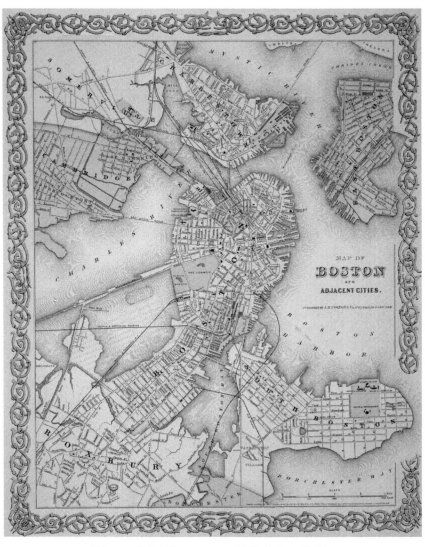

Figure 34 - Boston and Vicinity 1850s

4.1 The Enclosure of the Back Bay

The adjoining map shows the filling in of the South Cove and the portion of the Back Bay adjoining the Boston Neck and the South End. The expansion of the Boston Neck to the east by the filling in the 1850s of the South Cove created the land for a large row-house development originally designed for the Yankee middle class that was called the "New South End." It contained the new land south of Dover Street where the old Boston Neck widened on its way to Roxbury on the mainland. A large house built on Washington Street near Dover Street in 1848 seemed to presage a district of luxurious country homes. This was not to be. The South End became developed with row houses with checkerboard streets interspersed with small parks in the style of Georgian London. Initially following the pattern of Beacon Hill with its squares, it was most typically characterized by mansard roofs, high stoops and bow fronts, the last a replication by speculative builders of the more elegant and wider Bulfinch Beacon Hill originals.

The filling in of the large body of increasingly noxious water called the Back Bay could also permit the widening of the neck on its western side. There were no longer any hills in Boston that could be leveled to provide land fill. It was necessary to bring gravel and soil from Needham by rail. The portion incorporating Columbus and Huntington Avenues to the east of the Boston and Worcester railroad tracks was under the control of the city of Boston; the western portion the responsibility of the Commonwealth of Massachusetts.

By the 1860s, houses in the South End were being sold to lower class mechanics. The housing with relatively narrow front width on Columbus Avenue was particularly problematic in its financing. Following the 1873 Panic and the bankruptcy of many of the mortgagees, the entire area became un-fashionable. The shortage of lower cost housing soon converted the South End to the rooming houses it continued to contain for the next one hundred years. The Boston City Hospital (BCH), built between 1861 and 1864, remains as one of the institutions then built as well as a number of Catholic institutions, including the Jesuit Church of Immaculate Conception in 1861 and the Gothic Holy Cross Cathedral in 1867.

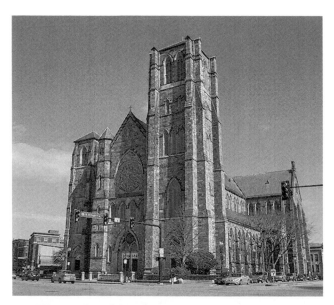

Figure 35 - The Cathedral of Holy Cross

Figure 36 - Boston City Hospital

Boston College was also founded by Jesuits in the South End in 1863, growing steadily to 500 students in 1905. The modern history of the college dates from 1907 when Thomas Ignatius Gasson became president. In 1911, he moved Boston College to its present site, the former Lawrence estate in Chestnut Hill in Brookline. It has grown to become one of the nation's leading Catholic institutions of higher learning.

The greatest accomplishment of this era was the completion starting in the 1860s of what became an upper class residential district delineated by the Public Gardens on the east, Beacon Street and the river on the north and the Fenway on the west. The entire area differed from that of the South End by its wider streets in axial lines that mimic Haussmann's Paris. Commonwealth Avenue was laid out as a Parisian boulevard two hundred feet wide with a median mall connecting the 1869 equestrian statue by Thomas Ball of George Washington in the Public Gardens to the park on the Fenway. Almost half the land in the Back Bay development was given over to parks and streets; twelve churches of various Protestant denominations and architectural styles filled the major corner sites starting with the spire of the former Federal Street Church at Arlington and Boylston Streets opposite the Public Gardens. The names of Newbury and Marlborough were given to the relatively wide streets laid out parallel to Commonwealth Avenue aligned with Beacon Street along the Charles River.

Separated by the railroad lines going to Providence and Worcester, the streets on the east of the tracks including Columbus and Huntington Avenues (under the aegis of the City of Boston) developed in relation to Washington Street. Along with the streets of the Back Bay district, they connected to the earlier city at a forty-five degree angle at Copley Square but not readily to each other at Berkeley and Dartmouth Streets and Massachusetts Avenue. The Boston & Providence tracks formed a long impenetrable barrier until streets could be cut through and Park Square replaced the Providence railroad station after the South Station was built in 1899.

The Back Bay District on the west (under the aegis of the Commonwealth) was enabled to develop as an upper class entity. No shopping place existed until the S.S. Pierce store opened in 1886 at the corner of Dartmouth Street fronting onto Copley Square. Appropriately in the mediaeval revival style, the store echoed some of the nearby mansions being built at the same time.

4.2 Frederick Law Olmsted and the Boston Park System

Figure 37 - Frederick Law Olmsted

Olmsted was one of the founders of the peculiarly Bostonian "American Social Science Association" (ASSA) whose charter stressed the "responsibilities of the gifted and educated classes toward the weak." He gave his famous address "Public Parks and the Enlargement of Towns" to the ASSA under the auspices of the Lowell Institute in Boston in 1870. He pointed out that life span is shorter; vice and crime, disease and misery greater in the town than the country. There is a hardening and a selfishness that occurs in the daily life of the streets. The antidote is to incorporate nature into the environs of the city. In founding the profession of landscape architect, beauty and appropriateness in landscape and architectural arrangements were not ends in themselves. They were but devices to secure moral aims; a means to promote human

> betterment, both physical and spiritual. Although most famous for his work in Central Park and Prospect Park and elsewhere, Olmsted lived and worked in Brookline adjacent to Boston and had a major impact on the development of Boston during his lifetime.

The appropriately named Muddy River provided the western boundary of the Back Bay. It also provided the opportunity for the firm founded by Frederick Law Olmsted finally to participate from 1878 to 1895 in creating a comprehensive park system for Boston. Credited with the emergence of landscape architecture as a profession in the United States, Olmsted's work incorporating nature into urban settings was based on the long held New England elite belief that American society needed to fortify itself against the crude and materialistic impulses of popular culture. He feared that immigration was overwhelming the cities with foreign ways and beliefs. The whole collection of city ills, its filth, ugliness and disorder, was thought to be causing a widespread disease across the entire society, leading to the social pathologies. Olmsted was part of the intellectual nativist elite that shared a commitment to focus professional intelligence on goals of social order and cohesion that underlay the Progressive movement.. He was however much more optimistic than others such as Henry Adams with the latter's bleak misgivings about the future of mass democracy.

Olmsted's first job in Boston in 1878 was to re-create a flowing stream from portions of Muddy River originally a salt water marsh that had become a sewer. He had the swampy area dredged to form a more sinuous river than even nature provided and placed intercepting sewers to divert the waste from entering the stream. The connection with the Charles, then still a tidal river, was regulated to maintain an even height and prevent overflow with high tide. The term he chose, Back Bay Fens, was an archaic word for a boggy marsh. The adjacent parkway became the attractive "Fenway." The now cleaned-up river emptied into the Charles at the Charles-Gate. By 1890, Commonwealth Avenue ran northwest from Massachusetts Avenue through what is now Kenmore Square and on to Brighton.

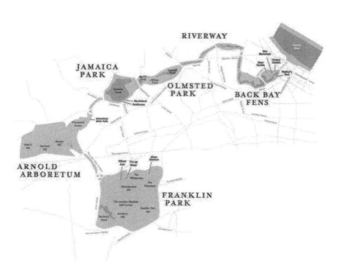

Figure 38 - The Emerald Necklace

Unlike New York's Central Park, the Back Bay Fens became part of what became a poetically named regional "emerald necklace" Actually planned by his young protégé Charles Eliot, it extended throughout the city from the Boston Common and the Public Garden. Born in Cambridge in 1859 the son of Charles William Eliot, Charles Eliot graduated from Harvard College in 1882. Intent on becoming a landscape architect, he studied at Harvard's Bussey Institute before becoming apprenticed to Frederick Law Olmsted in 1883. While there, he started work under Olmsted on the Arnold Arboretum that incorporated the Bussey Institute as well as the other components of the Boston Park system. He initiated in 1891 the "Trustees of Public Reservations," the first organization designed to hold land in trust that was of scenic beauty like a library would hold books and a museum would hold art. After work on his own, he became a partner in the Olmsted firm before dying of spinal meningitis at a young age in 1897.

After his work on the Fens, Olmsted designed the Arnold Arboretum on the grounds of the country estate of Woodland Hills originally laid out by Samuel Bussey. The funds for its development as a study center came from the bequest to Harvard by James Arnold, a New Bedford merchant, long interested in horticulture. A public park from 1882, the maintenance and policing of the Arnold Arboretum are the responsibility of the city; the choice of trees is that of Harvard botanists. Reflecting its dual origins in both science and art, it served as a study center for botanists and for amateur landscape gardeners. The road through the stands of trees still follows the "natural" 19th century classification based on the arrangement of leaves proposed by Bentham and Hooker from London's Kew Gardens but also meets artistic considerations by being lined by picturesque flowering shrubs.

In the winter of 1881 while visiting his friend H.H. Richardson in Brookline, Olmsted decided to move from New York to that town. It seemed to epitomize the new concept of a "suburb." It was a place that combined urban services such as sewers and other municipal services of high quality while retaining a rustic charm complete with "The Country Club," progenitor of all others. His Brookline home-office called "Fairsted" (named after his ancestral village in Essex) became his headquarters for the next half-century. Brookline was the preferred home of the Boston elite fleeing from the city they could no longer control. The "country improved," it was a model of the pastoral suburb that the Olmsted firm would export to many other American cities during the next generation.

To his surprise, Olmsted had now been entrusted in the 1880s by the Boston Park Department under the Irish-born Mayor Hugh O'Brien with the design of an entire park system, the first in the country so envisaged. That same year the president of the Bostonian Society, in his annual remarks, marveled at the completion of the additional lands that changed the entire appearance of what had been the small pear-shaped Shawmut peninsula. The design of a park system seemed timely. The Arboretum and Fens would unite with other waterways and roads. A large "kettle hole" where glacial ice had once settled called Jamaica Pond was the centerpiece of its adjacent flatland named Jamaica Plain. This area became connected to the remainder of the "Emerald Necklace" by parkways such as the Jamaica Way and received the name of Olmsted (Jamaica) Park in 1900. Skirting the western border of the city with Brookline, the Jamaica Way ran on the Boston side past the shamrock incised shutters of the iconic home of Boston's perennial mayor, James Michael Curley

The capstone of Olmsted's work in Boston was Franklin Park carved out of a mainly cleared farm land valley in West Roxbury. In his preoccupation to incorporate nature into the experience of town dwellers, he designed one part to remain an old-growth stand of trees.

His major concern was to protect a contemplative pastoral "Country Park;" an open expanse of sloping lawn enclosed by woods. The other portion was converted to active recreational space called "The Ante-Park" including a Playstead for active sports by young boys that increasingly encroached on the former more natural area. To insure the rustic integrity of Franklin Park, an active recreational area called Franklin Field opened farther down Blue Hill Avenue in an area considered unbuildable by Olmsted. However, Franklin Park never accomplished Olmsted's over-riding goal to reform the urban masses by their connection with nature. Rather by the 1890s, it became the site for a golf course and bicycle races as well as a wild animal zoo and, later even a formal rose garden.

Even beyond the boundaries of the city that lies in a sunken basin surrounded by hills with its crest at Franklin Park, are the parks that reflect the natural characteristics of these hills. To the south, the Blue Hills Reservation with the Great Blue Hill and the Neponset River Valley. To the north are the Middlesex Fells with Bear Hill and the Mystic River Valley. Saved by the Metropolitan Parks (now District) Commission in the 1890s, Revere Beach was in addition an improved strand of public beach to the north; Nantasket Beach to the south.

4.3 The Back Bay and the American Renaissance

Figure 39 - The Trinity Church

Replacing the original destroyed in the Great Fire of 1872, the Episcopal neo-Romanesque Trinity Church by Henry Hobson Richardson built in 1877, was one of the first reflecting a more European sensibility. The Congregational-Unitarian evolved into the Anglican and Anglo-Catholic among fashionable Bostonians of religious bent. Its rector Phillips Brooks. of proper Bostonian stock, was born a Unitarian and descendant of John Cotton to become a bishop of the Episcopal Church. Architecture during the post-Civil War "Gilded Age" was eclectic in that any single building might contain a mixture of styles derived from the past. Influences from abroad could include the French Second Empire or the German Rundbogenstil (round arch style). Richardson combined elements of all with the Romanesque into a monumental massive style that expressed "grandeur and repose" that transcended its sources to form a totality that was American in expression.

HENRY HOBSON RICHARDSON

Born in 1843 near New Orleans, Henry Hobson Richardson came to Harvard College in the class of 1859. A member of the Porcellian Club, his connection with the elite stood him in good stead during his prolific career in Boston. After training at L'Ecole des Beaux-Arts, he worked in New York before moving to Boston in 1874. His Trinity Church followed the nearby Brattle Square Church (now First Baptist). The tower of Trinity Church was based on the Cathedral at Salamanca; the church on a French Romanesque model from Auvergne. The Greek cross interior introduced the Byzantine influence. The eclecticism of the entire design permitted John Lafarge to carry out his interior art in terms of the Spanish Romanesque. Meeting the constraints of cost and time, Lafarge met the Richardsonian goal of a "color church" shared with Phillips Brooks, the rector. The Trinity frescoes were the first of such magnitude by an American artist. It has been compared with the interior of St Mark's in Venice. The brownstone neo-Gothic New Old South Church at Dartmouth Street with its campanile formed the other end of what, first called Art Square, later called Copley Square to honor the 18th century Boston artist.

The Boston Public Library (BPL) was the first free municipal public library in the world when it was founded in 1854. By the end of the 1850s, it had already outgrown its quarters on Boylston Street on the present site of the Colonial Theater. In recognition of its fame as the first public library, a great building was called for. Based on his Italian Renaissance Villard Houses in New York, Charles McKim, educated at Harvard's Lawrence Scientific School and Leola des Beaux-Arts in Paris, provided the massive horizontal Renaissance Florentine palace of the BPL. Although practicing in New York, McKim had apprenticed under Richardson in Boston and was married to an Appleton from Boston.

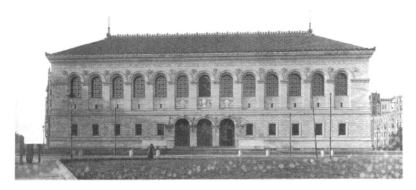

Figure 40 - The Boston Public Library

The centerpiece that completed the square, it was the manifestation of the civic consciousness of Boston; in America like Europe, the city can be a work of art. It was a "palace for the people." It was also the forerunner of the principle of the coming together of the architect, painter and sculptor that would epitomize the "American

Renaissance" of the 1893 Columbian Exposition in Chicago in 1893 and the Jefferson Building of the Library of Congress in the later 1890s. In accordance with its palatial character, statuary flanking the entrance was to be provided by the sculptor Augustus Saint-Gaudens; murals in the front lobby by John Singer Sargent and Edwin A Abbey and Puvis de Chavannes. The grand central reading room was named after the early major benefactor Joshua Bates who, born in Weymouth Massachusetts, made his fortune as a partner in London's Baring Brothers.

The Museum of Fine Arts (MFA) was one of the first free standing art museums in the country. It stood astride the square on land given by the city that was formerly the Boston Water Power Company, now the site of the Copley Plaza Hotel. Its building preceded the completion of the adjacent Trinity Church. Founded in 1870 in what was then in the neighborhood of the Natural History Museum and the Massachusetts Institute of Technology (MIT). Reflecting the extensive connections of the founding Perkins family, the MFA brought together the entire cultural establishment. The trustees included representatives from the Harvard Corporation, MIT, and the Lowell

Institute as well as the Mayor of the City of Boston and the Superintendent of the Boston Public Schools.

The MFA arose directly from the art gallery of the Boston Athenaeum. As early as the 1820s art exhibitions and an art collection began as part of its overall mission to develop into an institution of broad learning. The Athenaeum's original Pearl Street home in 1822 contained plaster casts of antique sculptures in the reading room along with a portrait by Gilbert Stuart of James Perkins, the building's donor. By 1828, Thomas Handasyd Perkins contributed an adjoining Fine Arts Building for what became for a time a series of popular annual art exhibitions. With the profits and by donation, during the 1830s the Athenaeum began to acquire a permanent collection including the "Athenaeum" portraits of George and Martha Washington by Gilbert Stuart, the Panini views of Rome and the Horatio Greenough bust of John Quincy Adams, all of which have since come on loan to the MFA.

At the time of the move of the Athenaeum to the new building on Beacon Street, an art gallery and sculpture gallery were included, taking up much of the space. After the move to the new building, during the 1850s the focus shifted to the expansion of the library funded by several new endowments. By 1866, the decision was made for the fine arts component to be removed to provide space for the expanding library.

In 1869, the unexpected bequest of the Lawrence Collection of Arms and Armor precipitated the decision to establish a new separate Museum of Fine Arts. The son of Abbott Lawrence, one of the largest textile magnates and the founder of Lawrence Massachusetts, Thomas Bigelow Lawrence had built his collection with wild abandon during his travels. His widow then added the funds necessary for it to receive prominent display in a new building, initiating the building drive.

The creation of the new MFA was the fruit of the continuing interest of the scion of the Perkins family, associated as had been his ancestors with both the Athenaeum and the first Fine Arts Building on Pearl Street. Thomas Callahan Perkins was the grandson of James Perkins and related to the entire family of Eliot's and Cabot's. After graduation from Harvard College in 1843, he spent most of the next decades living in Rome in pursuit of training in art and music and as a patron of artists. Living in Florence in the late 1850s, he found his true métier as an art historian, with focus on the sculptors of the Italian

Renaissance. The large number of French Barbizon paintings by artists such Francois Millet that entered Boston collections, and thus the MFA, also owe their popularity to Perkins's advocacy.

The focus of the new MFA was to be education in the spirit of London's South Kensington Museum (now the Victoria and Albert). The Art School remains one of its important components with the wide ranging collection also becoming more prominent over time. The final home of the MFA faces Huntington Avenue as designed by Guy Lowell. The great staircase and the Ionic façade in its subsequent new wing facing the Fenway are perhaps the fullest expression of the neo-Classical style in Boston.

Figure 41 - Huntington Avenue Entrance of MFA

Figure 42 - Fenway Entrance of MFA

The extraordinary world class collection of the MFA reflects the dedication to art of the Boston elite. As an example, Edward Sylvester Morse, engaged by the Japanese government to found the Department of Zoology at the Imperial University of Tokyo, in addition to his own pottery collection, was ultimately responsible for bringing its collection of Japanese art to the MFA. He recommended, on the advice of Charles Eliot Norton, Ernest Francisco Fenollosa, to become Harvard's professor of philosophy and to attract William Sturgis Bigelow to create their own collections. The large collection of portraits by John Singleton Copley is of course reflective of the great 18th century Boston merchant families that continued to support their own museum. Coached by Mary Cassatt, many of Boston's elite also collected 19th century French art with names like Lilla Cabot Perry, John T Spaulding and J. Montgomery Sears the provenances heavily sprinkled amongst the listings of paintings by Manet, Monet, Pizarro, Degas, van Gogh and Cezanne. Most famous is perhaps the Renoir *Le Bal a Bougival*.

The extensive Martha and Maxim Karolik Collection consists of three phases. The first collection focused on the high quality furniture and paintings that might have existed within families such as her own among the Boston elite in the 18th century. Their subsequent collections ranged much farther afield both in provenance and selection of artists to include the 19th century American school even to the extent of folk art. Maxim Karolik was a young Jewish tenor trained in pre-Revolutionary St Petersburg; she a much older descendant of Samuel Derby of Salem, America's first millionaire. Their joint interests increasingly reflected his leadership to consider the art of the middle and lower classes that had been neglected during the era of Colonial Revival by collectors such as that of the DuPont's.

Huntington Avenue served as an appropriate boundary for the fashionable Back Bay District by its width and by its being graced by substantial buildings representing significant cultural activities. The northwest corner of Massachusetts Avenue has the Massachusetts Horticultural Society and southwest corner Symphony Hall. The latter, by Charles McKim, reflects one of Boston's most notable ongoing claims to fame. Although founded in the 1830s, the Boston Academy of Music did not have a permanent ensemble. Founded in 1881 by Major Henry Lee Higginson as the nation's first with a permanent ensemble, he followed a single minded goal to create a first-rate professional orchestra. Higginson sustained the Boston Symphony Orchestra (BSO) unilaterally throughout his life from his income as a partner in the investment firm of Lee, Higginson and Company.

During its first years, starting with Sir George Henshel, German conductors reigned over the BSO until the first World War when the last was interned in a prison camp and then deported. Pierre Monteux succeeded in the 1920s, allegedly imparting a "French sound." Serge Koussevitsky, the long lasting music director during the 1930s and 1940s, brought the BSO national recognition by radio concerts and the summer Berkshire Music Festival. The popular (pop) concerts led by Arthur Fiedler helped sustain the BSO by the millions of records sold. After retirement in 1949, despite Koussevitsky's recommendation, his protégé Leonard Bernstein was not appointed but rather Eduard

Munch. After several others in succession, Seiji Ozawa was the longtime director from 1973 to 2002.

Figure 43 - Henry Lee Higginson

Born in 1834, his mother was descended from the Cabot and Lee lines. Higginson grew up in Boston where his father founded the important family brokerage and banking house. Higginson withdrew from Harvard College to study music, first in Dresden and then Vienna. He returned to Boston in 1861 to join the Union Army in the 2nd Massachusetts Regiment and then, before being severely wounded, reached the rank in the 1st Massachusetts Cavalry by which he was addressed for the rest of his life.

Appropriately close by on Huntington Avenue is the cluster of buildings of the New England Conservatory of Music. Founded in the 1860s, the main concert hall Jordan Hall is named after Eben D. Jordan its donor, the heir to the Jordan Marsh department store. It was dedicated by a concert by the BSO in 1903.

"Proper Boston" resembled its New York and Philadelphia counterparts but was even more exclusive, more English and more intellectual in tone, at least more literary. The previous terminology applied to the Federalist (or Whig) aristocracy was now characterized by Oliver Wendell Holmes Sr in the *Atlantic Monthly* as the "Boston Brahmins." The analogy was to the caste that ruled the Hindu culture and with Boston, the Hub of the Solar System from which all light emanated. The *Atlantic's* first editor was Ralph Waldo Emerson and its writers have reflected since its origin in 1857 not only its Boston roots but a continuing Boston headquarters for its editorial offices until 2005.

The Brahmin policy of providing public services while minimizing waste and corruption had made Boston a relatively well-governed city under their control. But the mid-1840s mark a turning point. After 1845, the trickle of immigration from Ireland turned into a flood. By 1850, fully one-quarter of the population was native to Ireland. Not just strangers, they were outsiders, felt by the nativist Americans to be different totally in culture and overwhelming the services to be provided to the "deserving poor."

Philanthropy had been one of the marks of the culture of the Boston elite. 1810 had seen for example an appeal to the community and not only the rich to fund the formation of the Massachusetts General Hospital. In the 1840s, the previous focus on philanthropy to the general community became limited to one's own. One example was the conversion of the McLean Hospital, the mental hospital branch of the Massachusetts General Hospital, into an increasingly private institution. Another was the overwhelming decision by the stockholders for the collection of the Boston Athenaeum to remain separate from the newly formed Boston Public Library. The division of the community into the rich and poor, the "Yankees" and the Irish Catholics became part of the hallmark of Boston, tempered only by such as the occasional gesture of an honorary doctorate extended to the Boston's Catholic Bishop Fitzpatrick in 1861, the first of Irish extraction.

4.4 Charles William Eliot and Harvard University

It is not incidental that the recognition by Harvard of Boston's first Irish Archbishop John Bernard Fitzpatrick was considered highly noteworthy. The formation of Boston's extraordinarily exclusive class structure in the early 19th century was intertwined with the growth of its cultural center across the Charles. During the half-century following 1800, Harvard began to achieve dominance among the American universities in terms of size of faculty, physical plant, its library and number of professional schools. This was buttressed by the size of its endowment augmented by fewer but larger private donations increasingly derived from a small number of families in the local elite. The wealthiest, most enterprising and most conservative elements of post-revolutionary Boston were the main support of their own cultural institution. Harvard in turn gave that class the intellectual sheen that lent it much of its claim to elevation.

Figure 44 - Harvard College in the mid-18th Century

In 1751, when John Adams enrolled, the three brick buildings (colleges) of Harvard Hall, Massachusetts Hall and Stoughton Hall comprised the "University at Cambridge." There, some ninety boys lived, ate and studied. Immediately to the west was the Holden Chapel, a small building emblazoned with the coat of arms of the donor on the east pediment. On Sundays, the entire student body crossed the street to worship at the First Parish Congregational Church on the corner of the Cambridge Common. A fence enclosed the several other buildings in the Yard (formerly the "Cow Yard"). Although no larger than Adams' native Braintree, Cambridge had a far greater air of distinction when persons from as far away as Philadelphia would appear at the annual Commencement.

There were two professors. Young Professor John Winthrop, by virtue of being the fourth in his lineage to carry the name in Massachusetts, had considerable leeway to explore his modern subjects of mathematics, physics, astronomy and geography. He held the chair of mathematics and natural philosophy. The more elderly Edward Wigglesworth was Professor of Divinity, responsible for the other classical two-thirds of the curriculum including Greek, Latin, Ethics and Rhetoric. Far more important, he trained the men who served as ministers for the Congregational churches of New England, the purpose of the college since its founding in 1636.

Particularly after 1830 and the accession of former mayor Josiah Quincy to the presidency, the governing body called the Harvard Corporation, rather than being made up of clergymen and faculty, increasingly reflected men of business. It also was made up of the "new men," of the new industrial fortunes derived from the textile mills being absorbed into the old mercantile group. Associated with the diminution in representation by the clergy on the Corporation, also came a greater focus on organization and precision of the "financial" administration and the secularization of the faculty and curriculum. There was particular enlargement of the scientific faculty with large new endowments going to the scientific schools. The carefully selected faculty mirrored both the politics and social connections of the "members" that formed the Corporation.

The student body similarly evolved. Expenses were high, almost tripling from the 1830s to the 1860s; scholarships were small and few. Under both President Kirkland (1810-1829) and President Quincy (1829-1845) student extravagance was encouraged. The requirement to pass an entry examination in the classics led to the need for expensive almost entirely private preparatory schools such as particularly the Phillips' Academies at Andover and Exeter. Admission was also possible from the Boston Public Latin School. Harvard became a school for the local and well-born. In 1865, the ancient connection between the Commonwealth of Massachusetts and the university was severed. Overseers were thenceforth elected by the alumni rather than appointed by the General Court. Harvard went on to remain the epitome of the upper class institution that maintained the status of the Boston elite and was sustained by it.

Having been turned down once before, Charles W Eliot was still opposed by many to be selected to be president on the grounds that he was neither a minister nor a classics scholar. The Lawrence Scientific School had been established in 1847 by the textile magnate Abbott Lawrence with the view of training engineers at Harvard to work in the burgeoning industry. An assistant professor of chemistry at the Lawrence Scientific School, Eliot represented the spirit of the new yet he nevertheless arose from the requisite family background. He traced his ancestry in America to Andrew Eliot, a shoemaker from Somersetshire who was a member of the First Church of Beverly in 1669.

His grandfather Samuel Eliot, born in Boston in 1739, was the founder of the family fortune. Educated at the Boston Latin School, he took over a large retail firm and grew rich during the era of the Revolution and the Napoleonic Wars. He established the Eliot Professorship of Greek at Harvard College in 1814. Having had his portrait and that of his wife painted by Gilbert Stuart, he left what up to then had been the largest fortune in Boston at the time of his death. His father Samuel A.(tkins) Eliot grew up in the family mansion across from Kings Chapel; entered Harvard with the class of 1817, and attended the Harvard Divinity School. Following his own father's premature death, he left school and married Mary Lyman whose family had been in the Northwest fur trade with China and had also invested in the new textile mills. The couple settled in a house adjacent to the State House at the top of Beacon Street paid for by the Lyman connection with summers at Nahant in a Greek revival cottage.

The second Samuel A. Eliot was mayor of Boston who abolished the riotous volunteer fire companies after the burning of the Ursuline Convent, introduced the teaching of music in the Boston public schools and was the treasurer of the Harvard Corporation from 1842-1853. A Whig congressman, he voted with Daniel Webster for the Fugitive Slave Law, to become known by its opponents as Samuel A.(abductor) Eliot.

Figure 45 - Charles William Eliot

An only son, Charles William Eliot was thus born in Boston in 1834 to members of the Boston Brahmin elite. Could not be ignored, however, was the effect on his development by the large port-wine birth mark that covered the entire right side of his face. That disfigurement led to gibes and his subsequent aloofness. He went to Boston Latin School as had his father, underwent what he considered its bleak narrow classical course of study but excelled in declamation in an effort to overcome his fear of appearing in public. His long career in education devoted to increasing the options for study by students was attributed at least in part as a reaction to that unhappy experience of a narrow set of choices at the Boston Latin School.

When he followed the family tradition to enter Harvard, seventy-two of the eighty-seven entrants to his Class of 1853 were from Massachusetts, six more from other parts of New England for a total of 93%. The curriculum, heavily weighted toward the classics, was very similar to what John Adams experienced when he had entered Harvard in 1751. Eliot roomed in a private house outside the college along with a first cousin. He did join a student literary group but found chemistry and mineralogy of particular interest, something to pursue on his own. This interest determined his startling choice of career to become a teacher of chemistry at the Harvard Scientific School. Despite his contributions to the department and the college, he did not receive appointment to the endowed professorship awarded to a more established figure. He then used a family legacy to spend several years studying the character of European technical education and published an article in the *Atlantic Monthly* of his recommendations that brought him to notice as a potential president of the college.

Eliot became president of Harvard in 1869. He added to the faculty, raised salaries and strengthened the graduate schools of law and medicine. Several of the dormitories like Weld and Thayer Halls in the eclectic Victorian style were added to the Yard as well as the grand Ruskinian Gothic Memorial Hall described as a "Valhalla" dedicated to the spirit of war. Some of the luminaries he hired included Henry Adams to teach mediaeval history, Charles Eliot Norton to teach art history and William James to teach physiology. Starting in 1879, arrangements were made for repetition of Harvard undergraduate's lectures to audiences of women students, to become Radcliffe College. He abolished Greek and Latin as requirements for admission as well as compulsory attendance at chapel.

Despite having become a professor of chemistry at M.I.T. at the time of his appointment to the Harvard presidency, Eliot failed in his several attempts to join the newly formed Massachusetts Institute of Technology to Harvard. William Barton Rogers was a Virginia-born geologist; his Boston-born wife brought him back there from Charlottesville on the eve of the Civil War. He designed a polytechnic school that opened in 1865 on land granted by the Commonwealth adjoining the Museum of Natural History in the newly reclaimed Back Bay. Then called "Boston Tech," expansion occurred in the early twentieth century on the Cambridge side of the Charles River near the Harvard Bridge. Designed in the grand manner by W. Welles Bosworth, the central dome is reminiscent of both the Pantheon and of the University of Virginia of the founding William Barton Rogers and was funded by the industrialists T. Coleman Dupont and George Eastman.

Figure 46 - Memorial Hall

Under President Charles William Eliot, the college entered upon its greatest period of growth and change. He introduced the "elective" system that permitted undergraduates to elect a wide variety of subjects, an antidote to the past rigid curriculum. Moreover, in 1872 he started the "Graduate Department" where one could earn a post-graduate degree aside from the medical, law and theological departments. In 1890, competing with the new highly successful Johns Hopkins University, it became the "Graduate School." Again, emulating Johns Hopkins, by 1901, the Harvard Medical School required a bachelor's degree and carried out the graded four year curriculum in magnificent new buildings in the Fenway funded by Junius Spencer Morgan. In his last years, Eliot founded the Harvard Business School. Despite the growth in professional education, in accordance with the anti-materialistic role of Harvard, poetry and literature were recognized apart from their usefulness.

Harvard was the place where eighteen of Franklin Delano Roosevelt's fellow Grotonians registered with him in 1900. Founded by the Anglophile Endicott Peabody, Groton epitomized the replica of the English boarding school. Like his distant cousin Theodore in the 1880s, FDR lived at Harvard on the "Gold Coast" of Mount Auburn Street in a three-room suite with private bath with a fellow Grotonian. In his address to the incoming freshmen, President Eliot recognized the forty percent of the students that came from public schools; the largest contingent (thirty eight) from Boston Latin School. However, those poorer boys who lived at the College in Cambridge lodged separately from the Gold Coast. They lodged in the Harvard Yard in the drafty unheated rooms with toilets in the basement.

The social life of the two segments of the class diverged as did their living quarters. The social hierarchy was rigid. The one hundred socially elect were identified from which were selected those eligible to club membership and from which the "final clubs" drew their membership. Even the patrician FDR was listed only in the 5th decade tier enabling him to enter the DKE but not the highest rung of the Porcellian, a defeat he never forgot. The rich and socially ambitious set the standard of nonchalance toward any academic interest. Although Harvard under Eliot was the most heterogeneous of the Big Three of the Ivy League, the background of the students was overwhelmingly Episcopalian, Congregationalist and Presbyterian. Despite presence in the Boston area, only 10% of the students were Catholic and slightly smaller number were Jews.

A generally liberal and tolerant man, Eliot was, for example, one of the leaders of the Anti-Imperialist League opposing the conquest of the Philippines and the Spanish-American War. He opposed restriction of immigration and, a genuine democrat, favored education as the bulwark of an enlightened citizenry. The long term president of the oldest, richest, largest and most prestigious university, he had much influence on the development not only of Harvard but, during these years of great growth, of many of the other American universities in relation to the creation of a meritocracy.

Lawrence Lowell, a supporter of the Immigration Restriction League, a representative of the exclusionary and conservative wing of the Protestant upper class was named his successor in 1908.

Figure 47 - A. Lawrence Lowell

Born in Boston in 1856, Abbott Lawrence Lowell carried the name of the two leading textile families. He had Percival Lowell the astronomer as a brother and Amy Lowell the poet as a sister. He entered Harvard College from Mr. Noble's private school closely associated with the college. He graduated cum laude in mathematics in 1877 and earned a law degree. Practicing law in Boston, he became a part-time instructor and then Professor of Government in 1900. Lowell continued and expanded Eliot's program to provide opportunities for a wider range of public school students to enter Harvard. By 1913, half of the approximately 500 entrants were from public schools. Boston Latin provided fifty three, Cambridge Latin thirty-five and Boston English seventeen, many of whom were sons of Jewish immigrant families.

To remedy the differences between students based on income and social standing, he required that all freshmen in 1912 live in the Harvard Yard. However, residential segregation within the Yard ensured that certain dorms were Protestant and others Jewish while excluding African Americans entirely thus obviating the stated purpose of increased communication. Racial differences were substituted to the stated goal of breakdown of differences between the rich and poor.

By 1918, in the context of the war and the heightened concern about "pure Americanism," the deans of New England colleges convened to deal with "the Jewish problem." In accordance with the Brahmin notion of assimilation to their culture as the goal, it could not occur if the number was too large to "absorb." Although Harvard retained a close connection with the elite of both Boston and New York, Lowell was explicitly and openly concerned that Harvard would lose that connection by raising its Jewish representation above 15%.

Inquiry began on admission applications as to ancestry that had previously probably been applied less formally. This same policy applied to the distribution of scholarships regardless of need. The policy of "selective admissions and scholarships," although thwarted initially by a faculty committee strongly influenced by former President Eliot, continued more or less in effect until the 1960s. A quota system was instituted not unlike the one that restricted immigration in order to retain the existing character of Harvard undergraduates rather than admission based on academic criteria. There was an absolute limit of 150 men identified as Jews out of a student body now fixed to be limited to 1000 freshmen. There were only a token number of blacks, perhaps two or three from politically highly prominent families.

4.5 Henry Adams and American History

The influence of the Adams family continued for the rest of the 19th century before coming to an end. John Quincy Adams was the erudite son and second president of the line who had acted on the basis

131

of principle. In the next generation, Charles Francis Adams carried on the family tradition of being minister to Great Britain. His activities during the Civil War prevented British intervention, a crucial component in Union victory. He also ran as an early candidate of the Free Soil Party and continued to represent his class and his New England constituency as the epitome of the "Liberal Republican" insurgency in 1872 against "Grantism."

Figure 48 - Henry Adams

In the next Adams generation, Henry Adams was born in 1838 at a time when his grandfather John Quincy, called by them "The President," still lived. One of his lasting memories was his grandfather's intervention in a forceful way in his grandson's life to insure that young Henry did not succeed in his rebellion against school. After graduating from Harvard College, Henry Adams entered a career as a writer, reinforced by reading Edward Gibbon's *Decline and Fall* while in Rome. He remained self conscious of his family's standing in history and for whom as New Englanders public service was not just a job but an essential moral and social task. On his return to Washington in 1868 to become a journalist,

He never recovered from his profound disillusionment about the post-Civil War era. He joined the insurgent Republicans in 1872 who by their upper class leadership sought to arrest the corruption of the American political structure engendered by the "new men" with their large industrial fortunes. Adams deplored the displacement of the selfless public servant who holds "his moral rules on the sole authority of his own conscience…indifferent to opposition," the Adams family self-description of their own role in American politics going back to the dynastic founder.

Appointed a Professor of Mediaeval History at Harvard, Henry Adams also served as editor of the *North American Review (NAR)*, the premier journal of opinion during the 1870s. Returning to Washington in 1878 with his new wife Marian "Clover" Adams, they built their town house on Lafayette Square designed by a Harvard classmate Henry Richardson. The coterie led by Adams and his wife prided itself on its intellectual pretensions and their breeding. They distinguished themselves from the "parvenus" that began to arrive in the 1880s distinguished merely by their money or official position. The "aristocracy of talent" to which the Adams's claimed to belong was reminiscent of the snobbery of their Boston connections. Grant and his wife were mocked. In his anonymous book on Washington society, Henry Adams uses James Blaine is the model for the villainous Senator Ratcliffe.

Ned (Edward) Beale bought the historic Decatur House on Lafayette Park with a fortune acquired in the gold fields of California. An old friend of Ulysses Grant, the house became the unofficial social center during the Grant Administration. Adams wrote about the "new men and their wives" in his anonymous satirical *Democracy: An American Novel.* As the leader of the so-called Lafayette Park "Antiques," he used the life of the Beale daughter Emily Beale McLean as the model for his character Virginia Dare. Emily Beale married John McLean, whose father, after making his fortune as a boiler maker, had come to Washington from Cincinnati seeking social recognition. One of the leaders of Washington society in the gilded age after the Civil War, the

McLean's had made the error in the eyes of Henry Adams in choosing to abandon Lafayette Park to build their mansion elsewhere.

"little Virginia Dare, who bubbles like the winds and the streams, with utter indifference about what she said or whom she addressed to bring choice bits of gossip...She has done nothing but scandalize every family in the city."

The great project of Henry Adams as a historian was his *History of the United States in the Administrations of Thomas Jefferson and James Madison Administrations*. He had grown up in the nest of Bostonian historians, possessing their own house organ in the quarterly NAR that he had edited. Despite the shock of his wife's suicide, he carried on. Work was his solace. In his ironic style, no leaders are great men even Jefferson and certainly not Madison although Gallatin remained his hero. Every judgment is wrong; all plans go awry. Worse, once in power, every leader betrays his principles. A scion of the house of Adams, the descendant of two presidents, arising from those who epitomized principle above all, he viewed with distaste from afar those who achieved the eminence he may have sought but thought undeserved to others. He met the model of the "Mugwump," that narrow segment of the elite educated class that looked for the moral in politics and found it lacking in meeting their standards.

By the time he completed his monumental work in 1891, the unchanging principles by which the Adams family and their class claimed to live were being challenged. He wrote in his masterful opening chapters in his *History* that Americans in 1800 still represented the hope of the world. He wrote with respect for their energy and willingness to work. His anger and hatred of the diverse new races, particularly the Jews he characterized as "money-grubbing," caused him to come to a bitter despairing end. He felt by 1900 that hope was destroyed by the unchecked material progress that left him and his kind behind to escape only into the Mariolatry of Gothic France.

Boston had been the epitome of a homogeneous society but was now no longer. There has been a long history of hatred between the Irish and the English. The Celtic Irish had been considered "a wild and undisciplined" people who resisted their English overlords. This was the attitude even before religious differences also arose following the separation from the rule of the Pope under Henry VIII. The nearly five hundred years of fighting reached a crescendo during the rule of

Cromwell in the 1640s when he settled Protestant Presbyterians on the land. By 1690, the Catholic Irish lost all civil rights; by 1800, the Anglo-Irish also lost their Parliament. It is not surprising that the Boston Federalist Harrison Gray Otis invoked this same term of "wild" when debating in 1798 the Alien Acts in the U.S. Congress in light of the recent immigration to Pennsylvania of "United Irishmen."

Even the entry of Protestant Ulstermen had been met with a hostile reception by the Puritans of the Massachusetts Bay in the 1630s. During the 18th century several hundred thousand Scots-Irish migrated to the colonies, relatively few to Boston. Moreover, beyond being anti-Irish, anti-Catholicism was even far more integral to the Puritan community established in the New World to escape such tendencies under the Stuarts. Irish Catholics were doubly damned since they were not only from an inferior race but adhered to a detested religion.

4.6 The Catholic Church and Boston

While allied during the Revolutionary War with Catholic France, a small congregation began to practice their religion openly. The Massachusetts state constitution in 1779 guaranteed freedom of worship for the first time. Father Jean-Louis de Cheverus, a refugee from Revolutionary France in 1798, become Boston's first bishop in 1808. The land enclosures post the Napoleonic Wars forced the very poor Catholic tenants from the south and west Ireland to immigrate. By 1830, there were 8000 Irish Catholics living in what had been a heretofore homogeneously Anglo-Saxon Protestant Boston. They worked mainly as day laborers on construction sites on the land being filled in surrounding the Shawmut peninsula and became voters for the Jacksonian Democratic Party.

The burning of the Ursuline Sisters convent in Charlestown in 1834 was a sign of the suspicions aroused by the influx that led to the worst arson in the 19th century history of Boston. A lurid tale of life behind the convent walls had sold thousands of copies. In addition, a nun who left the convent sought shelter in the hostile surrounding Protestant community but then returned to the convent following a meeting with the local bishop. A mob surrounding the building to "free the returned nun" lit a bonfire to bring the firefighters to the scene. The scenario then becomes unclear. However, although it appears that members of the fire companies did not participate as units in the riot, they did nothing either to prevent it or put out the fire that engulfed the building. Indeed, they offered refreshment to the rioters.

When a fungus infestation struck the potato crop starting in 1846 coupled with the repeal of the Corn Laws that had assured an English market for Irish grain, the evicted peasants either starved or left. Landowners even subsidized travel with rates for transatlantic travel reduced to $17. The number of immigrants from Ireland increased to a total of a million and a half during the next fifteen years. 37,000 came to Boston in one year alone, carried there by mail ships directed to come there as the shortest distance from England and Canada to America. Others going to Halifax on even cheaper transport also eventually found their way to New England and to Boston. They came to Boston and stayed; they had no choice and no place better to go. Only among the Irish did emigration necessitate settlement under the unfavorable conditions dictated by Boston's economic and social structure.

The "Famine Irish" came needy and ill as well as poor; living in the congested dock district, they were, according to the disdainful Yankees, turning Boston into a "moral cesspool." Alcoholism and public drinking was rife. The saloon was the social and political center. The position of the Irish in Boston was in many ways even lower than that of the few blacks. Unskilled jobs were few, yet that is all for which most could qualify. Irish girls worked as domestic servants in middle-class homes. A large number of men worked as stable hands; others were waiters. They provided the needed surplus labor for construction projects elsewhere throughout the country, frequently leaving women and children behind to shift for themselves. The surplus labor enabled the growth of the factory system in the Boston area for ready-made clothing and shoes that competed with New York. Moreover, in response to their appearance, in 1852 the nativist American (Know Nothing) Party elected the Massachusetts governor, all the state officers, the entire state senate and the mayor of Boston.

Nevertheless, by 1866, there were 300,000 Catholics in Boston, second only to New York; in 1875, Boston was raised to the level of an archbishopric. St John's Seminary was opened in Brighton in 1884 staffed by Sulpician priests from France. That same year, the Third Plenary Council of the Catholic Church in the United States meeting in Baltimore commanded parishes to build their own schools. There initiating a major effort in Boston where the common schools were felt to endanger the Catholic souls of their children. The way up for the Irish frequently depended on their rapid naturalization and their participation in elections. Organized by their ward bosses, jobs "on the city" were the goal for security.

In 1895, the population of Boston approached 500,000 with nearly half of Irish ancestry, mainly children of immigrants. The birthrate of the "strictly native New Englander" had fallen while many of the more fruitful Yankees went west. For the first time, there were also large numbers of foreign-born Jews and Italians living mainly in the North and West Ends, recently vacated by the Irish. There was a high of 40,000 foreign-born Jews in Boston in 1910 and an equivalent number of foreign-born Italians somewhat later by 1920. There were as many as 10,000 Blacks centered on Joy Street and the African Baptist Meeting House dating from the 1830s that were now moving to Roxbury and the South End.

By the 1880s, the first American-born Irish generation crossed out of the old slums to East Boston, Charlestown and South Boston, with the last the most populous Irish district. The Carney Hospital was founded in South Boston by an Irish-born businessman to provide care to the working class inhabitants. It was staffed by the Sisters of Charity with their gull-like headdresses. There were jobs as police officers and firefighters and blue collar jobs with the telephone company and other utilities. Hugh O'Brien became the first Irish Catholic Boston mayor in 1884 during a presidential election when the Republican James E Blaine lost to the Democrat Grover Cleveland. Blaine lost votes when labeling the Democratic Party one of "Rum, Romanism and Rebellion." With assimilation, came the rise of middle-class Irish leadership that would translate into political power. Nevertheless, the *Boston Social Register* of 1891 that defined the eight thousand "Proper Bostonians" listed fewer than a dozen with Irish names.

Just as bibliophilia had once been the hallmark of the cultivated Bostonian and a mark of class identity, the post-Civil War era extended into the more highly developed cultural areas of music and art. The leader in this seemingly uniquely Bostonian recurrent effort to divert American culture from its materialism was Charles Eliot Norton as Harvard Lecturer on the Fine Arts from 1874 until 1898. He was the arbiter of American high culture standing between America and Europe, and between New England and the rest of America explaining and evaluating each to each.

4.7 Charles Eliot Norton and the Pursuit of Art

Figure 49 - Charles Eliot Norton

Born in Cambridge in 1827, his father Andrews Norton was the Dexter Professor of Sacred Literature at Harvard; his mother the daughter of Samuel A. Eliot and the sister of Harvard President Charles William Eliot. He graduated from Harvard in 1846 and travelled in Europe where he came under the influence of John Ruskin and Thomas Carlyle. Secretary of the "Loyal Publication Society" during the war, he wrote and distributed propaganda for the Union cause. During these years, he was also editor of the *North American Review* and helped found *The Nation* in

1865. During his career at Harvard, Norton organized exhibitions of the works of Turner and Ruskin and brought English and American men of letters together based on his personal friendships. Mediaeval Florence was his model of integrity, beauty and civic pride, all of which he found missing in America.

Returning to Boston from Europe in 1873, his voyage had enabled him to have an extended conversation with the aged Ralph Waldo Emerson. He found, however, the latter's seemingly naïve optimism echoed what Norton had himself believed that the Civil War would bring about a great renewal in the North and the country as a whole. He thought that the removal of slavery would also lead to removal of the materialism and "mass of ignorance" that pervaded the country during the previous generation. He had devoted himself to writing in favor of the war and had been disappointed by the political scandals and the even more evident materialism of the "Gilded Age." The sacrifices during the Civil War had not seemed to divert the United States from a headlong flight into "unrestrained individualism."

Norton would recommend dipping more deeply into an understanding of other cultures both in the present and in the past. The study by the better educated such by the men of Harvard of the art of the Old World, the beautiful in the culture such as the churches, he thought would lead to the understanding of ideals and aspirations of its source as an antidote of the general vulgarity of taste.

The culmination of the influence of Norton in the creation of a group of Boston cosmopolites was the Isabella Stewart Collection and her Museum in the Fenway. During her early days of collecting in the 1870s, she was one of Norton's first women students at a time when women's education was new at Harvard. Born in 1840 in New York City, she was the only surviving daughter to a self-made Scots grocer claiming descent from the royals. She married John Lowell (Jack) Gardner in 1860 and moved to his native city of Boston where she was considered very much an outsider. After the death of their only son in 1865, the couple began to travel from their home at 152 Beacon Street where Isabella Gardner had also begun a contemporary art collection

Figure 50 - Isabella Stewart Gardner

aided by her artistic friends John Singer Sargent, James McNeil Whistler and Anders Zorn.

"Jack" Gardner, one of Boston's most eligible bachelors and attentive clubmen, came from wealthy Salem-based maternal antecedents. After attending Harvard College, he entered the family East India shipping business. He also was an investor in Michigan copper mines and the Chicago, Burlington & Quincy Railroad. Beginning in the 1880s, the Gardner's travelled in Europe and the Middle East, with Venice their center. They visited frequently at the Palazzo Barbaro. Its ballroom was famous with its stucco ceiling and paintings by Tiepolo. This palace, owned after 1885 by the expatriate Boston Curtis family, became the focus of the American artistic and literary colony in the late 19th century. Henry James stayed there and made it the setting for the American heroine of *The Wings of the Dove*. The Gardner's knew Henry James as well as the Curtis family and rented the palace on one of their several visits to Venice. The Venetian palace of Isabella Stewart Gardner in Boston's Fenway is its spiritual continuation with its added indoor atrium and garden.

After her father's death in 1891, Isabella Gardner had the means to buy art more actively. After the death of her husband in 1898, she began the Gardner Museum in the Fenway to house their extraordinary collection. Her good friend Henry James gave her the enviable accolade of a "true Bostonian" for opening her museum to the public in "the fine old disinterested tradition of Boston."

The first and for long the largest private collection in the New World; the only one named for a woman, it was largely amassed by the aid of her protégé Bernard Berenson. He was born in 1865 in a small village forty miles from Vilna, the center of rabbinical study in what was then the Tsarist Russian Empire. The family immigrated to Boston's North End in 1875 and lived in the West End. Like so many others with his background, his father Albert was an unrecognized intellectual, speaking of Voltaire and the Enlightenment while working as a tin-peddler. They lived near North Station alongside the railroad tracks where freight trains rumbled through the night. The first born, Berneson was especially favored by his mother, the first of a series of adoring women.

A voracious reader, Berenson was a constant visitor to the Boston Public Library, then unique in letting readers take books home. After a short stay at the Boston Latin School, Berenson enrolled at Boston University for a year before transferring to Harvard, sponsored by a wealthy fellow-student. Central to his career there was his participation as an editor of the *Harvard Monthly* along with his lifelong close friend George Santayana. He became for a time one of Charles Eliot Norton's art history students but was rebuffed for being a devotee of Walter Pater. Moreover, he became ultimately part of Isabella Stewart Gardner's social circle. Having shorn his rather threadbare Judaism for Episcopalianism, appropriately for his aestheticism baptized at the Trinity Church, he nevertheless wrote his senior thesis on a Jewish Biblical subject.

Supported by a small stipend provided by his friends, Berenson was able to travel in Europe initially in fruitless pursuit of a literary career. Finally in 1888, he arrived in Italy where he found his home and his career in connoisseur of Italian Art as well as his new found Catholicism. In 1894, his first major work *The Venetian Painters* echoed the favorite Italian city of his Boston' patroness. That same year, with the purchase of a Botticelli painting for Mrs. Gardner, he began the career as the great Italian Renaissance art historian, an area then relatively unappreciated in America. As a mentor to Isabella Stewart Gardner and as her agent, he brought for her Italian masterpieces such as the great Titian *Rape of Europa*. Bought for the then astounding sum of $100,000 that painting still makes her collection famous.

It is not fortuitous that the only major religious movement that originated in the United States in the post-Civil War era originated in New England and was the only one that was led by a woman. Its explicitly "Mother" Church built in the Back Bay in 1894 and the adjoining 1906 neo-classical Extension are part of a monumental Christian Science Center that is its world headquarters in Boston.

4.8 Mary Baker Eddy and the Mother Church of Christ, Scientist

Figure 51 - Mary Baker Eddy

Mary Baker Eddy was born in 1821 in Bow New Hampshire the youngest of six children in a highly traditional Congregational Calvinist home against which she rebelled to believe in a "God of Love." Afflicted by various illnesses from childhood, she eventually found relief in a moment of revelation in 1866 when reading about the miracles wrought by Jesus. She wrote *Science and Health with a Key to the Scriptures* in 1875 before founding in 1879 the Church of Christ, Scientist. Despite much antagonism from the existing churches and ridicule from the medical profession, she gathered several hundred thousand adherents and respectability particularly evidenced by her publications such as the *Christian Science Monitor*.

She can be considered to be a representative of her New England religious background. From its beginnings in New England, Puritanism had held that man's central duty was to live one's everyday life as though in the Kingdom of God rather than be concerned about the hereafter. This was modified by the Transcendental movement that also found religious experience in the immediate possibilities of experience of nature rather than in some future realm. Christian Science claims to grasp Biblical revelation as demonstrable for use in the present day; spiritual truth is knowable through prayer and the immediacy with which spiritual healing exists that denies the presence of matter.

The other New England tradition from which Mary Baker Eddy can be said to derive in her own life and that of her religion is the commitment to equality of the role of women. Margaret Fuller served as a forerunner who expressed within the Transcendental movement her aim to be recognized as an equal, although a woman, by the leading intellects of the age.

Figure 52 - Margaret Fuller

Born in Cambridge in 1810, Sarah Margaret Fuller was taught to read by her congressman father at a young age and introduced to a rigorous education "fit for a boy" that included Latin and the study of world literature. Her father had definite views on education and applied them to his first born without regard to her difference from the gender he had expected. By the 1830s, Margaret earned the reputation of being the best-read person in New England. She was the first woman permitted to enter the precincts of the Harvard Library. By 1839, she began to lead her "Conversations with Women" designed to serve as an alternative to the lack of higher education for women. Having come to the attention of Ralph Waldo Emerson, Margaret Fuller became a member of the Transcendental Club and (unpaid) editor for a time of its journal *The Dial*.

She wrote "The Great Lawsuit", on the rights of women; in 1845, she published it as *Woman in the Nineteenth Century*. Considered even now the manifesto of the feminist movement, it can be seen as the result of her experiences within the transcendental movement colored by the idea of self-perfectibility and her work with women in that same vein within her "conversations." The method of the latter provided opportunities for self-expression rather than merely opportunities for passively receiving higher education per se. It was her opinion that it was the thwarting of women in their self-expression that was characteristic of the times. In the contemporary abolitionist context, she likened the situation of the married woman to the black field slave.

She started work as the first woman book reviewer and an editor of the *New York Tribune*. Sent abroad as its foreign correspondent, she met an Italian revolutionary Giovanni Angelo Ossoli with whom she had a child and eventually married. They drowned in 1850 on Fire Island on their way back to the United States. Her biography, written in 1852, was the best-selling of the decade. She became the exemplar of the independent woman in her advocacy for women being equally qualified for any job taken by men. Emerson described her as having "both strength of mind and good of heart...a right brave and heroic woman."

This was a recurrent theme of the entire career of Mary Baker Eddy who continually urged on her mainly women early followers for whom she also provided a means for an independent income as a "reader." She admitted no failing on their part on the grounds that one was "only a woman" and that things were weighted against her gender. Her own imperiousness belied any suggestion that men would take control of her movement as they did in other religious groups; rather she sought equality between the sexes and opportunities for men as well as women.

Her Godhead incorporated both the feminine and the masculine, the "Mother-Father God." Nonetheless, she also found it not fortuitous that it was a woman, such as she, who had discovered the feminine nature of God and the primacy of the contributions of women in the Bible to its spirituality. She was, however, not an avowed feminist even in the context of her own times. She was uninterested in women's suffrage and dealt with the prevalent concept of the "inferior materialism" of the female versus the "superior spirituality" of the male by denying the existence of the body, indeed of all matter. Although during her life she denied any explicit avowal of herself as the re-incarnation of Jesus, she lies buried beneath a neo-classical Roman temple suggestive of that of the Vestal Virgins among the galaxy of great Bostonians in Mount Auburn Cemetery.

By the turn of the century, the political alliance between the largely Irish voter and the Brahmin leadership of the Democratic Party in Boston had begun to fray. The American-born generation of the Irish immigrants was ready to take power in its own right. The election of John F Fitzgerald as mayor marked the changeover.

4.9 John F Fitzgerald and Boston Politics

During the Civil War, the Republican Party was the heir of the long standing Whig program for "internal improvement" and centralization that passed Congress in the absence of the representatives of the Southern states. Factories proliferated, mechanization spread through the industrial system, a national currency and a national banking system supported the growth of "Big Business" exemplified by the transcontinental railroads. Supported by a more centralized government, a more highly industrialized, more capital intensive national business structure arose. The outmoded and parochial economy of Massachusetts with its limited and stagnant wealth invested in family trusts fell behind. With it, the social and political leadership of Boston would also fade, hindered even more by the ethnic divisiveness in the city between the old Boston Brahmin elite and the dominant Irish political class.

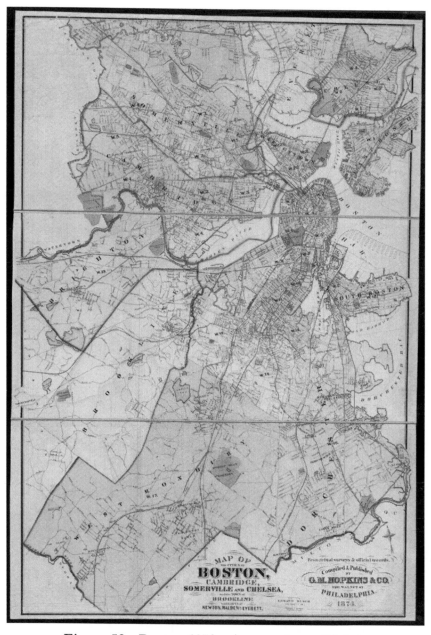

Figure 53 - Boston 1870s, Annexation of Brighton

The population of Boston did not rise in the post-Civil War era as quickly as other American cities. Boston did expand its population incrementally during the early post-Civil War years by the annexation to the city of Roxbury including Jamaica Plain and West Roxbury along with Dorchester and Brighton, all by 1874. The adjoining map shows the annexed area with the beginning of platting of the street system of Dorchester.

That tactic of annexation worked only as long as the Yankee inhabitants thought they were able to maintain control of the city government. It ceased when Irish political power appeared to become more dominant. In 1874, Brookline refused to join the city although surrounded on several sides. The state government remained Yankee and Republican intent on retaining control of the Boston police and schools under the guise of "metropolitan" government as the nativist Protestant middle class moved to the surrounding suburban towns. By 1910, although the population of "greater Boston" approached one and half million, that of the city was only 670,000 while integration increasingly occurred of metropolitan transportation, water, sewer and park systems.

By the end of 1850s, nearly half of Boston's population was foreign born, nearly all Irish. The great wave of Irish immigration began to recede in the 1860s. The subsequent much smaller but still significant immigration from Italy and of Jews from Eastern Europe came after the 1880s. During the interim, an uneasy alliance endured while the ruling Democratic Party held a coalition of Irish voters still deferential to Yankee leadership. The 1884 campaign for mayor marked the end of Boston Brahmin control of the mayor's office. Irish-born five term alderman Hugh O'Brien ran against incumbent Augustus Martin, a Yankee Mugwump during the crucial year when the Blaine nomination split the Republican Party. After several terms in which O'Brien demonstrated that he was not a creature of the machine, a truce was declared in which ethnicity was not used to divide the ruling Democratic political coalition.

Members of the Brahmin elite continued to head the ticket while Irishmen led by Patrick Maguire's Democratic City Committee organized the vote. Democratic Party identity that crossed religious and ethnic boundaries served to blur these differences. The alliance of some upper class ancestral Whigs and lower class Irish Democrats arose in their joint distrust of the reformist elements in the 1850s that coalesced in the anti-slavery Republican Party. This continued alliance

148

that lasted until the death of Patrick Maguire in 1896 did much to mediate the ethnic transition that occurred within the city before the election of Irish mayors after 1900 occurred under the direct auspices of the ward bosses.

Figure 54 - John F Fitzgerald

John Francis (John F.) Fitzgerald was born in 1863 in Boston's North End inhabited by recently arrived Irish. The trajectory of his life and that of his family illustrated that of the Irish American of the first native-born generation. Thomas, the Irish-born father of John Francis, prospered in the grocery cum groggery business to the extent of owning several tenement buildings. John F, the smallest of nine brothers, became a champion runner. His success as a runner created a sense of accomplishment that carried him through the rest of his life. More energetic and quicker in school than his other siblings, he graduated grammar school, then the Boston Latin School before entering the Harvard Medical School. He left prematurely to care for his mother and family after his father's death in 1885. Tribe and family dwarfed his own personal ambitions.

A protégé of the local North End ward boss, John Fitzgerald succeeded him. In the absence of entry into Boston's tightly controlled business circles, politics was the Irish road to success and power. Gregarious, Fitzgerald was elected to his first office in the State Senate in 1892 and then to the U.S. Congress in 1894. At that time, Fitzgerald was one of the only three Catholics in the Congress and the only Democrat in the Massachusetts delegation. In Congress, he was a strong opponent of restricted immigration, championed by many of the Boston Brahmins led by Henry Cabot Lodge.

Fitzgerald was elected to Congress with the support of the Democratic Party machine and the other ward bosses. The latter included Patrick Joseph Kennedy of neighboring East Boston, the father of his eventual son-in-law Joseph Patrick Kennedy. Like Fitzgerald, Kennedy was the son of Irish immigrants. He quit school at age fourteen to support his widowed mother and his three sisters. After working for a time on the docks, Kennedy prospered with the ownership of taverns and a liquor importing business. He established the Columbia Trust Company in East Boston in 1892 that provided in 1914 a springboard for the business career of his son Joseph P. Kennedy.

Fitzgerald ran successfully in 1905 in the Democratic primary. Although he was himself one of the "bosses," he ostensibly ran against the "machine" in the person of the West End boss Martin Lomasney. Although Hugh O'Brien was the first Irish Catholic mayor elected as early as 1885, John F. became the first Boston-born Irishman elected mayor. "Fitzgeraldism" denoted the rule by the Irish Democratic Party machine with city jobs the payoff. The worst fears of the Brahmins were realized. Taking office on January 1, 1906, in a way that seemed to presage the ways of his grandson as president, John F.'s closest confidantes during his mayoralty were his brothers. With his administration tainted by corruption by an investigation instigated by the Good Government Association (GGA), he managed to avoid prosecution only by courting a perjury indictment.

A fight had first erupted over the control of the public schools and jobs for Irish Catholic teachers. The politicization of the schools was joined in the context of the long festering antagonism between the Yankees and the Irish, no longer mediated and contained within a Democratic Party alliance. Just prior to the 1910 election, in an attempt to break the power of the "bosses," a new charter had been voted in with a much strengthened mayoralty, a smaller Council elected at-large; all consistent with the recommendations of the National Municipal League and the GGA.

Although Boston had been relatively well governed, there was a mainly Yankee group that sought reform and efficiency in accordance with the Progressive ethos of the times. Although not significantly corrupt in comparison with other cities at the time, the city property owners was heavily taxed. Expenditures had increased under the aegis of the fragmented aldermanic system that depended on patronage for its sustenance.

Stoking the fires with accusations of anti-Catholicism as well as great wealth, Fitzgerald managed to regain office in 1910 in a close race against James J. Storrow, the last Brahmin to be a candidate for mayor in Boston. Although indeed very wealthy and a poor public speaker, Storrow was actually very civic minded in having led the battle for the Charles River Dam and Embankment that now carries his name as well as chairing the Boston School Committee. Fitzgerald ran as a "man of the people," a product of his Irish heritage as opposed to the wealthy Storrow. One of the most significant city elections, it set the stage for the relationships that would dominate the character of Boston politics for the next fifty years.

Subject to a threat of blackmail by fellow Irishman James Michael Curley implicating him in a sex scandal, Fitzgerald withdrew from the race for re-election in 1914. Although making many attempts, he never again was elected to office. He eventually took on the role of the benign grandfather to the Kennedy brood. It was characteristic of Fitzgerald and his times that in order to assuage the concerns of Boston's Catholic Archbishop and his own political future, John F. sent his favored eldest daughter Rose to the Convent of the Sacred Heart rather than her preferred but non-Catholic Wellesley College.

His fellow ward boss, East Boston's Patrick Joseph Kennedy, sent his only and highly favored son Joseph Patrick Kennedy to the public Boston Latin School and then Harvard College, class of 1912. There, despite his popularity in his class and his strong friendships, young Kennedy was severely disappointed when not elected to any of the "final clubs." Merely the first of the many snubs experienced at the hands of the Boston Protestant establishment, Joseph Kennedy's exclusion, based on his Catholicism, was significant in creating the resentment that marked his driving ambition. Ward politics like his father's career would not bring the power he wanted; that would come with wealth and through his progeny.

Immigration to Boston continued after 1880 but shifted to include for the first time larger numbers from Italy and Eastern Europe. After having undergone the large Irish Catholic influx and having escaped to a large extent to the suburbs ringing Boston, those original native Protestant Yankees who remained now once again felt overwhelmed.

Between 1900 and 1910, 150,000 Italians entered Massachusetts superimposed on those who had arrived in the North End and East Boston starting in the 1880s. Although Catholic in their religion, they differed from the form practiced by the Irish. Fond of street processions and also somewhat anti-clerical, they much preferred their own Italian-speaking churches such as St Leonard's in the North End founded on Prince and Hanover Streets as early as 1873. Extraordinary animus toward Italian immigration had arisen due to their large scale importation as contract laborers. They were known as "birds of passage" not committed to staying in their new country. Emphasis on the imposition of literacy tests first arose in that context.

Moreover, the Chicago Haymarket Riot in 1885 when police and workers clashed and the threat of class-based violence aroused nativism. Fears for social stability were particularly projected onto the immigrant anarchists that would appear in Boston and affect its Italian community in the North End.

The other large-scale "new immigrant" group was Jewish. Unlike many other American port cities where Sephardic Jews (of Spanish origin) had settled in the 17th and 18th centuries, no organized Jewish community existed until the rather small German Jewish immigration to Boston in the 1840s. The first synagogue *Ohabei Shalom* (Lovers of Peace) was founded in 1843. Also unlike other centers of German

Jewish immigration, the congregants came from the portion of western Poland around Posen annexed by Prussia. Those far fewer coming from other areas such as southwestern Germany seceded from *Ohabei Shalom* in 1853 to found *Adath Israel*. In the 1870s, the latter became "Temple Israel" when it adopted the Reform more mainstream German liturgy.

The original synagogue of Polish origin remained more traditional until a generation later at the turn of the 20th century when it too affiliated with Reform Judaism. This combined "German" Jewish community was very small and was soon engulfed by the East Europeans arriving after the 1870s. To a degree unusual compared to other cities like New York, Philadelphia and Baltimore, the two strands coalesced under the leadership of members of the earlier community like Jacob Hecht. For example, in 1895, confronted by the barriers erected to outsiders, coupled with the intrinsic religious-based anti-Semitism, Boston was the first place where both strands united to develop a community-wide federated Jewish charity drive that still is a model for the entire country in its universality.

The Jews thus came late and in relatively small number to what had been a homogeneous Christian city. Boston indeed had not welcomed the Irish immigration that at least did speak a common language and shared the Christian religion. Now by 1910 as many as eighty thousand East European Jews lived in Boston. After also settling first in the North End, the East European immigration moved to the West End along Cambridge Street and then to the Dover Street area of the South End and Roxbury. Across the Mystic River by means of a three-cent ferry ride lay Chelsea until a devastating fire in 1908 drove many of its Jews to Dorchester and Mattapan to be enclosed by the city line from moving farther south to the adjoining suburban towns.

Their foreign appearance and language of these "new immigrants" appeared to foretell to observers like Henry Adams and Henry James the loss of their old more defined Boston. James particularly noted when observing Italian immigrants walking from the North End "where now no sound of English escaped the lips of a procession of persons on Beacon Hill." The loss of their faith in the ability of the political and cultural elite to impose their values led such as Henry Cabot Lodge and other Brahmins to form in Boston in 1894 the "Immigration Restriction League."

4.10 Henry Cabot Lodge and Immigration Restriction

Figure 55 - Henry Cabot Lodge

He was born in Boston in 1850 in the family house in Winthrop Place in the fashionable area then near Summer Street. His mother traced her ancestry to the *Mayflower*. The Lodge side of the family was more recent in its arrival. His most significant maternal ancestor was the Beverly merchant George Cabot, the founder of the fortune of what was Boston's First Family. Wealthy from privateering in the Revolutionary period, George Cabot was in 1801 a Federalist senator from Massachusetts and a member of the "Essex County Junto" that ruled Massachusetts politics. A strong supporter of Alexander Hamilton, Cabot remained the leader of the New England Federalists concerned about the dilution of their power in the new republic. He is quoted as saying "I hold democracy in its natural operation to be the government of the worst." He presided at the

Hartford Convention in 1814 where he wisely counseled moderation rather than secession.

Known as "Cabot," Henry Cabot Lodge grew to maturity in the family home on 31 Beacon Street on the crest of the hill near the State House. His father died early in 1862 and young Cabot was favored by his long widowed mother. Summers were spent in fashionable Nahant on the North Shore. The abolitionist Senator Charles Sumner was a family friend and frequent visitor. Lodge attributes his anti-slavery views that reached their pinnacle in the Federal Elections Bill of 1890 to his early connection with Sumner. Part of an overall national Republican Party strategy, this last attempt to provide Federal supervision to enable Southern black, presumably Republican, voting in Congressional races was in the spirit of Sumner's espousal of the 15th Amendment. Cabot Lodge never again took an interest in black civil rights.

He entered Harvard in 1868 after preparation along with his friends at the private Latin school run by Mr. Dixwell, formerly the head master of the public Boston Latin School. A member of the exclusive Porcellian Club and the Hasty Pudding, he graduated from Harvard College in 1872 and Harvard Law School in 1874 before joining what later became the blue-blood law firm of Ropes & Gray. He then received the first Ph.D. degree in Political Science from the newly established Harvard Graduate School. A student of Henry Adams in history in his senior year at college, he remained his lifelong colleague. They shared views as to Anglo-Saxon superiority and the fixity of the racial characteristics of what he considered the eminently undesirable recent immigrants.

Characteristically, Henry Cabot Lodge's first publication was of his great-grandfather's letters. In reviewing his ancestry in his own memoir, Lodge noted the absence of the clerical strain; he prided himself on the abundance of ship-owners and merchants, men of action. In his memoir, Cabot Lodge described his early life in a much smaller Boston of the 1850s among a closely knit society, transformed completely in the past seventy years by the enlargement of the city he had known. Once a small merchant seaport, it was now the center of an industrial metropolitan region sprawled over a ten-mile radius. In accordance with his conservative Boston Federalist/Whiggish antecedents, on one hand, he decried the power of the very rich plutocrats concerned only with money; on the other, he saw socialism as an evil in seeking to guarantee equality of result that arose from the foreign-born working class who then largely inhabited the city.

In light of his own ancestry, he felt that neither the large-scale capitalist nor the immigrant held the commitment to the "public good" in the old New England sense. His doctoral dissertation at Harvard on the Germanic origins of ancient Anglo-Saxon government may have informed his later legislative concern with maintaining the racial purity of the American "stock." He considered Anglo-Saxon origin as the basis for a commitment to political freedom as opposed to that of the immigrant voter to "boss rule" that he saw in the Boston of his time.

After serving in the Massachusetts General Court, Lodge was elected to the U.S. House of Representatives in 1887 and to the U.S. Senate in 1893. A "regular" Republican, he carried on the Federalist and Whiggish tradition by maintaining the gold standard and "sound money." Rather than joining the "Mugwumps" in 1884 in opposition to James Blaine, their joint commitment to their party brought him into close association with Theodore Roosevelt, from then onward a close political ally and family friend.

Lodge took a particularly strong interest in restriction of immigration with an article so entitled published in the *North American Review* in 1891. He argued for a literacy test that would reduce overall immigration; that the recent increased immigration particularly from eastern and southern Europe with whom "we have never previously amalgamated" was relatively inassimilable, made up of radicals and illiterates who also undercut wages. It is interesting that he tempered his previous Boston Brahmin concern about the Irish immigration in light of his even greater concern about the "new" immigration. The republic seemed to have survived the Irish; it was not clear that it could do so in face of the new arrivals.

Lodge was the public voice of the Immigrant Restriction League formed in 1894 by several Harvard men of the class of 1889 dedicated to closing "the unguarded gates." Evoking the example of the Chinese Exclusion Act of 1882, they believed strongly that through these still open gates came a flood of illiterates, paupers, criminals and lunatics. In turn, these immigrants created crowded warrens in the large cities that bred social unrest as well as actual disease. Invoking data from the eugenicists, the high birthrate of the immigrants was diluting the Anglo-Saxon American genetic stock. All these issues seemed to be particularly true to members of the Brahmin elite in Boston in the 1890s that were acutely aware of their low birth rate while being engulfed by the large number of eminently distasteful immigrants and their many children.

Immigration restriction had several sources with a long history in Boston. The belief that foreigners were a source of radical ideas had surfaced during the 1790s in the wake of the French Revolution particularly related to the immigration of the radical nationalist "United Irishmen." It had resulted in the Alien and Sedition Acts of the Federalist Adams administration that found ready support in pro-British Boston. Anti-Catholicism also had surfaced there in the wake of the Famine Irish invasion of the 1840s to coalesce into the highly popular "Know-Nothing" movement of the 1850s. Restriction of immigration never reached the level of action in Boston as it had elsewhere such as Baltimore and Philadelphia tempered by an overriding belief in democracy by such as Ralph Waldo Emerson. The issue receded in the generation after the Civil War. Immigrants had fought bravely to save the Union. The peopling of the west and the absorption of low wage industrial workers by the expansion of industry allayed fears that immigration had adverse effects.

Now in the 1890s, these same old concerns resurfaced, once again re-amplified in the light of the labor troubles following the Panic of 1893. The Yankee Protestant ruling group felt particularly beleaguered in their native city. Their political power was threatened by the rule of the Democratic Party based on the immigrant vote. Harkening back only to the great ante-bellum era of New England flowering as the mark of American civilization, the immigrant, like the Southern Negro and the rude Westerner was outside the pale of civilization for the class-ridden Brahmin. Since "racial" characteristics were fixed according to the racialist eugenic theories of the time, the only salvation for democratic society was the exclusion of the non-Anglo-Saxon.

Representative of the founders of the Immigrant Restriction League was Charles Warren. From a family with an old Colonial name, he had argued while at Harvard College in his Commencement speech that immigrants voted for taxes they did not have to pay; needy to receive patronage, they supported boss rule and were unfamiliar with democratic procedures and their role in government. Concerned with the depravity of American life following the industrial revolution, descendants of the "Liberal Republicans" of the 1870s and the Mugwumps of the 1880s, those opposed to immigration were never a mass movement. The Immigrant Restriction League nevertheless established branches in New York, Chicago and San Francisco. Via a press campaign, the short term goal was to impose a literacy test on immigrants; but only as a step toward the greater end of totally restricting immigration.

In 1895, the recently elected Republican Congress offered hope for success in the League's legislative campaign but the bill was successfully vetoed by President Cleveland. Lodge repeatedly introduced legislation in the House to impose the literacy test. A senator from 1903, from 1907 to 1911, he was an active member of the bi-partisan Joint Congressional Dillingham Commission. The Commission was intent on restricting immigration, particularly of those coming from eastern and southern Europe. The Dillingham Commission specifically singled out Italians, especially from Southern Italy, when it not surprisingly concluded that such immigration was detrimental to the "American way of life." Presidential vetoes successively defeated the literacy requirement until 1917; the wartime fears of anarchist activity then took hold.

An absolute annual limitation of 150,000 coupled with a national quota system based upon the census of 1890 took effect after the First World War. To remain in force until the 1960s, immigration legislation succeeded in bringing an end for a generation to the arrival of foreign immigrants to Boston. The incidence of foreign-born and foreign parentage fell in Boston to a low of 13% in 1970 but still did not lead to any change in the city's persistent inter-ethnic residential segregation.

The other thread in Boston's political and intellectual life was represented by the reformist Republicans who broke with the regular Republicans such as Henry Cabot Lodge over the Blaine nomination in 1884 and helped elect the Democrat Grover Cleveland. The derisive term "Mugwumps" was applied to them by their enemies inferring that they were "high and mighty" above the dirty work of politics and the spoils system. They were not only in favor of civil service reform but also free trade and came to oppose imperialism. A continuation of the "liberal" abolitionist strand that made up the original Republican Party coalition that had elected Lincoln in 1860, they had been evident in the unsuccessful "Liberal Republican" candidacy of Horace Greeley opposed to "Grantism" in 1872.

Particularly strong in the Boston-Cambridge area, the Mugwumps of 1884 in turn included Harvard President Charles William Eliot and Harvard Professor William James along with a number of other members of the Harvard faculty. One of their most activist leaders was the relative outsider Louis D. Brandeis.

4.11 Louis D. Brandeis and the Boston Reformist Tradition

His original law partner was his law school classmate Samuel Warren, a leading member of the "Mugwump Reform Club" and the "New England Free Trade League". Samuel Warren's brother Fiske also brought Brandeis into the "Anti-Imperialist League". Growing out of the moral impulse of the 1893 World Columbian Exposition and the "Boston Municipal League", George Read Nutter, another of the Brandeis law partners, was a founder in 1903 of the "Good Government Association" (GGA). Noted for his fierce morality, he carried as had his ancestor "Hate-Evil" Nutter. The reformers saw themselves to be the modern version of the virtuous civic leaders of early republican Boston.

Brandeis was in the center of the reformers, sharing throughout his life an over-riding concern for "good government." His concern with Blaine's reputation of corruption had initially led him to support Grover Cleveland and to his continuing membership and support of the Boston GGA. The Mugwump economic stance of free trade was also compatible with the business interests represented by the Brandeis law firm. The original law firm of Brandeis and Warren found its clientele mainly among the social and business connections in the paper industry of the Warren partner. Sam Warren was a Harvard graduate, a member of the Porcellian and the Hasty Pudding Club. Brandeis was a southerner and a Jew, not even a graduate of Harvard College. He was reluctant to join Warren unless as an equal. He was invited by Warren to be his partner but was not necessarily a close friend, presumably at the instance of Warren's wife, not even invited to their wedding. Although a member of the Dedham Polo Club and the Social Register on the strength of the Warren connection, neither Brandeis nor his family were ever welcomed in Boston Brahmin social settings.

Figure 56 - Louis D. Brandeis

Born in 1856 in Louisville Kentucky to a prosperous Jewish family, Louis Brandeis grew up in a setting of liberal politics exemplified by the 1848 revolutions; their failure had caused his parents to flee from Bohemia. His maternal uncle Lewis Demnitz, a lawyer of great principle active in liberal branch of the Republican Party, was a major influence on his nephew's development. When Brandeis came to Harvard Law School in 1875, he thus joined a setting compatible with his own upbringing. After graduation as first in his class, he was appointed, by Harvard President Charles William Eliot, considered the "king of the Mugwumps," to give courses at the Law School.

The specifically Brandeis clientele and social circle were among the German Jewish mercantile community with such persons as Edward Filene of the department store and most importantly Jacob Hecht in the boot and shoe business and other members of the "Boston Merchants Association" (BMA). Although the major concern of the BMA was the rising real estate tax rate, they were also interested in free trade. For example, the Brandeis clients in shoe manufacturing sought low tariffs for raw materials they imported such as hides, whereas the protectionist textile manufacturers were allied to the regular Republicans. Although he had many non-Jews as his clientele, his was known as a "Jewish firm" and did not represent any of the non-Jewish large family trusts nor the large capital banks, railroads or textile manufacturers.

These several factors of social isolation and absent business involvement in these larger areas of the Boston economy brought Brandeis to his independent commitment to social action beyond the bounds of his previous political allies in the reform movement. When in 1897 the newly organized Boston Elevated Railway gained the franchise to tunnel under the Boston streets to build the Tremont Street Subway, Brandeis and Edward A. Filene organized the "Public Franchise League" (PFL) to fight against private control of the city streets. They succeeded in imposing the PFL plan on the transit company to insure cheap domestic transportation like their previous commitment to free external trade. Brandeis chose to conduct his campaign under more populist, democratic and militant lines as only an outsider would do; the charter for the transit line imposed a short lease and a five cent fare that lasted until 1919.

Brandeis then went beyond his anti-monopoly efforts to support the interests of labor unions. He came to this stance after the Homestead strike of 1892 via meeting with Irish labor leaders and the example offered of enlightened employer-employee relations by the "Filene Cooperative Association." He also helped his shoe manufacturing clients improve their employee relations by solving problems of intermittent work-layoffs and cooperation on the workshop floor. He then applied the same principles in creating a model for the garment industry in 1910 that also marked his first large-scale involvement with East European Jews.

The nativist tinge to the Mugwump-based Reform Association by its connection with the Immigration Restriction League led Brandeis by 1905 to resign to join the Progressives and their Economic Club. Thus further isolated from his earlier Brahmin connections, he became more closely identified to his Jewish roots. For the first time, he addressed a Jewish organization in the context of the 1905 municipal election in opposition to the overtly Irish Catholic John F Fitzgerald. However, he spoke to enlist the Jews of Boston in support of a Yankee candidate, good government and quality public schools. His increasingly national and even international role as head of the American Zionist movement after 1914 took him out of his work in Boston. His last connection with the city took place in 1916 when the antipathy he had engendered in the Brahmin elite throughout his career manifested itself in their widespread and deep opposition to his appointment to the Supreme Court. Such opposition was led by Henry Cabot Lodge in the Senate and President A. Lawrence Lowell of Harvard in Boston.

4.12 William Monroe Trotter in "Freedom's Birthplace"

The black population of Boston has been historically low. In 1860, the approximately 2000 inhabitants comprised somewhat over 1%; in 1930 the 20,000 represented 2.6%. So far north, the opportunities for unskilled migrants from the south were limited and the competition fierce for jobs with the concomitant large number of European immigrants. The black community was based on the relatively free ante-bellum welcome for fugitives and then the migration of freed slaves to a city noted for its support for black rights. The population tended to be heavily made up of persons born in the north; migrants came mostly from Virginia and were more likely to be light-skinned. Although socially racially separated from the start, housing and school segregation was not absolute on Belknap (Joy) Street on Beacon Hill and later in the South End but was part of the overall pattern characteristic among the various ethnic enclaves in Boston.

The black population of Boston, albeit small, was highly significant in national black circles. Although by the Centennial in 1876, Boston welcomed representatives of former Confederate units from Charleston South Carolina and Norfolk Virginia, the city was also unique in recognizing its black Revolutionary War martyrs such as the slave Crispus Attucks and its Civil War black Union veterans in the 54th Massachusetts Regiment. It also still had a number of active descendants of its Garrisonian white radical abolitionists. For example, Francis Jackson Garrison, William Lloyd Garrison's youngest son was still available to serve as the first president of the NAACP branch until his death in 1916.

The Boston black elite were a model for the entire nation. They were made up of about 20 mainly light-skinned families that socialized and intermarried with each other. They summered at Oak Bluffs on Martha's Vineyard and prayed at the Charles Street A.M.E. Church in the West End and the Twelfth Baptist Church in the South End. The latter was known as the church of the fugitive slaves when it was founded by Leonard Grimes. Born free in Loudon County Virginia in 1815, he used his hackney coach to transport slaves from there to freedom on the Underground Railroad in Washington DC until caught and imprisoned. In 1854, he moved to Boston where he participated in the activities of the Vigilance Committee to safeguard fugitive slaves. He founded the Twelfth Baptist Church and remained its pastor for the next twenty-seven years.

Although freed blacks were able to attend white churches, they did so infrequently. The first African Meeting House arose in 1805 on the north slope of Beacon hill and was of the Baptist confession. Known as the Joy Street Church, it was called eventually St Paul's Baptist. The first black Methodist Church was founded in 1818 and, in 1838, joined the African Methodist Conference. In the 1870s, the congregation purchased the Charles Street Meeting House at the corner of Charles and Mt Vernon Streets. It remained known as the Charles Street A.M.E. Church even as it moved from that area to the South End and then Roxbury.

The 15th Amendment in 1870 that seemed to assure suffrage and recognition of black males as full citizens was celebrated in Boston at a large inter-racial meeting at Faneuil Hall. The densely populated sections of Ward Six on the north slope of Beacon Hill and adjacent West End contained about fourteen hundred blacks. The potential black electorate of somewhat over 400 coupled with their high rate of turnout could make a difference in legislative races. An inter-racial Republican Party flourished. Its high point was when Clarence Mitchell, a veteran of the black Massachusetts 55th Regiment, was elected in 1866 to the Massachusetts House from Ward Six and the black lawyer Edwin Garrison Walker from all-white Charlestown. Blacks were recurrently elected to the Massachusetts legislature from the district that contained Ward Six. However, the end of Reconstruction in 1876 marked the reduction of the influence of blacks in national politics and a concomitant rise of the Democratic Party in local Boston politics. Black men nevertheless continued to try to exert their power through the political process in loyalty to the increasingly impotent Republican Party in Boston.

One of the leaders of the black community during its post-Civil War era was George L Ruffin. Born in Richmond Virginia of free blacks, he moved to Boston in 1853 in order to receive an education. Unable to serve because of poor eyesight, he actively recruited for the U.S Colored Troops during the Civil War. He was a pioneer when he graduated from Harvard Law School in 1869 and carried on a criminal law practice. He was elected to the state legislature for one term and also to the Common Council of the city in the 1870s. Superintendent of the Twelfth Baptist Sunday School, he also mixed easily with the white community and was appointed as a municipal judge by Governor Benjamin Butler in 1883 to serve in Charlestown before dying at a young age because of kidney disease.

His wife, Josephine St Pierre Ruffin, the descendant of a free black father in Taunton Massachusetts, along with her daughter Florida Ruffin Ridley, founded the "Women's Era Club" in the 1890s and edited a journal of that name. She also helped found the "National Association of Colored Women" (NACW) whose first meeting took place in Boston in 1895. Black women's clubs carried out literary and other activities but also social welfare. In the 1890s, inspired by Ida B. Wells, they took the lead in exposing the largely economic basis for the lynchings in the South and were concerned broadly with women's issues such as the funding of kindergartens and women's suffrage. They also supported, for example, the "New England Hospital for Women and Children" that accepted patients and nursing students regardless of race.

Committed to the Republican Party as the party of emancipation, the black elite were one with the Boston Brahmin Henry Cabot Lodge in his advocacy of the Federal Elections Bill in 1890 to ensure freedom for voting in the South. The failure of the bill and consequent final failure to create a Republican voting presence in the South marked the beginning of the end of the long liaison of the Republican Party and the black voter. Orphaned by the federal government and isolated even within the Republican Party, blacks were also abandoned by Boston Brahmins such as Henry Cabot Lodge and such other formerly noted racial liberals like Thomas Wentworth Higginson.

A supporter of John Brown's Raid, Higginson had commanded one of the original black regiments and written of the valor of his troops. He represented those Brahmins whose commitment to black rights began to wane in favor of the "Liberal Republican" priority for civil service reform in 1872 over "Grantism." Higginson then wandered farther from his abolitionist roots in 1884 in favor of other issues during the split over the nomination of James Blaine. More locally, in 1895, the Democratic legislature gerrymandered the Boston black and Republican West End district effectively ending black representation in city politics in favor of the Democrats.

Despite the ongoing opposition of Bostonians like Trotter and Harvard-trained W.E.B. Du Bois in their fight for civil and political rights, Booker T. Washington led many of the black Boston elite to focus on self-help during the period after 1890. Born in slavery, Washington spoke on behalf of the needs of the rural Southern disenfranchised black. However, he was actually very much at home in Boston. His wife had attended the Massachusetts Normal School in Framingham as a protégé of a Boston Brahmin; the Booker T. Washington family summered on Boston's South Shore. Indeed, his message of self-help arose from his teacher at Hampton Institute, the son of Boston missionaries. His Tuskegee Institute was supported by such neo-abolitionist Boston capitalists as Henry Lee Higginson. It was therefore appropriate that he called the first meeting of his "National Negro Business League" in Boston in 1900.

The effects of race riots in Atlanta and lynchings elsewhere, the action of President Theodore Roosevelt in relation to the expulsion of black soldiers at Brownsville Texas as well as the advance of the Jim Crow laws even into the north led to the eclipse of Booker T. Washington within Boston. There was the concomitant rise of William Monroe Trotter at the turn of the century as the voice of its black community.

Figure 57 - William Monroe Trotter

His father James Monroe Trotter was born in slavery in Mississippi one of three sons of a slave woman and her slave master. Freed by their father, Trotter was living in Cincinnati Ohio during the Civil War when he enlisted in the 55th Massachusetts Regiment. One of the few blacks promoted to officer rank, he led the fight to achieve parity of pay for the "U.S. Colored Troops." Moving to Boston after the war, he worked in the postal service. The leading New England black Cleveland Democrat, he was appointed in 1884 during Cleveland's first term to the lucrative post of Recorder of Deeds in the District of Columbia. This was the salient federal patronage position offered to blacks, long held by Frederick Douglass under Republican Party auspices.

His son William Monroe Trotter grew up in Boston. Graduating as valedictorian of his all-white class at Hyde Park High School, he graduated from Harvard in 1895 while earning a Phi Beta Kappa key. Believing in the principles of the meritocracy he had experienced while at Harvard, he refused to accept the limitations in ambition that Booker T Washington espoused. Prospering in the real estate business despite the difficulties encountered by blacks even in Boston, he and his wife were members of Boston's small black elite society. They lived in a private home in a multi-racial neighborhood in Dorchester. Throughout his life, he remained committed to temperance and was active in the Twelfth Baptist Church.

In 1901, he founded *The Boston Guardian* in opposition to the self-help position taken by Booker T. Washington. He personally opposed Washington when the latter spoke in Boston in 1903 at the Columbus Avenue A.M.E. Zion Church (the "Boston Riot"). Imprisoned for a month as a result, his support never reached the level of the "Bookerites" although providing an impetus to W.E.B. Du Bois to inaugurate his black-led Niagara Movement as a precursor to the NAACP. He worked in 1915 with De Bois in protest in Boston against the showing of the film *The Birth of a Nation*. In the spirit of his idol William Lloyd Garrison and from the same building, Trotter carried on his crusade for equal rights as editor of his weekly newspaper.He drove away potential political allies such as Du Bois and the Niagara Movement and then the NAACP, thus dividing the already small black community. In opposition to what he considered the white-led NAACP, he founded in 1908 the "National Independent Political League" (NIPL) as an alternative black-led organization to participate in elections. Rather than be in the pocket of one party, he advocated playing off one party against the other. However, after supporting the Democrat Woodrow Wilson in the election of 1912, he was confronted by an even more segregationist administration than that of the Republican William Howard Taft. He had attacked the latter based on President Taft's refusal to rescind the decision re the court martial of the black troops in Brownsville. Despite the advance of Jim Crow, from his unique stance in Boston, Trotter still believed in the political power that could be generated among blacks themselves.

The Boston branch of the NAACP was still the largest in the country until exceeded in 1918 by the far larger black community of Washington DC. With a heavy sprinkling of Yankee Protestants, it still represented the Boston abolitionist tradition along with the descendants of the elite black community. After 1920, the white membership yielded to black leadership even in Boston. Nonetheless, even after the migration that occurred during the First World War, with a population of ca 16,000 in 1920, blacks represented only 2% of Boston's population. Power shifted within the national stage and within the NAACP to Chicago, Philadelphia and New York as much larger centers of black population. The old black elite that considered themselves as "Black Bostonians" did not unite with the newly arrived southern migrants nor with the West Indian immigrants. The disenfranchisement of the black community occurred even more as the Irish-led Democratic Party took power.

Chapter 5 The Immigrant City 1914-1965

Introduction

The adjoining map shows Boston at the turn of the century when South Station has been blocked out to consolidate the railroad lines going south and west. By the turn of the century, the expansion of the population of the city no longer depended upon the filling in of the coves but upon those living in the annexed adjacent areas on the mainland and access by streetcars. By streetcar, a worker could reach his office downtown from Dorchester, annexed in the 1870s, as easily as from the Back Bay. Electrification enlarged the range for commuters farther to six miles from City Hall. Street layout was primarily the result of the action of developers sub-dividing their holdings; their small scale operations necessitated frequent deviations from the grid. With little municipal control over building, the development of the streetcar system defined the growth of the city for the next generation.

The steam railroads from the 1840s enabled businessmen from as far as five miles out to access downtown. Passenger transport became increasingly important as a source of revenue to the railroads. As soon as 1837, the Boston & Lowell (B&L) began to add an intermediate stop in Woburn; the Boston & Worcester (B&W) did as well by its "Newton Special" starting in 1843. Supported by the entry of "commuters," buying "commuted" reduced fare season tickets, country estates in the peripheral towns became subdivided into building lots with Newton the most prominent railroad suburb. Newton Corner, Newtonville, West Newton and Auburndale were all separate railroad stops around which houses clustered.

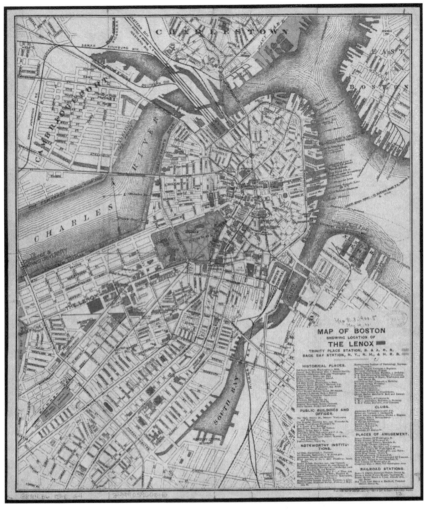

Figure 58 - Boston 1898

170

5.1 The Streetcar System

The first horse car line reached Roxbury Crossing from the South End in 1857. With development occurring along street car lines, the horse car enabled the development of the closer-in South End in the 1850s and 1860s and of Lower Roxbury and Dorchester in the 1870s, all within four miles of downtown. Boston experienced a great burst of building activity in the late 1880s and early 1890s. The population rose from 450,000 in 1890 to 560,000 in 1900. These immigrants, mainly English-speaking Protestants from the Maritime Provinces of Canada, were prosperous enough to take advantage of the newly established electrified streetcar lines in the 1880s and 1890s extending six miles from City Hall. They dispersed into the newly annexed areas of Dorchester and Jamaica Plain to build detached houses on larger lots, farther from downtown.

One area of development in Dorchester was near the First Church on Meeting House Hill that can serve as an example.. One such transition was that of the Dyer estate. Micah Dyer sold his house on South Union Park in the South End in 1865 to buy and build in Dorchester near Meeting House Hill. A graduate of Tilton Academy and the Harvard Law School, he was a pioneer in women's professional education as president of the New England Female Medical College in the South End. His wife was a descendant of early Dorchester settlers and one of the founders of the New England Hospital for Women and Children, connected to the Women's Medical College. The hospital provided professional opportunities for female medical graduates.

By the 1880s, Dyer subdivided his estate on Jones Hill overlooking Dorchester Bay near Cushing Avenue. He built his own family house in which his son lived until the latter's death in 1918. Other buyers included men such as James Humphreys Upham, the last chair of Dorchester's Board of Selectmen and a descendant of the family for which nearby Upham's Corner was named in 1800. Another was Sylvester Pashley, one of New England's leading builder-contractors. St Mary's Episcopal Church along with the Methodist Church associated with the Dyer family gave gravitas to the neighborhood. At the top of the hill was St Mary's Infant Asylum (later St Margaret's Hospital) that attracted prosperous Irish Catholics in the next generation associated with the hospital. Columbia Road was later laid out in 1897 as a parkway to connect this area of substantial architect-designed detached houses to the entrance to Franklin Park.

With electrification after 1887, there was a merger of the existing lines such as the Metropolitan Street Railway into the West End Street Railway Company (WESR), founded by the financier Henry M. Whitney that had extended the lines as far as six miles from City Hall. He built the first electrified line out Beacon Street in premier upper-class Brookline in conjunction with the development of that street. Originally planned for mansions, it was eventually lined with apartment houses. Frederick Law Olmsted had been innovative in designing that street as a wide boulevard with a central reservation for the streetcars as he did Commonwealth Avenue west of Kenmore Square.

In 1894, the Boston Elevated Railway Company (BERY) was formed to build rapid transit elevated tracks and subways to deal with the problem of downtown traffic. In 1897, the BERY also acquired lease of all the surface lines to create a coordinated system. To the surprise of outsiders, conservative Boston was the first in the country to open an underground route. The rationale for that decision was compatible with the antiquarian character of the city. The subway line in the model of London and Paris rather than an "el" would be used from Park Street along Tremont and then Boylston Streets to skirt but not desecrate the sacred Boston Common. The Common had ceased to be common pasture land in 1831 and became America's first public park. The choice of a "subway" rather than an unsightly "el" respected the Common while freeing up clogged Tremont Street from its streetcar traffic.

Figure 59 - Boston 1910 Tunnels and Subways

The Washington Street "tunnel" (note the difference in terminology) was built but then extended in both directions from downtown as an "el." To the south, it ran from the South End to Dudley Street in Roxbury, the secondary commercial shopping district. Then despite strenuous objections, the "el" was extended in 1909 along Washington Street past Egleston Square station to a terminus at Forest Hills. Adjacent was the Forest Hills Cemetery, established in 1848 by the Town of Roxbury analogous to the earlier Mount Auburn Cemetery to create landscaped burial grounds to comfort mourners and elevate the public taste. With the cemetery a forerunner of the landscaped public parks, the adjacent Franklin Park became the cemetery's successor and substitute.

In 1912, an elevated route also opened from Haymarket to Lechmere Square in Cambridge; in 1914, the original Tremont Street line extended beyond the Public Gardens to Kenmore Square. By 1914, the combined BERY system carried nearly 350 million passengers a year, never to be exceeded as the automobile took hold and the money inflation of the First World War occurred and upped the five cent fare. Starting in 1922, busses began to replace the streetcars. "Public control" starting in 1919 guaranteed a specified return on the BERY securities. The fare was immediately raised to ten cents by the end of 1919 and remained at that level for many years.

The publicly-owned Metropolitan Transit Authority (MTA) took over the Boston Elevated in 1947; extensions to Revere and Riverside came about in the 1950s. The Massachusetts Bay Transit Authority (MBTA) took over in the 1960s to create, by incorporating the earlier railroad commuting lines in the following decades, a truly regional system by the South Shore Extension and the incorporation of the Old Colony Railroad; the Cambridge Extension to Alewife from Harvard Square and other extensions to the east from East Boston including Logan Airport.

The re-aligned Orange Line built in the 1980s from Back Bay Station to Forest Hills enabled the removal of the elevated structure that had darkened Washington Street since the first decade of the 1900s. In explicit recognition of the spirit of the Emerald Necklace, a linear "Corridor Park" was created above the swath through the city taken during the 1950s and 1960s to become the aborted "Inner Belt" of I-95. The mainly underground redirected Orange Line runs from the South End through Roxbury and Jamaica Plain. Local residents, called "user consultants," participated in the design of the decking where there would be access accorded between the South End and the Back Bay, divided by the building of the railroad in the mid-19th century.

5.2 Dorchester: The Jewish Streetcar Suburb

In the first decade of the new century, Boston's population rose to 670,000, with the continued increase of the poorer "new" immigrants mainly clustered in the central city tenements. More affluent German and Canadian immigrants continued to diffuse to the suburban areas of West Roxbury and Jamaica Plain served by streetcars. The population reached near its height at 750,000 in 1920, augmented by the "new immigration" and their natural increase, mainly Italian and Jewish. The increased prosperity of the latter particularly enabled them to disperse from the tenements of the West End and the South End. However, because of Catholic parish territoriality, they were free to move only into the empty area of Roxbury and South Dorchester to make these areas far more densely populated than before.

Once relatively thinly settled with estates on the minor hills, the Bowdoin Hill portion of South Dorchester became subdivided and synonymous with "Jewville." At the turn of the 20th century, the East European Jewish community, formerly in the North End and then the West End, moved to the lower reaches of Blue Hill Avenue in Roxbury and Warren Street at Grove Hall. The Stanetzsky Funeral Home at Grove Hall remained its centerpiece for the next half-century. Centered by 1906 around the Orthodox *Congregation Adath Jeshuran* at the corner of Brunswick Street, the movement of Boston's immigrant East European Jews to that area accelerated following the 1908 Chelsea fire. Extending south along Blue Hill Avenue, they moved into the then last open area south of Roxbury adjacent to Franklin Park.

West of already settled Upham's Corner, Blue Hill Avenue ran on the edge of Catholic parishes relatively distant from their churches. The area of Jewish settlement then extended along the three-mile spine of Blue Hill Avenue from just south of Dudley Street in Roxbury through Grove Hall. The street widened south of Columbia Road in Dorchester to lead eventually to the southern border of the city in Mattapan (Roxbury-Dorchester-Mattapan). This "RDM" area of

Jewish settlement thus skirted Franklin Park and Franklin Field had been designed by Olmsted long before in the 1880s, in then rural West Roxbury.

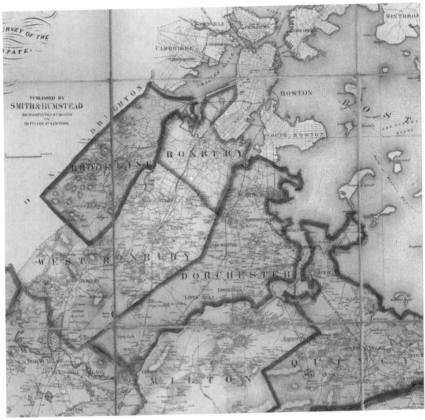

Figure 60 - Roxbury-Dorchester-Mattapan

The Washington Street "el" brought commuters to Egleston Square from downtown and the South End. The trolley then ran in a reservation for a distance along the northern edge of Franklin Park along Seaver Street's well-tended low rise apartments, many with discreetly advertised ground floor physician office. Humboldt Avenue led to the earlier settled upper middle class area of Roxbury Highlands/ There was the Young Men's' Hebrew Association (YMHA) in a sprawling converted mansion.

Farther on was the 1925 Greek temple of the Conservative *Congregation Mishkan Tefila* at the corner of Elm Hill Avenue. The third of Boston's synagogues, *Mishkan Tefila* was a result of the merger of two of the orthodox synagogues organized in the 1870s when both *Adath Israel* and *Ohabei Shalom* moved to a Reform mode of worship. First in the South End, it then moved to Moreland Street near Dudley Street in Roxbury where it introduced family pews. This was in the manner of the Conservative movement with rabbis trained at the Jewish Theological Seminary in New York. Family pews were a hallmark of that movement as it modified Orthodox practice in adaptation to American norms but retained Hebrew to a greater extent than Reform.. The move to its Greek temple in the Roxbury Highlands in the mid-1920s was recognition of the prosperity and size of the new community.

The streetcar then turned to join Blue Hill Avenue close to Columbia Road at the grand entrance to Franklin Park. The Franklin Park Theater at the corner was the centerpiece of a block of stores. Its upper floor was the focus of the *Arbetyr Ring* (Workmen's Circle) that represented the secular Yiddish speaking descendants of the Jewish Socialist Bund of the Jewish Pale. Once prominent, it disappeared as the original Yiddish speaking Socialist immigrants were succeeded by their English speaking Democratic Party children. Franklin Park provided a rose garden, zoo and a promenade, the sections mainly utilized by the local community but shared with the entire city. The popular golf course was not a preoccupation of the mainly working class Jews of RDM. During the dark winters of the Second World War, walking in the park could make one subject to wandering toughs hyped up by followers of Father Coughlin and his sermons about the Jews.

The trolley line then ran in a reservation in the center of the wide street south along Blue Hill Avenue and the eastern edge of Franklin Park. The American Legion Highway that ran along the southern boundary of Franklin Park led to the Hecht Neighborhood House. First founded as the Hebrew Industrial School for vocational training for girls in 1889 on Chambers Street, it had moved from the West End in 1936. It was there, during the 1940s and 1950s alongside the YMHA that young men played basketball and billiards and learned to dance with the local girls by big band music provided by a juke box. These more secular informal settings were joined by an entire range of organizations sponsored by B'nai B'rith and the American Zionist Organization (AZA) but not by the religious organizations.

The American Legion Highway then led to Morton Street that split the extensive grounds of the Boston State Mental Hospital. Close to Morton Street on Blue Hill Avenue almost exactly in the center of RDM was the large G&G Delicatessen, the social center of the entire neighborhood. On the eve of Election Day, the local political candidates would pay a courtesy visit in an open air rally adjacent to the restaurant to this bastion of the Democratic Party in Ward 14.

The southern border of RDM was just a few blocks north of Mattapan Square at the bridge over the New York and New England Railroad line that ran through the steeper upland route through central Dorchester from Readville to Boston. Near that border, just a block south of Wellington Hill Street was Hazleton Street, notable for its detached houses and the very attractive Palladian windowed Mattapan Branch Library built in the last flush years before the Depression took hold. There were a few more blocks of low-rise well cared-for apartment houses culminating in a large park well-equipped with tennis courts superior to those in Franklin Field.

The frequently contested ground of Franklin Field between the Codman Square working class Irish at Talbot Avenue and Jewish Blue Hill Avenue was the recreational center with a large clubhouse of 1890s vintage. The Catholic Irish gangs to the east along Talbot Avenue near Codman Square would descend intermittently to disrupt the Jewish boys playing ball. A deep depression (formerly a peat field) served as a running track oval that was flooded in winter to provide a skating rink. On the higher ground was a bevy of asphalt-lined tennis courts bereft of nets and basketball courts. Men in white visors played bowls with ritually polite murmurs on the exquisitely green lawns kept smooth by concrete rollers immediately in front of the clubhouse. This was also the site of the 4th of July fireworks and other festivities where ice-cream cups would be freely given out. Memorable was the trip in an open-air car down Blue Hill Avenue past Franklin Field that Franklin Roosevelt made during his 1936 presidential campaign.

Blue Hill Avenue was also well-equipped with second run movie theaters at Franklin Park, Morton Street and the Oriental motif theater at Mattapan Square, the last with a ceiling with small lights that twinkled like stars. The smaller Liberty Theater intermittently showed Yiddish films. Saturday matinees had a full bill of a double feature, serial and newsreel for a theater-full of young shouting children where fantasies thrived while Fred Astaire and Ginger Rogers danced in formal attire. Weekday matinees raised attendance by giving out dishes but it was the uniquely air-cooled interiors that drew patrons in the summer.

Figure 61 - The Boston Three Decker

For the next fifty years until the 1960s, a Jewish community of Roxbury-Dorchester-Mattapan (RDM) with a population approaching 80,000 lived within this three square mile area. They lived in apartments and detached houses but mainly in traditional closely packed wooden "three-deckers." A streetcar-suburban detached adaptation of the fashionable trend to horizontal living in French flats; it is characterized by "flats" of up to six or seven rooms on each floor. Relatively inexpensive to build, they provided light and air and front and rear porches. With two rents to insure pay-back of mortgage loans, they furnished working class or lower middle class families with decent if modest living quarters.

The widespread frame triple decker built in Boston during the era of 1890-1920 can be described as follows: Each building is self-contained with a separate entrance from a public hall and a stairway in front and often with a similar entrance from a small staircase in the rear. A dwelling with as few as five rooms and a bathroom would contain a small private hallway from which would arise on one side the parlor, bedroom and dining room, On the other side the private hall

179

leads into a second bedroom and bathroom; at the end is the door leading to the kitchen containing set tubs and a cook stove with an adjoining water heater, at the other side of which is the entrance from the back public stairway.

Unlike other areas of the city, there were very few barrooms. The numerous small stores that served every need were strung along one side of Blue Hill Avenue. The few restaurants were Kosher as were the butcher shops. It was scandalous when an ostensibly non-Kosher Chinese restaurant called "Ye Old Brown Jug" opened in the neighborhood on the corner of Morton Street. Reflecting the densely populated and segregated RDM neighborhood, the many local public schools named after such Yankees as William Bradford, Pauline Agassiz Shaw and Roger Wolcott were almost entirely Jewish in their student body but almost entirely Irish Catholic in their teaching staff and even more clearly Christian in their culture leading into the Christmas season. Christmas Carols were sung as a matter of course. At Christmas, the sole Christian family of the local Greek shoe repairman on one of the blocks living near Morton Street stood out with its windows alight with electric candles in a sea of darkness. There were just a few non-Jewish students in the elementary schools on the High Holidays. On those days, the streets near the numerous Orthodox synagogues on Woodrow Avenue were closed off to traffic. Few cars drove along Blue Hill Avenue while the young people dressed in their holiday best stood along the stone wall that enclosed Franklin Field.

The elementary schools fed into junior high schools that also reflected the segregated population. The mainly Jewish Solomon Lewenberg Junior High School on Wellington Hill Street served upper Dorchester and Mattapan; the Frank V. Thompson the area around Morton Street; the Patrick T. Campbell School the area of Grove Hall. Few Jews went to the local Dorchester High School for Boys; more to Dorchester High for Girls. Jews were far more in evidence at Roxbury Memorial High School for Boys and the Jeremiah E Burke School for Girls. The central city Boston English High School had a substantial number but the clearly college-bound went to Boston Latin School in the Fenway. For the first generation of native English speakers, college was almost a universal goal. However, the holy grail of Harvard was particularly available only to those from the Latin School.

Gerrymandered within Ward 12 and Ward 14 and a single state legislative district, their representatives traded their vote for petty favors. In the face of the overwhelming Irish hegemony in Boston and the at-large election to the City Council, RDM could not exert influence that the number of constituents might warrant city-wide and even state-wide. The police and school systems were Irish. The Boston Public School Committee candidates boasted of their parochial school credentials rather than their interest in public school education. Enclosed by the actions of the local banks and the anti-Semitism of the neighboring Irish clustered protectively around their parish churches, the lines were clearly drawn block by block, street by street, even building by building as though enclosed by a ghetto wall.

Throughout this era, the socio-economic level of the Jewish area was higher than the Irish Catholic area to the east. This began to change after the Second World War; by 1960, the more affluent Jews had moved out of Boston to adjoining suburbs like Brookline and Newton, as had such important congregations as *Temple Mishkan Tefila*. In the early 1960s, the YMHA close by the long standing African American neighborhood near Townshend Street closed, merging its assets with the Hecht House. Those 50,000 Jews remaining that had become mainly working class unable or unwilling to support the community facilities. The population moved out en masse with the arson and street attacks when subjected to the block busting of the late 1960s. Even the landmark G&G closed in 1968. The Jews were able to disperse to live in many of the surrounding towns like Milton, Sharon, Randolph and Stoughton from which they had previously been excluded or not chosen to live. However, an entire generation had managed to enter the professional class via entry to Harvard or Boston University with many finding opportunities in their dispersal throughout the country.

As an example of the deterioration of the community, the southern edge of Franklin Field became the site of poorly built temporary veteran housing for Jewish veteran families. More permanent public housing replaced in 1954 the temporary buildings. Welcomed at the time, faulty construction coupled with the low-lying character of the site bedeviled those living there after heavy rains. Rats were a problem. Although initially entry in the project required an income higher than the surrounding area, the inhabitants became increasingly foreign to the racial and lower-middle-class social character of the neighborhood on which it was imposed. The housing project eventually contributed to the disintegration of the surrounding community. Conversely, without its own commercial strip, the departure of the Jewish inhabitants and Jewish-owned businesses on Blue Hill Avenue in the 1960s contributed to the destruction of the public housing project without a community structure of its own.

The varied American response to immigration seemed to play out particularly in Boston. The creation of the "new American" in the melting pot in which differences will be burned away was a somewhat generous and idealistic response to the large number of immigrants in the nineteenth century. Although mainly of British origin in Boston itself, there were from the start elsewhere in the country in the 18th century also Dutch, Swedes, French, German Protestants and Scots-Irish. Boston remained different in its almost universal British stock. The process of seemingly effortless "Americanization" that had transpired seemed unlikely with the settlement by the large number of Irish Catholic immigrants in cities like Boston. The "Know-Nothings" had as elsewhere a significant impact in Boston in the early 1850s in response to the Irish influx. Nevertheless, those such as Ralph Waldo Emerson maintained a generous opening to "all the European tribes"… even extending to "the African, Polynesian and the Cossack." The nativist response to the increased diversity in the 1850s seemed to dissipate following the Civil War in an uneasy truce in Boston as a Democratic Party coalition of the Irish and the still ruling Yankees lasted for a generation.

The response originating among the Yankee elite in Boston of immigration restriction in the 1890s was based on the persistent underlying belief in Anglo-Saxon racial superiority coupled with the seeming unlikelihood of its imposition on the large number of the newly seemingly inassimilable masses. A continuing single-minded commitment to "Anglo-conformity" led to bigotry, the proliferation of patriotic societies, restrictive covenants, and restrictive quotas. However, an alternative that also arose was to mitigate the unilateral application of Anglo-conformity as the measure of "Americanization." The "triple melting pot" maintained the idea of the amalgamation of nationalities but accepted for the first time the possibility of an "American" whose religion might be other than Protestant to include not only Catholics but Jews. The rubric of a "Judeo-Christian" society appeared to offer equality to the entire range of white European immigration in the latter half of the 20th century.

Starting in 1915 in a series of articles entitled "Democracy versus the Melting Pot," Horace Kallen offered this concept of a federation or commonwealth of national cultures united under the aegis of a common language and common American political and economic system. Democracy for the individual could also by extension mean democracy for the multiplicity of groups. The metaphor of an orchestra playing a symphony was offered rather than a melting pot, of a harmony of voices rather than in unison. To counter the enhanced commitment to "Anglo-conformity" and immigration restriction, "cultural pluralism" also arose as an alternative within Boston. This latter concept arose in the context of the explicit tension offered by the existence of immigrants in Boston and their existence at Harvard, the bastion of the Boston Anglo-conformity.

5.3 Horace Kallen and Cultural Pluralism

In 1906, Kallen helped found the "Harvard Menorah Society," the first of its kind in the United States serving to sponsor Jewish cultural events among college-level students. His initial academic career, after a short period at Harvard, was at the University of Wisconsin from 1911-1918 where he failed to achieve tenure. A brilliant thinker, he remained relatively unrecognized. His major academic position was at the somewhat irregular "New School for Social Research," which he helped found in New York and where he taught from 1919 until his retirement in 1952.

Kallen's interest was in the secular, non-theological aspects of Jewish tradition. Ethnic identity, he asserted, can provide the individual with the will to persist in the rootlessness of modern life. Zionism, as a secular Hebraic ideal to renationalize the Jewish people, became his replacement for the religious tradition he no longer accepted. It was also a means by which he could reconcile his membership among the Jewish people with his adherence to American principles. For example, becoming a Zionist was fully compatible with being an American since the Bible was the foundation for the formation of a free society with guarantees of liberty and justice for all - the American idea. Support for the formation of a new society in Palestine devoted to these same ideas would make one a better American as well. This same idea provided the basis for Louis Brandeis to reconcile his American identity with Zionism.

Figure 62 - Horace Meyer Kallen

Horace Meyer Kallen was the son of an orthodox rabbi of Lithuanian background, born in 1882 and brought to Boston in 1887. He rejected his father's insistence on the primacy of religious training in favor of secular education. He eventually graduated from Harvard where he was a student of George Santayana as well as William James and a colleague of Alain Locke, the black intellectual. He also rejected his father's orthodox Jewish religion in favor of what he later called "atheistic humanism."

Nonetheless, he did not discard his Jewish identity. Under the influence of Mugwump Barrett Wendell, one of his Yankee Harvard teachers, Kallen was able to reconcile his Hebraic inheritance to his American identity and his Harvard education. Wendell was a Professor of English at Harvard, a member of the Boston Athenaeum and the Massachusetts Historical Society. He represented an ongoing liberal strand of thinking among Boston Brahmins that believed the development of America was based on the effect of the Hebrew Bible on the Puritan mind. Moreover, Kallen was a student and protégé of William James at Harvard whose philosophy of "pragmatism" offered the sense of options, of alternatives based on respect for differences in experience and culture. Although James accepted Darwinism, he did not accept the derivative Social Darwinism that provided a justification for Anglo-Saxon claims of superiority. With a newly minted doctorate, Kallen was chosen by William James to edit for publication his last work entitled Some Problems in Philosophy.

Kallen used the Jamesian thinking that was prevalent during his time at Harvard as part of his justification for cultural pluralism as an alternative to the idea of the "melting pot." In America, he stated, Jewish Emancipation is not the suppression of differences as was the case in Western Europe. In accordance with the Declaration of Independence, it was the liberation of differences. He reiterated these ideas toward the end of his long life America represented to him " right to be different...That law and government are devices to secure this right...to convert feelings of exile into sentiments of freely belonging...It is Emancipation for rather than from, creative rather than defensive."

5.4 Sacco -Vanzetti and "Americanism"

Coupled with the nativist response to the Jewish immigration to Boston was the response to the one from Italy. The newly arrived, unskilled and speaking a foreign language, came as had the Irish from the poorest rural areas of their country. Afflicted by famine and disease as well as natural disasters, the Italian immigrants had in many cases a sense of helplessness and hopelessness. They once again inhabited the North End but soon spilled over to the West End starting in the 1890s and to East Boston connected in the 1930s by the Sumner Tunnel; then to Somerville and elsewhere where they too lived segregated from the Irish Catholics as well as the Yankees.

185

Most men and their first generation sons worked as laborers in construction, as fishermen and in the fruit and produce stands and as barbers. Many of their daughters worked in the needle trades. To an extraordinary degree, the first American-born generation continued to live within the Italian community and work in family businesses. It was only the next post-Second World War generation that had more access to post-secondary education that moved away, to the lamentation of their parents.

It is important to note that the term "Italian" was not used initially; the immigrants identified themselves by the locale from which they had come. Even as later identified as "Italian" to outsiders, they continued to identify themselves to each other by their locale. The country had but recently been politically unified, but not so culturally. Significant divisions remained between the northerners and the much larger number of southerners; between those from the Italian mainland and those from Sicily. Identification was with one's family and one's fellow villagers with whom one lived, married and worked as well as shopped and prayed. By 1920, thirty thousand Italian immigrants lived in the North End, mainly in cold water tenements with hall toilets, creating a population density that rivaled that of Calcutta.

Because of the expected temporary nature of much of the early Italian immigrants; unlike the Jews, they had a low rate of naturalization and thus low level of political power. By 1900, only 36% of the eligible Italian inhabitants of the North End were citizens, even fewer were registered to vote. Despite strenuous efforts, James Donnaruma, the Republican publisher of *La Gazzetta del Massachusetts* was never able to induce a significant number of voters to follow his recommendations. Although socialists saw the ballot as a basis for reforming society, there were others politically conscious who eschewed the ballot box as a farcical exercise in futility. Although frequently the nativists lumped together all political radicals as "reds," they considered those calling themselves anarchists particularly dangerous and alien. The anarchists questioned the very existence of private property and sought to undermine the government by singular acts of violence designed to foment revolution. An active effort was made by nativists to brand all immigrants as radicals and even further as "anarchists" and thus incompatible with American ways. Boston's North End was considered their center.

In 1919, labor unrest erupted. Four million persons went out on strike. The Bolshevik revolution in 1917 seemed to presage world revolution. In Boston, even the police went out on strike. The social order seemed to be collapsing. Many robberies had occurred during this year immediately after the end of what was then still called the Great War. On the 15th April 1920, two men were robbed and killed carrying a $16,000 payroll for a shoe factory in South Braintree near Boston. This robbery led to the arrest of a pair of Italian immigrants, known to be anarchists. The trial was unfair impugning their Americanism rather than their guilt and full of error. They nevertheless went to their execution in August 1927 despite protests from the world over. The high point of nativism known as Anglo-conformity that denigrated all foreign characteristics in the name of "Americanism" seemed to be epitomized in a cause célèbre that branded Boston a center for bigotry.

Figure 63 - Sacco - Vanzetti

Known to be followers of a particularly charismatic preacher of violence living in Boston's North End, they were nevertheless men with a gentle nature. Nicola Sacco was considered a skilled and dependable worker who made soles for shoes. Married to a fellow anarchist, he had a child with another on its way. Bartolommeo Vanzetti had left Italy deeply embittered by the injustice he himself had suffered; not doing well in the new country, he chose to work as a fish peddler to permit greater freedom to carry on his life as a thoughtful autodidact. They were portrayed by their supporters as merely "philosophical" anarchists whose character could not have led them to a violent act. Nevertheless, they had lived among a close group in Mexico during the First World War some of whose underground members were clearly involved in attempted assassinations. In addition to still unresolved questions as to their guilt or innocence is the validity of the judicial process by which they were convicted.

The "Sedition and Espionage Acts" passed in 1917 during wartime reflected that immigrants, already viewed as inferior and a drag on wages, were also seen as potentially dangerous. Hundreds of anti-war and radical immigrants were arrested and deported. Foreign-born members of the Socialist party were targeted as was Eugene Debs, their native-born leader. Suppression of free speech continued even after the war ended. The anti-radical branch of the Department of Justice, the General Intelligence Division, was headed by J. Edgar Hoover then at the start of his career. A specific target of Attorney General A. Mitchell Palmer was the followers of the anarchist Galleani, which included men like Sacco and Vanzetti. The infamous Palmer Raids in early January 1920 rounded up suspected radicals throughout the country; eight hundred in New England alone were marched through the streets of Boston in chains to be imprisoned under brutal conditions.

When arrested, no specific evidence tied Sacco and Vanzetti to the robbery and murder in South Braintree. However, when arrested in a roundup of other persons thought to be involved in a series of bombings, they were found to be armed and evasive, lying in reply to questions. They later claimed they had been evasive and fearful because they were in the process of distributing anarchist literature that might be considered subversive. The prosecution had a weak case tying either of them to the robbery; witnesses did not identify Vanzetti despite his distinctive handlebar moustache and Sacco was identified, perhaps erroneously, because of his close similarity to others. Eyewitnesses putting the pair at the scene of the crime did so on very shaky evidence.

Questioned mainly during the first few days about their beliefs and affiliations, it appeared that they were being tried and convicted because of these beliefs rather than any actual guilt in the robbery. This seemed to be confirmed by the actual trial when foreign culture and particularly those who were Italian speakers were treated contemptuously. The issue of the men's political beliefs was brought in by the judge as "cognate" with the crime. Their patriotism impugned, they were goaded into a defense of anarchism as a political philosophy. The defense attorney also worked to turn it into a political trial, of who the men were rather than what they may have done. Responding to the political implications of supporting patriotism versus these immigrant anarchists, the jury convicted the men within a very short time. The prosecution found additional continued support in the recurrent (seven) appeals heard by the same presiding judge who had intervened so boldly on the behalf of the prosecution in the original trials.

The case had now become a cause far beyond the fate of the two men. Artists and writers intervened in their behalf. The funds necessary for their defense came not only from their poor Italian core supporters but from a wider range of labor organizations, even the conservative American Federation of Labor. The Sacco-Vanzetti Defense Committee enlisted a number of Boston liberals led by Mrs. Glendower Evans and William Thompson, his last defense attorney. The novelist John Dos Passos was an active defender as was Felix Frankfurter of the Harvard Law School publishing an article in *The Atlantic Monthly* and an editorial even in the conservative mainstream *Boston Herald* (for which it received a Pulitzer Prize). Detractors of the atheistic foreign radicals spanned the range of evangelical and nativist organizations starting with the *Boston Evening Transcript*, the voice of Brahmin Boston, extending to the American Legion and the evangelist Billy Sunday.

The Commission set up by the Cadillac car dealer and Republican Massachusetts Governor Alvan T. Fuller offered great hope and led to even greater disappointment. It was headed in practice by the highly respected but also highly conservative Harvard President Abbot Lawrence Lowell. The sometime representative of the Brahmin class in protecting free speech and academic freedom, he also represented in his career the abdication of that class from its abolitionist past to its more insular characteristics of anti-Semitism and anti-immigrant bias.

The execution was no longer merely the workings of bigoted backwater officials but was now stamped by the seal of Harvard. The failure of the "Lowell Commission" to prevent execution drove many of the educated class into a subsequently more radical political and social stance in despair of what they had hoped to be a vindication of the American judicial system.

During the days leading to their execution, the streets of Boston were filled with protesters; hundreds were booked at the Joy Street police station of persons such as Edna St Vincent Millay and many others who were proud for the rest of their lives of having participated in these protests. Alfred Dreyfus, among many other foreign intellectuals and political leaders, signed a petition making clear a connection with his own politically-motivated trial. After their execution, the two lay in state at the Langone Funeral Home in Boston's North End, making explicit their connection with the local Italian Boston community. They were recognized by many of their fellow countrymen as having been executed based to a great extent on their Italian identity. The trial and its aftereffects exposed the deep rupture in America of two nations, confirming the nature of Boston in its inability to evolve into a more inclusive city.

With the turn of the century and men like John F Fitzgerald as mayor, power had clearly shifted. No longer need Catholics be deferential and accommodating to the Protestant establishment. David Walsh had been elected governor in 1914 and then re-elected for the next thirty years as the Massachusetts Democratic senator. One of the leaders of the ascendant Irish during the 20th century was their militant archbishop William O'Connell. He announced triumphantly in 1908 at the time of the centennial of the church in Boston: "The Puritan has passed; the Catholic remains." To illustrate its wealth and power, a new diocesan chancery was built in the 1930s in the Italian Renaissance style in Brighton alongside a palazzo for his residence.

5.5 Cardinal O'Connell and the Boston Catholic Church

Figure 64 - William Cardinal O'Connell

William O'Connell was born in 1859, the eleventh child of a devout Irish Catholic couple who had emigrated from County Cavan in 1850. The father worked as a brick mason in Lowell until his early death from throat cancer; the mother held the family together. A bright student, young William found school much more congenial than work in the mills. He went to St John's College, the Sulpician seminary in Baltimore and graduated from the Jesuit Boston College. He studied for the priesthood at the North American College at Rome and was ordained at St John Lateran in 1884, the seat of the Bishop of Rome. His first pastorate was at St Joseph's in the slums of Allen Street in the West End, with which he stayed identified as he rose in stature. He was chosen as rector of the North American College replacing the "Americanist" Denis O'Connell, a protégé of Cardinal Gibbon of Baltimore. The Boston O'Connell was a safe "Romanist" who would support papal supremacy.

Favored by Pope Pius X and other high ranking church officials, he moved up quickly. Several other candidates were passed over when he was appointed Bishop of Portland Maine in 1901. In 1906, he was appointed bishop coadjutor, with right of succession, to the ailing Archbishop Williams of Boston. On his accession in 1908, the archdiocese covered 2500 square miles and contained 850,000 Catholics. There were 200 parish churches, six hundred priests and sixteen hundred sisters of various orders. By his death in 1944, many more parishes existed as the Catholic population spread throughout the north and south of Boston. Illustrative was the activity during his first eighteen months when there were thirty-one new parishes, twenty-nine new priests, nine more parochial schools and three new orders of nuns. In recognition, he was appointed cardinal in 1911, considered a particular mark of favor by all Boston Catholics.

O'Connell prided himself as being a modern day manager who personally controlled all the activities under his direction; described as "arctic," he brooked no delays or insubordination. The exalted churchman dressed in elaborate robes, speaking in lordly phrases and conducting himself with grave solemnity; he gave vicarious dignity to his working class parishioners. *The Pilot,* an independent pro-Irish paper once edited by the poet John Boyle O'Reilly, became the official wholly owned diocesan newspaper. St John's Seminary in Brighton, no longer under the direction of the Sulpician Fathers, came under Cardinal O'Connell's personal jurisdiction. His influence extended far beyond the diocese into all aspects of the political life of Massachusetts and the American Catholic Church as the leader of one of the largest sees.

During his tenure, the local parish church, co-terminus with the entirely Catholic neighborhoods separated only by ethnicity, was pervasive in the life of its members. The educated parish priest was an ever present authority in the midst of his uneducated flock. "Your parish speaks not only in your pastor and Bishop but in the name of the Holy Father who speaks in the name of God." Pictures of the Holy Family in every home were to be a universal model for the working class family. Special devotions took place at specific churches; particularly popular was the Mission Church founded originally by German Redemptorists on Parker Hill in Roxbury. Made of the Roxbury puddingstone quarried nearby, it is the site of popular novenas in honor of Our Lady of Perpetual Help.

Neighborhood, parish and religion were intertwined throughout the calendar. To encourage separatism, the faithful were warned to avoid all non-Catholic activities including funerals and other such semi-social occasions. Although heavily Irish in membership and management, ethnic parishes did exist where French, Portuguese, Polish or Italian would be spoken. There were particular differences between the Italian parishioners and the Irish hierarchy as well as between the two Italian parishes. The first Italian national parish was St Leonard's founded with its own building in the North End and an Italian priest in 1873. The Sacred Heart Italian Church in North Square founded in 1888 by Northern Italians of the Societa San Marco is unique in being under the control of the lay board rather than the Archbishop.

The separateness extended to all other ethnic groups; the Jews were a particular target. Father Coughlin's political party received its largest vote anywhere in Boston in 1936, affecting even Roosevelt's huge majority; Coughlin's newspaper *Social Justice* attacking the "Jewish moneychangers" was sold alongside the diocesan weekly *The Pilot* on the way out of Sunday Mass. In Boston, three o'clock on Sundays was sacred; schoolboy football games took a recess in order to listen to Coughlin's radio sermon. Cardinal O'Connell acquiesced to the appearance of Father Curran, the pro-Coughlin editor of the diocesan *Brooklyn Tablet*, at a civic ceremony in 1942 when Father Coughlin had himself been silenced for his Fascist sympathies. Jews in Dorchester were being attacked by Irish toughs even as they were being attacked and killed on the streets of Nazi Europe.

Under Cardinal O'Connell, Boston Catholics were engaged in a "cosmic" battle between the forces of darkness and light that seemed to echo the pervasiveness of religion in the early history of Calvinist Boston. Thousands marched through the streets of Boston behind bands in celebration of various anniversaries; the golden jubilee of O'Connell's ordination included a solemn High Mass attended by thousands followed by a "civic ceremony" that filled Fenway Park.

Italo-Americans also marched, united in defense of Mussolini and the Church; Irish joined them in defense of Franco and the Church and against godless Communism. Despite the fall-off in immigration after 1920 and particularly in the 1930s; by the time of his death in 1944, the Boston archdiocese passed a million mark and was third in the country after New York and Chicago.

This same generation of emerging immigrant Irish took delight beholding James Michael Curley, one of their own, resplendent with his pearl grey cravat, tailored morning coat and elegant striped trousers. Once elected mayor in 1914, he was re-elected either to Congress or state-wide office or as mayor intermittently for the next thirty four years. His funeral was the largest in Boston history, witnessed by a million on a November day in 1958. His career had witnessed an era of ethnic politics in Boston in which the Irish had triumphed at the cost of polarization that would begin to come to an end only with the election of a Catholic president who ran as everything James Michael Curley was not.

5.6 James Michael Curley and Boston Politics

Figure 65 - James Michael Curley

James Michael Curley was born the second son in 1874 in Roxbury to parents who were both immigrants from County Galway who met and married in Boston. His father literally worked himself to death from the exertion of lifting a curbstone at age thirty-four; his mother washed floors to support the family. The story of the Irish Catholics of Roxbury was imbedded in persecution; the building of their first church required defense by armed men to protect the construction site. Active in his local parish organizations and the Ancient Order of Hibernians, young Curley worked sixty hours a week and attended high school at night.

Trading on his gregariousness, in 1889 he was elected to the 75 member Common Council and became the leader of the Democratic Party organization in the Seventeenth Ward, the youngest of the city's political bosses. He founded his own local "Tammany Club." He was first elected to Congress in 1910 where he distinguished himself as had his predecessor John F Fitzgerald as an opponent to those seeking restriction of immigration by imposing the literacy test advocated by Henry Cabot Lodge.

Imprisoned for fraud for sixty days in 1904 for blithely taking a civil service exam for a constituent, he was nevertheless re-elected to office on the nine-member Board of Alderman after having been given a rousing send off to prison. As a "champion of the people," he was to be excused because after all he was merely taking care of one of his own. Despite his bravado, this imprisonment forever tainted his political ambitions. His reputation of petty graft and corruption never left him as he encountered recurrent legal difficulties.

The new city charter of 1910 placed him in the mayor's office in 1914 in control of far more patronage, stripping the former ward bosses of their power. Cultivating a reputation of "taking care of the people," he reinforced the sense of victimization that led to the bitter divisiveness that characterized Boston for the following generation. Mayor from 1914 to 1917 and again from 1922 to 1926, he took office again in 1930 at the start of the Depression. He could no longer as before provide the jobs and the public works he promised; the jobs were provided by the federal government through the New Deal and the hostile Republican state government prevented him from raising taxes. Although Massachusetts's governor from 1935 to 1937, he failed for the first time in his attempt to win the mayoralty in 1937 against Maurice J Tobin, once one of his lieutenants. The latter formed a new coalition of the now middle class Irish, Yankees and many of the assimilating Jews.

A national laughing stock, with any legitimacy withheld by the dispossessed Yankees, Curley became ever more desperate in his demagoguery. By his last campaign in 1945, he had become an embarrassment to the Cardinal; his trans-ethnic mainly Irish personal coalition had begun to fall apart. Boston's tax rate had gone far higher than other cities as unskilled jobs and manufacturing businesses began to migrate out of New England. He was finally defeated when John Hynes ran successfully in 1949 "to restore Boston's good name" after Curley once again returned to Boston after a federal prison term.

Curley was however perhaps more truly a champion of the people than his enemies would credit. He advocated improved workers' rights. His term of office as mayor during the prosperous 1920s was characterized by extensive public works spread throughout the city. The new tuberculosis hospital in Mattapan offered "fresh air" therapy to replace the far poorer one on Long Island that seemed to lead directly to the cemetery. The bathhouse at the L Street Beach in South Boston was another popular lasting example of his largess. Branch libraries appeared in the last burst of prosperity before the Depression set in.

James Michael Curley built several buildings at the Boston City Hospital (BCH); the one named after his sainted mother was the pediatric unit. It was not unusual that both patient care and building maintenance to suffer subsequently since funds had been expended for shoddy construction and hiring incompetent staff as political patronage. Nevertheless, during this era, the BCH was one of the leading hospitals in the country. The Thorndike Laboratory, established in 1923 under Harvard auspices, was the first clinical research facility in a municipal hospital. Its first directors Richard Minot and William B Castle carried out the work establishing the treatment for "pernicious anemia," earning the Nobel Prize as well as defining many of the basic principles for establishing the specialty of hematology.

Just as the earlier tide of Irish immigrants had been considered inassimilable, so the "new immigrants" with their strange appearance and particularly their Hebrew religion and its writing were categorized as "incompatible to the American way of life." Assailed during the debate about immigration restriction and in the 1920s by Henry Ford and other nativists and in the 1930s by Father Coughlin, they lived isolated within the ghetto of RDM. The Hebrew Teachers College, embedded in RDM, was the capstone of Hebrew education carried out in Hebrew schools that met after public school hours.

There were no Jewish day schools, which might be considered divisive. The Jewish Philanthropies and *The Jewish Advocate* weekly newspaper united the community in its march to Americanization. In 1923, it was symbolic that the Jewish Philanthropies raised a million dollars to move the Beth Israel Hospital from Townshend Street in the Roxbury Highlands to Brookline Avenue alongside the other Boston hospitals and the Harvard Medical School. The Reform *Temple Israel* built its synagogue on Commonwealth Avenue, its Meeting House adjoined Longwood Avenue in Brookline. The goal was acceptance; quality education was the means for entry into the Yankee world where commitment was also to things of the mind.

5.7 Boston Latin School and Harvard '53

Figure 66 - The Boston Latin School

The long established Boston Boys Latin School had moved to the Fenway in the 1920s across from the scholastically equivalent but far smaller and less prestigious Girls Latin School facing Huntington Avenue. Starting in 7th grade in 1943 to enter the class of '49 as an alternative to the local junior high school, there was no question but that the goal would be entry to college, possibly Harvard. In my case, there was no paternal hesitation to signify that intention as a perquisite to enrollment in what was supposed to be a school for those college-bound. It had been founded in 1635; by going there, one therefore partook of an eminently honorable tradition; the culture of Boston seemed compatible with a scholarly rabbinical familial tradition.

Coming from a three-decker from the center of RDM on Blue Hill Avenue near Morton Street, I had a 45-60 minute commute twice daily in the grey cold days of the Second World War. One was starting on a route out of the ghetto of RDM into the larger world. The journey to be taken was a long one. It started by streetcar along Blue Hill Avenue to Egleston Square; by Elevated to Dudley Street; then, rushing down the stairs to the bus to go to Brigham Circle through Roxbury past Eliot Square with its New England spire on the old Congregational Church and then past Roxbury Crossing on Tremont Street past the Roman Catholic semi-Romanesque Mission Church on Parker Hill to Brigham Circle. One would then walk the half-mile along Huntington Avenue to the Latin School past the buildings of white marble neo-classical court of the Harvard Medical School and a cluster of other medical institutions suggesting one's possible ultimate professional goals. The relatively recent red brick long-windowed two-bay school building of the Latin School built had a portico with pediment and Ionic capitals on a street named after Louis Pasteur.

The curriculum was essentially unchanged since the days of Charles William Eliot a century earlier of the class of 1849. One started Latin in 7th grade (Class Six); the only choice offered in 10th grade (Class Three) was for German or Ancient Greek. French was a requirement from 9th grade (Class Four); taught by men successively named Murphy, Sullivan and Fitzgerald with a singular teacher called Levine. Reading and writing grammatical French was taught, not conversational French. Science was taught for one year in 12th grade only (Class One). In Latin class, one read Caesar's *Gallic Wars* in 9th grade, Cicero in 10th, Livy and Ovid's *Metamorphoses* in 11th and Vergil's *Aeneid* in 12th. For those far fewer such as I who elected Ancient Greek rather than German, one read Xenophon's *Anabasis* in 10th and 11th and Homer's *Iliad* in the 12th grade. The students merely read and translated; there was no attempt to interpret or place the readings in their social or historical context. English did include stories such as Edith Wharton's dark *Ethan Frome*; novels such as *Lorna Doone* and *Mill on the Floss*. Grammar was taught but poorly. American History was an annual affair; starting each year with the explorers and petering out in the sands of the Civil War but never extending beyond Reconstruction told from the "Lost Cause" perspective. Questions were to be narrowly answered; discussion was discouraged. Declamation still carried on but much attenuated from the time of Eliot in the 19th century.

Several of the masters had Ph.D.s and were relatively well-trained to be high school teachers as a residue of the Depression era. They were likely to be the best in the school system in this the most prestigious of the public schools. Many, however, awaiting retirement, merely parroted the earlier versions of textbooks. Moreover, the entirely male instructors were usually limited in their commitment to their school jobs; they felt themselves poorly paid as prices rose with the post-war inflation while salaries did not. Aside from the athletic coaches who did so only fitfully, few led extra-curricular activities while seeking after-school jobs. One English teacher stood out. He ran a Music Appreciation Club where one could listen to classical records and invited a group of students to his apartment overlooking the Charles River for lemonade and cookies.

Some formality persisted; one still stood to recite; the master sat on a dais and was addressed as "sir." He addressed the student by his surname rather than his given name. The rules for coat and tie were, however, no longer enforced. The building was large, holding well over twenty-five hundred students in its six grades; the time for transfer between classes was only slightly longer than that in Eliot's time, of which he had complained. The impressive assembly hall frieze had lined in gold a litany of the great names of those who had gone before and a Roman statue of *Alma mater* stood at the front entrance.

The student body was however far different from the time of Eliot. It was split almost evenly between the sons of second generation white collar Irish government workers and teachers mainly from West Roxbury, a sprinkling of Italians, even fewer Greeks and the large number of first generation American-born East European Jews from RDM. There was but a single black student from Roxbury along with one who was a descendant, appropriately named John Winthrop, who provided continuity with the original Protestant families. Although there was no active animosity between the Jews and the non-Jews as there had been apparently between the Jews and the residual

Protestants reported in the 1920s, the long commute and the long hours for homework precluded an active extra-curricular life. Yet somehow, the replacement of Cardinal O'Connell by Archbishop Richard Cushing in 1945 (later Cardinal in his own right) ushered in a warmer climate in Catholic-Jewish relations that filtered down throughout the city into the student body.

There was strong discipline with "misdemeanor" marks given for minor infractions; a "censure" for those more severe infractions such as cheating. Expulsion could follow one or more censures. Far more likely, students would withdraw to enter their local high schools which were on occasion co-ed and offered a less stringent course. This was more likely to be true for the non-Jews; the Jewish students tended to excel; they persisted and formed the largest percentage of those eventually entering Harvard.

Harvard opened its golden door in 1949 for a large part of the class. Latin School provided as usual the largest public school contingent for H'53. Probably the high water mark of the post Second World War era, there were over seventy Harvard entrants out of the two hundred graduating. This was Harvard's first post-war class with only 55 veterans. Its size had been reduced to 1100 from the abnormally large post-war classes designed to accommodate returning veterans. Accordingly, the class statistics recorded that students were admitted from a more narrow selection of schools than the year before. The statistics reported that there were an equal number of public and private school boys.

There was of course some departure from the entering class of Charles William Eliot in 1849, when 90% of a class of eighty-seven came from New England. Similar to the last pre-war entrants in 1941, the class entering in 1949 contained only 60% from the New England states. However, there had been a reduction from the previous year from 19% to 16% of those from the Middle Atlantic States consisting mainly of those from the New York metropolitan area. 12% persisted as coming from the quaintly called "Old Northwest Territory" of Ohio, Indiana, Illinois and Michigan. The only change from those entering in the last pre-war fall of 1941 was a 25% increase in the still small number overall coming from the Pacific States and the West.

The passage of a "Fair Educational Practices Act" in Massachusetts and the changing climate regarding anti-Semitism in the post-war era may have exerted some slight change in Harvard's admission practices. However, there was still a series of questions on the admission application designed to elicit information as to ancestry. By the time of the entry of the class of '53, Harvard had begun to return to peacetime status in retaining its preferences for "legacy" admission from the eastern elite who were both "paying guests" and probable donors while also pursuing "geographic diversity" in its continuing efforts to restrict the number of Jews, albeit more subtly and perhaps more generously than in the 1920s and 1930s.

There was also subtle but definite segregation in the placement in upper class houses. Somehow, there was a majority of Jewish students who were not acceptable to one of the Colonial revival Houses lining the Charles River. They were required to live in the older apartment houses (appropriately called outhouses) that lined Mount Auburn Street for at least a year of purgatory before being admitted. This seemed to be true even for several who were very wealthy. Despite high grades and even a demonstrable commitment to a "broad education," entry into the Harvard Medical School was also problematic. However, there were alternatives unlike the pre-war situation when rigid quotas existed everywhere. The high tide of post-war prosperity lifted all boats and, moreover, offered opportunities elsewhere outside of Boston. We did feel fortunate.

Just as the election of John F Fitzgerald in 1905 had marked the rise to power in Boston of the first American-born Irish generation, the election of his grandson and namesake John Fitzgerald Kennedy to the presidency in 1960 marked the rise of the next generation to the pinnacle of American politics. The triumph was far more than a personal one; it was of a family and a people. It was particularly sweet that it transcended the limitations offered by their family's roots in Boston's rocky soil.

5.8 The Kennedy Family and American Politics

Figure 67 - The Kennedy Family

The life of John Fitzgerald Kennedy and his family is a saga that that has never exhausted the interests of Americans. More practically, the rise to power for the Kennedy family; and it was as a family that it rose, is an exemplar of the rise to affluence and influence of the Irish Catholic immigration epitomized by his Boston origins.

The two children of the only sometimes allied Boston politicians from the North End and East Boston met and, despite opposition from the maternal John F. Fitzgerald, Rose Fitzgerald and Joseph Patrick Kennedy married in 1914. Illustrative is that the upwardly mobile young couple chose not to live in Boston but in Brookline. The formation of the biological Kennedy family proceeded rapidly; the first was the namesake Joe, then the more sickly John Fitzgerald (Jack) and then Rosemary all born while the family was living in suburban Brookline during the First World War. Rosemary, born during the flu epidemic was found to be brain injured and was later institutionalized. A prefrontal lobotomy carried out to control her outbursts of temper and irresponsible behavior unfortunately caused serious brain damage.

By 1920, there was a fourth child, another daughter called Kathleen. Joseph Sr was making money in the stock market through his job and by trading on his own account at the blueblood firm of Hayden, Stone and Company in Boston. By 1921, there was a fifth child Eunice, named after Rose's sister dying of tuberculosis. The two parents seemed united in creating a strong family based on their Catholicism and subordination of the children's lives to the family destiny. The sense of isolation and the need to make the family a bulwark was strengthened by the failure of Joseph P. Kennedy to be admitted to the Cohasset Country Club during the summer of 1922, again he felt based merely on his Catholic religion.

Patricia was the next daughter. A third son Robert was born in 1925, now making seven in all. Coincident with the increase in the family was an increased fortune accomplished by insider trading on Wall Street. A millionaire by 1925, he entered the movie business in Los Angeles, eventually creating RKO Pictures. Tired of his exclusion from the inner sanctums of Boston society despite his wealth, in 1927 Kennedy moved his family to Bronxville in the New York City suburbs. An eighth child, a daughter named Jean was born. Returning to the bosom of his family after his affair with Gloria Swanson, a ninth and final child was born in 1932, called Edward but known as Teddy.

Returning from Hollywood, in the midst of the great Bull Market of 1929, Kennedy had the foresight to liquidate his stocks at the top of the market but made his real fortune by selling short, betting that the market would fall. Having joined the 1932 presidential campaign of Franklin Roosevelt, in 1934 Kennedy became the first chair of the Securities Exchange Commission (SEC) designed to regulate the markets he had known so well how to manipulate.

In order to equip them to enter the precincts he had not been permitted to enter, Kennedy prepared his sons at Choate School, patterned on Groton. Joe Jr went to Harvard after a year at the London School of Economics under the tutelage of Harold Laski; Jack started at Princeton to be out of the orbit of his elder brother but left school because of illness and eventually also went to Harvard. Still highly connected with Roosevelt during the 1930s, Kennedy became head of the Maritime Commission and finally Ambassador to Great Britain in 1938. The first Irish-American to fill this most prestigious of diplomatic posts, Kennedy brought his attractive family to London and created a successful social splash. The international situation was tense; Kennedy supported Prime Minister Neville Chamberlain and his policy of appeasement of Hitler. Kennedy firmly believed that it was in America's interests not to join the war, regardless of the nature of Hitler. In an interview after his return from England, he was quoted as saying that "Democracy is finished in England." The resultant storm ended his public career. From then on, having prepared each of them with wealth and self-confidence, he lived for the political advancement of his sons, to make up for his own failures to enter the top rungs of the American social ladder.

Although Joe Jr had been the more successful, meeting all his parents' hopes, he had died in the war. Jack Kennedy, sicklier and less driven, now carried the family's hopes. Equipped with a heroic war record and aided by his grandfather's political allies, he easily won when running for office in his grandfather's solidly Democratic old congressional district in 1946. However, John F. Kennedy differed from his antecedents. Not the corny backslapping Irish politician arising from the streets of Boston like his grandfather, he represented for the now largely but not entirely middle-class Irish the sort that reflected their own strivings for upward mobility. Moreover, the elder Kennedy's wealth gave his son the social status and the resources that translated into political success. During his three terms in Congress, reflecting the advice of his father, he was only a "bread-and-butter" liberal while representing what was overall a poor working class district. He supported, without taking on the liberal ideology, the needs of his constituents for extending Social Security and raising the minimum wage.

During the 1930s, the image of American Catholics had changed. Representation in film brought new images of an American community that included Catholics. During the New Deal, the new ethnic and class identities challenged the Anglo-American Protestant middle-class culture. Moreover, the post-war nationalist Cold War consensus was devoted to material abundance and entertainment. Religion, home and family were now the sources of personal happiness that Catholicism also fostered. In his national political career, John F. Kennedy also broke away from the pugnacious Catholic public personas of Senator Joseph McCarthy and Father Coughlin. He was calm, self-assured and pragmatic. He represented the suave young Catholic priest played by Bing Crosby in the extremely popular 1944 *Going My Way* that made being Catholic seem so "American".

John Kennedy's good looks and poise also seemed to fulfill every Irish mother's dream and titillate their daughters. Hidden was his ill health, particularly his dependence on daily doses of cortisone to deal with his adrenal insufficiency. His actual performance in Congress was lackluster; his ill-health and womanizing took up much of his limited interest in life. However, by the 1950s, although strengthened by his family, John Kennedy had become a person in his own right. His irony, intelligence, and charm had arisen in the context of his position in the family striving to counter the role of the perfect elder brother. Now, without strong ideological convictions, he was the glamorous exciting political celebrity brought into people's homes by television. Moreover, he could use ideas from divergent views and surround himself with persons of intelligence and strong convictions.

The 1952 race for Senator against the Brahmin Henry Cabot Lodge Jr was not only symbolic but key to his political rise to national recognition. He won overwhelmingly aided by his father's money, his mother's and sisters' teas and his brother Bobby's management. The family team was formed that would carry him to the presidency. His marriage to Jacqueline Bouvier in 1953 was the society wedding of the year; it made him more acceptable as a politician on the national scene. His Senate career was once again affected by his ill health, this time by recurrent operations for his back problems, complicated by his treatment for his hidden adrenal insufficiency. His over-riding familial loyalties were revealed by his failure to vote for the censure of Joseph McCarthy.

The presidential campaign of 1960 can be said to have started in earnest immediately after the Democratic Convention in the summer of 1956. Then, the possibility for the vice-presidential slot opened up when Adlai Stevenson declined to make his preference known. Kennedy's near win, then graciousness in defeat, brought him the national attention on which he would capitalize in his run for the presidency in 1960. Despite the support engineered by his father Joseph P. Kennedy of the old-time Catholic party bosses in the Bronx, Buffalo and especially Chicago, young Kennedy had to prove he could win despite his youth and Catholicism. The Kennedy money made his campaigning in the primaries such as Wisconsin far easier than that of Hubert Humphrey, his poorly funded rival. The numerous Kennedys multiplied his impact across the state. After Wisconsin, came heavily Protestant West Virginia where his family wealth again won the day.

Television had begun to play its role in projecting youth, attractiveness and charm rather than content. The extremely close 1960 election marked the continuing dominance of the Democratic Party based on the ever shakier coalition formed by Franklin Roosevelt in 1932 of both the Solid segregationist South and the immigrants of the northern cities.

It's the old story. For one of your own to be elected, he has to go out of his way to prove he is not just one of your own. Invented as the first Irish Brahmin, Kennedy suggested a means of reinvention and identification for millions of upwardly mobile others. Also reflecting the old Boston mode of operation, but on a national stage, he enlisted men with names like Archibald Cox and McGeorge Bundy and others from the faculties of Harvard and MIT to bridge the gap between the Irish politician and the Boston intellectual elite.

Figure 68 - President-elect Kennedy and family, 1960

Chapter 6
The New Boston 1965-2010

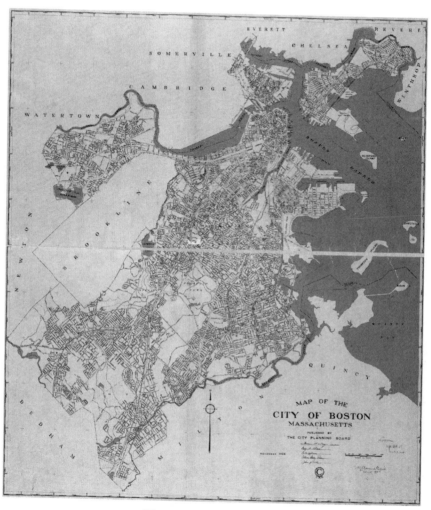

Figure 69 - Boston 1926

Introduction

Boston ceased growing as early as 1930. The attached map shows Boston at its greatest extent in the 1920s. It had experienced the closure of its boundaries in large part by the 1870s following the annexation of Brighton, West Roxbury and Dorchester. The subsequent population growth had occurred in these streetcar suburbs mainly by the filling in by the immigrants moving from the tenements of the West End and South End.

With the closure of major immigration in the 1920s and the start of shift to the South of the textile industry and the departure of the shoe and boot industry, Boston and New England entered a period of economic stagnation. No new office buildings arose in Boston during the 1920s following the Custom House Tower that topped off at twenty-six stories in 1913-1916. This was in an era when Boston native and MIT-trained Louis Sullivan in Chicago pioneered the iconic steel-frame American skyscrapers ending in New York's one hundred-floor Empire State Building in 1930. The first all steel frame building actually appeared in Boston's Winthrop Building (once called the Carter Building) in 1886 prior to those of Chicago. However, it was 1939 before the New England Mutual Life Building on Boylston Street used a floating steel platform that could enable buildings to rise on the made land that underlies so much of Boston.

6.1 Greater Boston/A Regional City

Although Boston had been the home of the first colonial newspapers and of many of the longest lasting, its multiple competing modern newspapers had little national significance. The *Boston Transcript*, the voice of the Boston Brahmins and the subject of the poem by T.S. Eliot, ended its run starting in in 1941 with the departure of its readership. The Democratic *Boston Post* broadsheet lasting until 1968 was balanced for most of its life by the Republican leaning combination of the morning-afternoon *Herald-Traveler* while the Hearst *Record-American* was a tabloid.

The most dominant and still extant paper of this era is the *Boston Globe*, a morning and Sunday only paper since 1979. Founded in the 1870s by Eben Jordan of the family owning the Jordan Marsh Company, it had a burst of excellence and market dominance following the 1960s. Published for over a hundred years by one family, it was acquired by the *New York Times* in 1993 at its height of influence only to be sold at a great loss in 2013 following the universal loss of print readership in the digital age.

Despite a relatively diverse economy and relatively high per capita income in 1929, Boston suffered high unemployment during the Depression with continued loss of manufacturing jobs, a disorganized political response to opportunities for federal largess and a pallid response to the opportunities for war-time prosperity. Its ethnic enmity undiminished, and its real estate tax rate even higher, the city faced a bleak future in the post-war era. Having reached its population height of 800,000 in 1950 in the post-war baby boom, its population had fallen to 700,000 by 1960 with no signs of leveling off while the population of the metropolitan area had increased by one-half million during that same period. The children who grew up in the three deckers in Charlestown, South Boston, East Boston and Dorchester departed from within the city limits to split level houses in the widespread suburbs. In doing so, they were following the long standing tradition of inhabitants spreading to Boston's periphery.

As early as the first quarter of the 19th century, independent towns with substantial populations had grown around Boston, limited as it was to only two square miles at the start of the century. Cambridge and Somerville were pioneers in independent growth but were not later annexed as had been Charlestown, Roxbury and Dorchester. The Cambridge Tory estates of the Lechmere and Inman families having been confiscated; the marshy land of East Cambridge lay available for purchase and platting. By 1815, bridges were built that connected both Charlestown and Cambridge to the original Shawmut peninsula.

During the next generation, food supplies would be raised and delivered to the adjacent city. As roads improved fresh milk supplanted cheese and fresh produce came for daily delivery to the markets. Slaughterhouses appeared in East Cambridge drawing animals from markets farther to the west in Brighton and even later, at what is now Porter Square, noted for its "Porterhouse" steaks. Almost all industry was by artisans in their own workshops with apprentices; factory work did exist in East Cambridge glass works and soap factories as well as brickworks as cropland receded to be replaced by other uses.

Omnibuses appeared on the Cambridge-Boston to run on a regular schedule for the first time on Harvard Commencement Day in 1834. Reduced price "commutation" tickets introduced the word "commuter" to describe those relatively well-off coming to and from the city daily. These developments increased in the 1850s when portions of mainland Charlestown split off to form Somerville while Boston itself became more crowded by Irish immigrants. Cambridge also acquired some of its neighbor's improvements in streets, fire services and enclosure of the Cambridge Commons near Harvard Square. It had evolved into a city by the 1840s with a city hall in the Central Square area in a fashion that would exemplify the other surrounding towns in Middlesex County.

Cambridge introduced the horse drawn streetcar in the 1850s from Central Square to Bowdoin Square in Boston that replaced the earlier omnibus and also replaced the longer distance more costly steam driven railroad. Still too costly for the working man, the streetcar enabled the middle-class white-collar clerk a daily commute to work. This mobility based on the horse cars established the "suburb." An independent entity eventually devoted to middle class, native-born residents but did not admit large scale commerce or industry. It was thus defined by both class and residential usage.

The term "suburb" came to signify the site for country estates noted for their cultivated appearance. Stimulated by such organizations as the "Massachusetts Horticultural Society", also founded in 1829, "Wellesley" was the country estate of the Hunnewell family; "Bellmont" the home of the Cushing family that gave their names to their respective suburbs. By 1860, the number of commuters had increased substantially with towns such as Somerville, Woburn and Medford growing along the line of the Boston & Lowell Railroad with its cheap five cent fare to East Cambridge. Somerville and Newton also became independent cities in the 1870's. Annexation to Boston did not proceed further save for Hyde Park in 1912.

The environs of Boston pioneered the parameters of suburban design. Brookline, the home of Frederick Law Olmsted, became the model he exported to cities all over the country of mainly politically independent towns based on persons commuting daily to the city. By the mid-19th century, many of Boston's leading families had built country homes as Beacon and Boylston Streets had been extended from Boston into the countryside. The large property owners succeeded in 1874 in preventing annexation by Boston despite the wishes of local businessmen and workers. By the 1880s, the segregation of metropolitan Boston between the residential nativist suburbs and the immigrant city had hardened.

The suburban parochialism of Boston was somewhat tempered. There had been the earlier development of metropolitan-based water, sewage, park and transportation services thus removing many of the incentives for annexation while allowing for the possible functional integration of the still remaining politically independent towns. The Republican-controlled state legislature in 1889 established the Metropolitan Sewerage Commission; in 1893 the Metropolitan Park Commission; and in 1895 the Metropolitan Water Board. All were merged into the Metropolitan District Commission (MDC) in 1919. Metropolitan Boston as early as 1910 was therefore far larger than the census figures would indicate for those within the boundaries of the city of Boston, approaching that of Chicago and Philadelphia. The ambitious "Boston-1915 Plan" drawn up in 1909 and successive reiterations were turned down by suburban jurisdictions suspicious of Boston politicians. The parkway system established by the MDC nevertheless defined a level of regional land use planning that has made Boston unique during the era of the motor vehicle.

By the middle of the 20th century, there were 21 cities and towns, each with a population over 50,000 that comprised the Boston Region with a total population of several million. Route 128, opening in 1951 twelve miles from downtown, was the first circumferential highway that served to unify the entire region in the age of the automobile. The prototype for such highways in other areas of the country, it also became the basis for a resurgence of the Boston area in the post-war era with technology companies incubated at the Massachusetts Institute of Technology.

In the first decade that followed, there were over 200 businesses located on Route 128; by 1967, there were over 700 with 65,000 employees. I-495 in the 1960s expanded the range of the region thirty miles from downtown with the growth of even larger technology companies on low-priced land dependent on the automobile. The post-war era had its golden age in the shadow of the new technology nurtured by the needs of the Cold War. The intimate relationship between the military and technology reflected the career of Vannever Bush and the Massachusetts Institute of Technology.

6.2 Vannever Bush and the Raytheon Company

The large expansion of MIT that occurred in the post-war era started much earlier. MIT in 1918 developed a Technology Plan to encourage large corporations like General Electric, DuPont and Eastman Kodak to fund scientific research. During the 1920s, the university developed a Division of Industrial Cooperation and Research to acquire industrial research contracts. Bush helped found Raytheon in the 1920s as a manufacturer of vacuum tubes for radios. During the war, that company manufactured radar; after the war, it

Figure 70 - Vannever Bush and the Differential Analyzer

Vannever Bush (1890-1974), born in Everett, Massachusetts to a Universalist minister, grew up in Chelsea Massachusetts where he attended the public schools, trained at Tufts College and at M.I.T. During the First World War, he worked for the Navy in techniques for submarine detection. Professor of Electrical Engineering and then a Dean at M.I.T., Bush was also founder of several industrial firms, one in 1922 the forerunner of Raytheon Corporation. His research led to the invention in 1927 of the differential analyzer enabling the solution of complex equations. It was useful in wartime in solving problems in ballistics, acoustics, and atomic physics.

President of the Carnegie Institution in Washington from 1935 to 1955, Bush led in the wartime coordination of scientists through the Federal Office of Scientific Research and Development (OSRD). Its accomplishments included the implementation of radar, the proximity fuse, early work on the atomic bomb Manhattan Project as well as techniques for the mass production of penicillin and sulfa drugs. The first scientific advisor to any president, he also helped move this large level of federal support into peacetime uses through the establishment of the National Science Foundation (NSF).

manufactured transistors and microwave ovens with Charles Francis Adams its head. Becoming also the prime government contractor for missile systems, it moved its headquarters from Cambridge to Lexington on Route 128. Names familiar to Boston such as Cabot, Cabot & Forbes developed the electronic plants along Rte 128 in preference to the deteriorating downtown Boston.

Lincoln Lab was established by MIT on the behest of the Air Force in 1951 to develop long-range air-defense warning systems and high speed digital processing. MITRE Corporation headed by Charles Coolidge of the blueblood law firm of Ropes & Gray was spun off to manufacture the products developed by research labs including those by the Air Force Cambridge Research Laboratories. Many for-profit companies were spun off by the thousands of scientists employed by the defense industry research entities creating the country's leading center for mini-computers. Called for a time the "Massachusetts Miracle," Digital Equipment Corporation (DEC) manufactured personal computers using old abandoned textile mills as did Wang Computers before being absorbed by competitors in the fast moving computer industry and ceding primacy in the 1990s to Silicon Valley in California.

6.3 The West End and Housing the Poor

John B. Hynes had been elected mayor in 1949 to succeed the discredited James Michael Curley, newly returned to Boston after having been released from prison. The center city had been stagnant. The only post-war building was the unimaginative twenty-six story John Hancock Building in 1947. In the first flush of post-war enthusiasm and the end of the Curley regime, many plans were made to rejuvenate the center city. The local bankers for the first time in more than a generation were interested in investing in Boston. The redevelopment with luxury housing and the destruction of the community that lived in the West End was one of the major achievements while also becoming a hallmark of the evils of urban renewal.

The West End was close to downtown. It ran from Bowdoin Square (adjacent to honky-tonk district of Scollay Square) to the Charles River and the Massachusetts General Hospital and from North Station to Cambridge Street. Mostly made land by the filling in of the Mill Pond, it was the first area for persons leaving the overcrowded North End in the 18th century. Fashionable for only a short time, the adjacent North Slope of Beacon Hill had an unsavory reputation and Joy and Phillips Streets became the site for the settlement for freed slaves after slavery was abolished in Massachusetts in 1789.

The main street led to Cambridge via the West Boston Bridge and the adjacent Craigie Bridge (now Charles River Dam) led to Lechmere Square. Cambridge Street defined the area as commercial and the home of working class immigrants rather than one of fashion. After 1880, the old originally single family houses were mainly replaced by four to five story walk-up tenements with or without central heat and indoor toilets. Bathtubs, if available, were usually used as coal bins. They housed the Italian and East European Jews that largely replaced the earlier Irish. The last maintained political control under the "Mahatma" Martin Lomasney who also enlisted the Jews into his political machine immediately on arrival as well as Italians, albeit the latter to a lesser degree. "West Enders," like "Southies," geographically and socially separated from the rest of the city evolved in a place that retained traditions inherited from their immigrant ancestors.

One of the few areas in Boston that contained a diverse interethnic community, the West Enders were powerless, perhaps for that very reason, to be represented within the dominant interethnic power struggles that characterized Boston politics. The Jews had largely but not entirely moved to RDM. Two synagogues and a Hebrew school remained. The Italian inhabitants of Boston did not reside only in the West End. Although the largest number, a larger proportion of the total lived elsewhere, in the North End and East Boston. Coupled with the traditional Southern Italian passivity and cynicism toward those in power, their representatives had little power in the overwhelmingly Irish power structure. Nonetheless, many of the West End's former inhabitants still nurse a sense of betrayal and nostalgia for their former home. The story of the West End and its dissolution illustrates the history not only of that particular area but the way the elite of Boston have dealt with the ambiguity of their responsibility toward the poor amongst them.

Based upon the view that poverty was mainly the result of willful indolence or indulgence in "spirituous liquor," the first almshouse in the colonies was constructed on the Boston Common in the 1660s. It was then replaced by a larger one in the 1680s associated later with a workhouse. In addition to such "indoor relief," the Overseers of the Poor primarily provided "outdoor relief" by committing funds to lodge the indigent with relatives. The limited facilities available for the "deserving poor" were situated on the edge of the settled area at the Common near what is now the Old Granary Burial Ground at Tremont and Park Streets.

In the 19th century, the view changed to include possible causes for poverty beyond the control of the individual. This new belief led to the idea that the proper environment might bring about a "cure." Like the contemporary development of the penitentiary and asylum, elimination of dependency was seen to require isolation from the crowded environment in which pauperism could flourish. The almshouse near the Common fell victim to gentrification and a new building, even larger than the new State House, was built at the then very edge of the settled area in the West End at Leverett Street at its northwestern tip.

To separate the "virtuous poor" from the "vicious poor", a "House of Industry" and an adjacent "House of Correction" were subsequently constructed in the 1820s in then far-off South Boston. By 1847, pressured by the adjoining inhabitants, the House of Industry for those deemed able to work was removed. Rebuilt in a turreted fortress on Deer Island at the very northeastern edge of Boston Harbor, the poor reached an apogee of concentration and isolation. With the overwhelmingly large increase in Irish immigration, such "indoor" relief could not achieve its stated goal of reform. The large institutions became custodial, increasingly dealing only with the sick.

The focus shifted to the large number of immigrant poor and to the improvement of their lot within the swath of tenement housing in which they lived. The motive was to prevent the apparent endangerment of the non-poor. The poor and their habitations were seen as a potential source of disease, criminality and "immoral behavior" that could contaminate the rest of the city. The tenement areas of Boston were next only to those of New York. Based on the law passed in New York the preceding year, the first Tenement House Law was passed in Boston in 1868, leading to successively greater degrees of licensure and inspections. There also were recurrent efforts by philanthropists to create "model tenements," regrettably too few in number.

In the 1890s, Boston Brahmins founded The Twentieth Century Club that conducted a survey of tenements under the leadership of Robert Treat Paine that finally drove the Board of Health to condemn buildings that had particularly egregious violations. The principle was nonetheless clearly established by now that the problem of the immigrant poor lay in the poverty of their "slum" environment where filth and disease co-existed. An improved physical environment, "slum clearance" would lead to the removal of these dangers to the surrounding population. The source for such improvement would increasingly lie with public rather than private funds. The West End was specifically identified as ripe for redevelopment as early as the 1930s with the formation of the Federal housing initiatives of the New Deal.

An intermediate stage was the settlement house that focused on the neighborhood rather than the individual building as the unit for housing reform. They also saw the need to include social and cultural change as well as improvement in architectural design to allow more light and air. Soon after Jane Addams at Hull House in Southside Chicago, Robert A Woods established the first settlement house in Boston's South End. Its initial name in 1891 was the Andover House, reflecting its origins in the evangelical Andover Theological Seminary. Called the South End House following 1895 better to reflect its neighborhood, it followed the pattern of the "Social Gospel" pioneered in Toynbee Hall in London's East End by which "theology was connected to life."

Born in Pittsburgh in 1865 and with a strongly Calvinist upbringing, Robert Woods attended Amherst College and then came under the influence of William Jowett Tucker at the Andover Theological Seminary. Although the origins of his work were in evangelical Christianity, Woods claimed his goal was to educate and not evangelize. He described himself as entering the neighborhood as a "wrestling Angel" to bring about change by virtue of example. That change was to bring about "American" standards among the immigrant; to encourage the uplift of the striving deserving poor. Woods wrote extensively and his South End House became the model for settlement houses elsewhere in his role as Secretary of the National Federation of Settlements. Still another such was the Elizabeth Peabody House, the first in the West End starting in 1901. Named after a pioneer in kindergartens and first devoted to providing services to young children, it was eventually the city's largest under the direction of Eva Whiting White called "The Light of the West End." Peabody House provided among many other activities, access to showers in a district without a municipal bath. (It moved, along with many West Enders, to Somerville in 1958.)

The schools were overcrowded; children frequently dropped out to go to work to help support their families. A serious group of Jewish teenagers that congregated around the corner near their school formed a club, found an adult representative and a room in which to meet. Calling themselves the "Excelsior Association," they then met at the West End Educational Union run by the Jewish Philanthropies. About to lose their clubhouse, the boys approached the Boston Brahmin James J Storrow who had become interested in their progress. The West End House was founded in 1906 by the extraordinarily public-spirited Storrow, a partner in the then leading firm of Lee, Higginson and Company, to be sustained almost unilaterally by him and his family until 1926.

Storrow hired Mitchell Freiman, a recent Jewish Harvard Law graduate and athlete, to run it. Succeeded by Jacob Burnes in 1916, it continued to focus on the moral development of the boys and on competitive athletics but also declamation as the ticket to success in life. After the death of Storrow, the West End Club alumni took responsibility for its support as its membership became more diverse. Its building at 16 Blossom Street still remains as one of the legacies of the old West End although the club itself moved to Allston-Brighton after the destruction of the West End community.

The difficulties, even the futility, of these generally well meant efforts to alleviate what seemed like intractable problems led to consideration of alternatives. One naturally occurring option was the gradual decentralization of population with the movement of the upwardly mobile to other less crowded districts. This occurred in the West End where its population fell from a high of 23,000 in 1910 to 12,000 in 1950. The former Jewish inhabitants largely moved to Roxbury by 1930 while the Italian population tended to remain, replenished by post-Second World War Italian immigration.

The other alternative was, by use of public powers of eminent domain, to carry out the physical destruction of the tenement districts for the inhabitants presumably to start anew in the same setting or in others with adequate sanitary facilities and light and air. With the federal housing initiatives of the 1930s, the stage was set for slum clearance and public housing to be the solution for the dangers offered by the poor. With the increased post-war availability of federal funds for "slum clearance," and the almost universal agreement that poor and crowded housing existed in the West End, there seemed little reason to postpone removal despite the insistence of some of the inhabitants that the low-rent West End was a "good place to live." One very significant concern expressed was the danger of fire and the inability of fire trucks to navigate the narrow streets.

However, satisfactory housing at equivalent rents was not available. The promise of priority in the replacement housing was not honored. The time elapsed before the housing was completed and its far greater cost made that promise a hollow one. High-priced park-like "Charles River Park" with a mix of townhouses and high rise apartments replaced the former narrow streets. The goal was clearly no longer slum clearance and replacement with better housing stock but replacement of low income with higher income residents to bring prosperity to the city.

The callousness with which it was done brought all subsequent slum clearance in Boston to a halt without the agreement of those affected. Future re-development of the Parker Hill neighborhood in Roxbury and the design of the ribbon-like park of the Southwest Corridor are offered as examples of the lessons learned from the West End.

Furthermore, the experience of the destruction of what was in retrospect a functioning community called "an urban village" has had long term reverberations in housing policy throughout the country. The failures of public housing have become clear in subsequent decades everywhere. Public housing segregated by income as a replacement for poor housing stock has also brought into question the definition of a "slum" based upon the age and quality of its buildings without consideration of the human network that maintained the safety of its inhabitants.

The Boston School Committee was almost exclusively Irish in its composition. It had long been a bastion for those seeking higher office while the quality of education had deteriorated. Ethnic housing segregation had been the norm that extended to the black population as it increased to 60,000 by 1960. During the 1960s, the School Committee under its chair Louis Day Hicks remained adamant in its refusal to respond to the NAACP requesting alleviation of segregated unequal education. For example, it was clear by official figures that expenditures per student were much lower in schools in Roxbury serving a mainly black student body than schools elsewhere. The buildings were frequently decrepit with broken windows covered with boards and overrun with rats.

A sticking point was the Committee's refusal to accept the premise that "de facto segregation" exists in the schools while admitting that de facto housing segregation led to the existence of predominantly black schools. The term "racial imbalance" was offered as a substitute. Starting in 1965, "open enrollment" was a voluntary program funded by black parents; another program to bus black students to the Brookline schools was at best an only partial solution to overcrowded and poorly equipped black schools.

6.4 South Boston and Louise Day Hicks

South Boston is a peninsula immediately to the east of downtown Boston separated by the narrow Fort Point Channel from the mainland and also forming the southern boundary of Boston Harbor. Called Dorchester Neck for its connection to the mainland of Dorchester to the south, the heights overlooking the harbor became the site for the gun emplacements that forced the British to evacuate Boston on March 17th 1776. That date is celebrated each year as a holiday unique to Boston not only as the first major victory in the Revolutionary war; it holds particular meaning as St Patrick's Day for the largely Irish inhabitants of South Boston. Its eastern end, known as "City Lands" ending at the beach at "City Point" was the site of a large number of municipal institutions in the mid-19th century. Finally removed at the behest of the other nearby inhabitants, their former presence nevertheless destroyed any likelihood that the area would be fashionable despite its sea breezes. That history engendered a tradition for the inhabitants of South Boston seeing themselves distinct and in opposition to the city authorities of "Boston proper."

The northern and western portion of the South Boston peninsula became the site for industry; and then for tenements to house those mainly Irish immigrants working there. The tenements remained even after the industry departed post-Civil War and the area became an Irish Catholic working class residential enclave. By 1900, this "Lower End" contained 80,000 inhabitants whose anthem "Southie is My Home Town" expresses their insularity and loyalty. Physically and psychologically, the fourth generation Irish of South Boston remained in an immigrant ghetto unable to leave where, for example, the local South Boston High School specialty was training in sheet metal work.

During the 1930s, the western Lower End was marked as the site of "blighted housing" to be a prime target for slum clearance and replacement by public housing along West Broadway. Coupled with its Irish identity and their political influence, South Boston early became the site of the largest concentration of public housing in the city. Two of the first five pre-second World War housing projects in Boston occurred in South Boston in areas where the poorest did not necessarily live; West Broadway around D Street continued to languish only to be leveled on the very eve of Pearl Harbor..

Delayed by wartime shortages, the area remained leveled as though by the blitz before public housing opened along West Broadway seven years later in 1949. None of those originally living in the West Broadway area were deemed eligible when it finally opened. Contributing to a sense of outrage, only veterans were eligible, and these not necessarily from South Boston. Like all post-war public housing, the at first carefully selected upwardly mobile white tenants of West Broadway were increasingly replaced by those of lower income and from less intact families. Those living in public housing were no longer upward striving but had themselves grown up in public housing. It had become what some called "generational."

The South Boston residents who had obsessively protected their district from outside control had also tried to insure that their government-subsidized public housing would serve only mainly Irish local white residents. They were now subject to federal guidelines for desegregation beyond their local control in schools as well as housing. The Boston Irish had always harbored among them the truculent xenophobic, ethnocentric and illiberal strains that had been expressed under Father Coughlin in the 1930s. Even while toasting the rogue progressiveness of James Michael Curley, there many who were still inclined to intolerance and reaction. Yet the overwhelming electoral support for the New Deal-New Frontier tradition of pluralistic tolerance and cooperation still had its long time adherents. The "Boston Home and School Association" was for example a multi-racial multi-ethnic group that worked for reform while opposed to busing.

Many others rightfully pointed to the unfairness of imposing busing on the poorest elements of the city's population while safeguarding those who lived in the suburbs. Yet the anti-busing movement did not seek as a possible remedy an increase in busing into suburban areas already being done voluntarily by several jurisdictions. Nor did they deal with the top heavy excessive number of administrators who held jobs to the detriment of the resources available to teachers and pupils. When the opportunity was offered, whites living in Dorchester refused to permit their children to be bused to a brand-new extraordinarily well-equipped school designed to encourage integration appropriately named after the liberal School Committee member Joseph Lee. Louis Day Hicks became a highly divisive figure; considered by her opponents as a "buffoon," an opportunist drawn far beyond her political depth by some observers who came from a background not dissimilar from hers.

In 1967, the state of Massachusetts passed a "Racial Imbalance Law" that required desegregation of schools if there was greater than 50% membership of any races in the classroom with withdrawal of state funds as the penalty. Boston along with Springfield and Cambridge were affected. This was the year when the federal government under President Lyndon Johnson was still pursuing black civil rights; the neighborhood schools for which Mrs. Hicks was fighting were no longer sacrosanct.

In 1972, the NAACP sued to force the highly recalcitrant Boston School Committee to implement that law; in 1974, Judge Arthur Garrity ruled in favor of the plaintiffs. Busing would be required as one of the remedies. Like the former West End, South Boston was the home of a white working class enclave living in blighted or public housing. However, unlike the West End, South Boston was Irish and rooted in the Boston political network that not only included Louise Day Hicks but both Billy Bulger as its state senator and his elder brother James (Whitey), the local mob leader and FBI informant.

The Bulger father had grown up in the North End as one of the few Irish left in a sea of Italians; his mother came from the strongly Irish working class enclave of Charlestown across the harbor. With the father's arm amputated in a railroad accident, the Bulger's considered themselves very lucky to be in 1938 one of the first tenants in South Boston's Old Colony Harbor federal housing project. Boston's first, it was built under the sponsorship of their congressman then Majority Leader John McCormack. Even when becoming Speaker of the House, McCormack continued to be helpful to the family, one of his faithful constituents. This continued even as the eldest son entered into a life of crime and was inmate of a series of federal prisons including Alcatraz. Aiding him in his rise among the mob was Whitey Bulger's corrupt connection with an FBI agent, a former neighbor at Old Colony Harbor. Apparently in complete contrast to his elder brother, his young brother Billy entered politics after graduating from Boston College High School, Boston College and Boston College Law School.

In 1967, Mayor John Collins decided not to run for a third term. The race was between Louise Day Hicks ("You Know Where I Stand.") and Kevin White ("anybody-but-Louise"). White won although Mrs. Hicks received the blue-collar vote, especially that of Southie. In 1968, state representative Billy Bulger received her much needed endorsement; in 1970 he moved up to the state Senate as she moved to the U.S. Congress, taking the late John McCormack's seat for one term. As brother Whitey became established both as a mobster and an FBI informant, his brother Billy was in the midst of the anti-busing movement along with Louis Day Hicks. In 1978, Billy rose to become senate president to the mutual benefit of both brothers since the politician could surreptitiously protect his mobster brother even as Whitey took over the drug trade in Southie as the community deteriorated further in the wake of busing.

Phase I of Judge Garrity's order required cross busing starting September 1974 of some 17,000 out of the then 94,000 students pairing schools in South Boston and Roxbury, each containing poor families and highly segregated public housing. Led by Louis Day Hicks and others of their political leaders such as Billy Bulger, many of the South Boston white students boycotted the transfers to schools in Roxbury. State police were ordered in to protect black students in October 1974 being bused to South Boston after the request for federal marshals was turned down by President Ford; the opposite soon occurred in Roxbury.

Figure 71 - Louise Day Hicks

The city noted for its commitment to the desegregation of schools based on race in 1855 became the center of one of desegregation's greatest storms as Louise Day Hicks came to represent the reality of the nature of Boston's highly segregated housing. Born in South Boston in 1916, Louise Day Hicks was the daughter of William Day. The son of poor Irish immigrants, a lawyer and the owner of the "Irish" bank and later judge, her father was South Boston's leading citizen. In young gangster Whitey Bulger's terms, they were one of South Boston's F.I. F's (First Irish Families). Trained in home economics at Simmons College, Louise Day received a teaching certificate from Wheelock College. After marrying and raising two sons educated in the Catholic schools, she completed Boston University Law School in 1955 and entered law practice in South Boston. In 1961, she was elected to the Boston School Committee running for office based on her role "as a mother."

Louise Day Hicks became the chair of the Boston School Committee and spokesperson in favor of neighborhood schools in opposition to busing to achieve desegregation. Her political career paralleled the rise of this issue in the 1960s and 1970s. At her height in politics, she was elected as the first woman to chair the City Council as well as member of Congress and ran several strong races against Kevin White as mayor. The two cultures of poverty, white and black, were pitted against each other.

Prior to school opening in 1975, one thousand persons appeared at a rally in Southie to protest busing. During this Phase II, Judge Garrity had increased the scope to 26,000 out of an expected diminished enrollment of 84,000. For want of any another, he used maps coding police activity. Thus, black areas of police activity were paired with equivalent white areas. One such pairing was between the Condon School on West Broadway in South Boston serving the public housing project on D Street and the Dearborn School in Roxbury adjacent to the all-black Orchard Park housing project near Warren Street.

However, the Dearborn School had an extraordinary cadre of dedicated teachers, several Ivy-League trained, that had created a sense of community and an oasis of commitment to excellence. Several of the middle school teachers had formed a strong connection with the students and their families led by a Harvard-trained English teacher raised in Jewish Roxbury. Harriet Orlov Schwartz had committed her life to being a teacher. It was all she wanted to be. Led by Harriet Schwartz, the teachers would go to their students' baseball games and visit around their kitchen tables after climbing the steps that reeked of urine and alcohol. On many Saturdays, they would bring students to sporting events, to museums and to "real restaurants" to raise their expectations for themselves as well as for their academic goals in the classroom. Among other things, they were taught grammatical Standard English as a key to entry into the wider world and how to read books and to write book reports at greater depth. They were tutored to receive acceptance into suburban busing programs or to the elite Boston Latin School where Harriet Schwartz herself had gone prior to Radcliffe.

When school started in 1975, fifteen hundred police were on hand; SWAT riflemen were stationed on the roof of Charlestown High School; fifty FBI men were assigned as were twenty-one clerics. The 82nd Airborne Division was on stand-by at its base in North Carolina. Only 72,000 students showed up, a 20% reduction from the enrollment in 1974. By 1982, total enrollment had fallen even further to 56,000 with white enrollment now dropped from 57,000 to 18,000 and black enrollment also down somewhat. The students that remained were apparently those who had no other choice. In 1982, the spokesperson for the black parents who initiated the suit asked Judge Garrity to step down and permit parents free choice, despairing of the original goal of integration.

Despite all the problems that made the experience so difficult for all concerned, there were some mitigating efforts that seem to have borne fruit. The teachers in the Dearborn Middle School set out to duplicate their work with their Orchard Park community with those students arriving from D Street. They arranged a series of meetings with the parents of the white students to be bused acquainting them with who they were and the goals of their school. Few parents came at first; more came later as the teachers persisted despite all obstacles. As a first step, students were brought together before school started from both communities for a cookout on an outing far from the city. Few white students first came to class; more came later. By the end of the first school year, one estimate is that as much as 60% of those on the list to be bused ended up attending. Despite the policy of the Boston schools cancelling all athletics, baseball teams were formed under the auspices of the Catholic parishes in the both areas of the city that helped bridge differences; a joint Dearborn marching band won a first prize in a city-wide contest. One possible measure of success was that far more of the white students from the originating Condon School ultimately remained in their classes at Dearborn than those bused to even newer school buildings.

Some of the white students, now with families of their own, speak of the lessons learned of quality education and the possibilities of setting higher goals for their own children as a result of their experience at the Dearborn Middle School. At the time of her early death, the funeral of Harriet Schwartz was attended not only by the Superintendant of Schools, Judge Garrity and the Deputy Mayor but by both blacks and whites in recognition of her sincere and steadfast attempts to carry out a commitment to education that also served to bridge the two communities at a time that few of the city's leaders did so.

6.5 The Great Migration and Mel King

A much larger increase in black migration to Boston in the post-Second World War era was part of the overall black migration into the north. Their number marked a rise from around 2% to 16% of the population as the white population left for the suburban belt while the black population grew both by natural increase and in-migration. The black protest movement in the 1960s brought new energy to the Boston black community previously the province of the NAACP under the influence of the "Black Brahmins." In the early 1970s, the election of five blacks to the Massachusetts lower house led to the formation of a Black Caucus and the redistricting under court order that could enable a black to enter the State Senate.

In 1977, a black guidance counselor did get elected to the School Committee with a solid black vote but also support from the white community based on his credentials. Despite this minor increase in representation and far greater militancy, there still has not occurred translation into political power in light of their relatively small number and the overwhelming white political hegemony firmly committed to their own local interests. This has been coupled with the overall commitment to the construction of a "New Boston" through urban renewal channeled though the office of the mayor.

Recurrent efforts at charter reform to eliminate at-large elections to the School Committee and City Council failed completely until 1981. The 1981 charter revision provided for election on the City Council of four at large and nine in districts, limiting black representation essentially to two seats incorporating the South End, Roxbury and portions of Dorchester. The Council president generally represented the white majority, sometimes based on anti-busing credentials. The same revision of the membership on the School Committee has brought about somewhat greater results with the selection of black school superintendents in the 1980s. In response, in 1990 an appointed school committee was substituted, with the support of black ministers accused by the political activists of being co-opted by the city administration.

In the absence of established political routes to power, the role of street protests became magnified and that of Mel King. Executive Director of the Urban League in 1967, Mel King changed the direction of the Urban League in Boston from providing jobs and training toward political protest in the name of "community development through community control" in the spirit of the "Black Power" rights movement. Community involvement in redevelopment was one issue; then jobs for local minority workers in the redevelopment process. Police brutality was another more generic issue. The Boston Public Schools were the only option for most black students and the plan by Judge Garrity for busing is a story told elsewhere.

The growth in the total population who were "of color" does not reflect a unified community. The in-migration of American blacks in the 1960s and 1970s was superseded by persons from the West Indies, and then from the Cape Verde Islands, then Haiti and Africa with quite different cultures and leadership. The opportunities and limitations of the political career of Mel King reflect these differences.

Figure 72 - Mel King

Born in Boston's South End in 1928, Mel King's mother was an immigrant from Guyana and father from Barbados. They had married in Nova Scotia before immigrating to Boston. Young King went to Boston Technical High School and then majored in mathematics at the traditionally black Claflin College in Orangeburg South Carolina. Returning to Boston, he taught mathematics at his own high school. In 1953, he worked with Lincoln House and then as Youth Director working with street corner gangs for other settlement houses in the South End. Becoming involved with community organization, his C.A.U.S.E. (Community Assembly for a United South End) worked for community control of the re-development of the "New York" streets of the South End where he had grown up. His first major effort was the sit-in at the offices of the Boston Redevelopment Authority (BRA) in 1968 and the "Tent City" at the site of a projected parking garage at an area of former housing in the South End.

King failed in his attempts at election to the Boston School Committee in 1961, 1963 and 1968 but was elected to the Massachusetts Legislature in 1973, serving until 1982. His 1979 mayoral campaign placed him to the left of the white candidates. Gaining 65% of the black vote, he threatened the future but not the election of Mayor Kevin White. In 1983, King reached the high point of his political career when he ran for mayor after the retirement of Mayor White He achieved for the first time a unified "Rainbow Coalition" but lost to Raymond Flynn. Retiring to create a fellowship program in the Department of City Planning at M.I.T., no subsequent black political structure has appeared nor any unifying black political figure.

In the post-Second World War era, it was plain that years of neglect, a decade of depression and generations of political feuding between natives and newcomers had taken its toll. Boston seemed to have no future. Drastic steps would need to be taken if the inner city was to be rescued from urban blight.

The election of John B. Hynes to succeed James Michael Curley was a start of change. The first major step actually occurred starting in the 1960s under Mayor John F. Collins with the building of Government Center to take the place of the tawdry Scollay Square area. The Prudential Center in the Back Bay arose based on a law that calculated tax revenues as a percentage of rental income rather than assessed value that penalized large scale investment. The Quincy Market was renewed in the 1970s by James Rouse under Mayor Kevin White in what became one of his most successful urban "festival" sites. Rouse had pioneered indoor suburban shopping malls but was now intrigued by reversing the trend to suburbia and envisaged an urban downtown mall that would extend from Government Center as a "Walkway to the Sea."

In 1970, the population of the overall area was around 3 million with the population of the central city only 22%, one of the smallest of any metropolitan area. While tensions that divide the population of Boston such as busing appeared in the 1970s to explode and as the population also continued to diminish, the central core city attracted new buildings and employment of high income professionals. Working in banking and money management, they commuted in and out of the city with the augmented transportation system. The Massachusetts Bay Transit Authority (MBTA) created a growing alternative to the urban sprawl of the automobile age extending its service to Worcester on the west, Haverhill and Lowell on the north and on the south to Plymouth and as far as the airport serving Providence Rhode Island.

Even more important in terms of generation of new industries is Boston's continued leadership in education and medicine. In addition to the continued leadership of the Massachusetts General Hospital are the other Harvard-allied Beth Israel/Deaconess and Brigham/Women's Hospitals in the Fenway area adjacent to the Harvard Medical School. The Boston Children's Hospital is world-renowned for its work in pediatric surgery initiated under Dr William E Ladd and raised to even greater heights under Dr Robert E. Gross.

In the 20th century, Boston University, founded in the 1871 by a trio of Methodist Boston merchants, created its first unified campus along Commonwealth Avenue. The Boston Theological Seminary was the first department of the new university to be joined by Colleges of Liberal Arts, Business Administration, Fine and Applied Arts, the last on Huntington Avenue as well as Law, Medicine, and Public Health. Incorporating the former Boston Braves National League Baseball Field as University Field on Commonwealth Avenue, the former Cottage Farm Bridge on the Charles River, now also carries the name of the Boston University.

Founded in 1864, the Boston City Hospital (BCH) in the 1970s became more closely allied to the Boston University School of Medicine (BUSM) in the South End as that area became renewed in its own right. Founded in the 1840s as the New England Female Medical College, the medical school became part of Boston University in 1873. First the Massachusetts Homeopathic Hospital, it acquired the Robert Dawson Evans Endowment in 1912 to establish a department of clinical research. The arrival of Dr Chester Keefer in 1940 as Physician-in-Chief of the "Massachusetts Memorial Hospitals" and Professor of Medicine at BUSM led to the recruitment of an entire cadre of specialists from the Harvard-affiliated Thorndike Laboratory at the BCH and marked the beginning of the growth of BUSM to first rank. Keefer was also heavily involved during wartime in the National Research Council and the Office of Scientific Research and Development in the production of penicillin and later as consultant to the first secretary of the Department of Health, Education and Welfare. Now the Boston Medical Center (BMC), the much enlarged campus incorporates the BUSM, the University Hospital and the Boston City Hospital (BCH).

The Tufts Medical School-New England Medical Center is a third medical campus between Chinatown and the Theater District in downtown Boston. It contains the Boston Dispensary first founded in 1796 even before the Massachusetts General Hospital. The Boston Floating Hospital was founded in 1894 as a healthier seaborne environment for sick children before becoming landlocked. The connection was first made in 1930 with the Tufts Medical School and the creation of the New England Medical Center in its present location in 1950 as one of the earliest medical centers drawing from a regional base. Its present "T" station site on Washington Street near Stuart recaptures the name of the South Cove that underlay this area before being filled in.

6.6 Boston Renewed and Tip O'Neill

Although the regional nature of the high quality water supply has been exemplary since the mid-19th century, the regional sewage system was not. Despite the needs pointed out in the innovative sanitary survey of the early sanitarian Lemuel Shattuck in 1845, there was no further progress until the 1870s. Beyond the aesthetic considerations, the putative link between disease arising from atmospheric emanations from putrid wastes had been instrumental in creating sewage systems, most eminently in London following the Great Stink of 1858.

Based on the strong repeated recommendations by the physicians employed by the Boston Health Department, Boston built a sewage system by 1885 that emptied wastes considered at the time to be far out in Boston Harbor; a complementary system under the auspices of the highly innovative Metropolitan Sewerage Commission (and later conjoined with the Water Board and then incorporated into the MDC) drained areas to the north and south of Boston. However, all of those introducing untreated wastes into the Harbor made it one of the most highly polluted areas in the country.

In the 1980s the Massachusetts Water Resources Authority (MWRA) was created, given independent budgetary resources and the political will to begin to reclaim Boston Harbor. In addition to the treatment of wastes, tunnels were built much farther out into Massachusetts Bay by which the treated wastes would be more widely diffused into ocean waters no longer dependent on the tides for removal.

In 1988, Massachusetts Governor Michael Dukakis, riding high based on the economic growth based on electronics encompassed in the "Massachusetts Miracle," was the Democratic candidate for the presidency. The Boston Harbor Project (BHP) had finally just gotten underway to clean up the harbor by the building of a treatment plant at Deer Island. Although there was much blame to spread around for the delays in implementation, the presidential campaign of George H.W. Bush chose to focus on the delay in Boston to demolish any claims Dukakis might have for his support of environmentalism. The BHP became a national campaign issue before receding with the defeat of Dukakis. It was finally deemed to be accomplished in 2000 when the gates that fed sewage to old Deer Island outflow were shut. Within minutes, for the first time in history, treated waste water began flowing through the tunnel that would bring it nine miles out into Massachusetts Bay.

The implementation of waste removal has brought back the marine environment and recreational areas to the harbor islands for the first time. The water supply system has been improved by an additional tunnel leading from the Quabbin Reservoir. Water wastage and utilization has been improved to the extent that there appears no need for additional water sources. Its unique success has been attributed by a long time board member to the fact that at least a majority of its eleven member board must be in agreement for any deciding vote. Because of the distribution of members with no more than three members from any one interest group, no one constituency can exert its will without enlisting the cooperation of others. It has been a model for the cooperation between the City of Boston and the almost fifty cities and towns that comprise its region that has long eluded the area and offers hope for the resolution of other problems.

Complementary to the cleansing of Boston Harbor, has been the creation, once again in the spirit of the original Emerald Necklace, of the "Rose Fitzgerald Kennedy Greenway" covering the "Big Dig." She was the mother of Senator Ted Kennedy who, along with Tip O'Neill had been instrumental in supporting the project. The Central Artery, named after Boston Mayor John Francis Fitzgerald, the father of Rose Kennedy, had been the prototype of the elevated highways that had ripped through the country's cities in the 1950s. The first elevated portion, built in the early 1950s, connecting to the Mystic River (Maurice Tobin) Bridge, isolated the North End from the market district and met with such opposition that its southern end in the later 1950s leading to Dewey Square and South Station was built below ground level. At the time, that mile of depressed highway was recognized as the most costly in history.

The subsequent cancellation of the Inner Belt Freeway (I-95) designed to channel traffic from the Massachusetts Turnpike caused the Central Artery to become unbearably clogged with traffic and made travel to East Boston and the Logan Airport highly problematic. The former elevated portion was taken down starting in the 1990s to be replaced, at an even far higher cost, by the "Big Dig" depressed below ground highway and a third tunnel that could funnel traffic from the south and west to East Boston and Logan Airport.

The feasibility and political skill necessary to create the "Big Dig" arose from the devotion of Frederick P. Salvucci to the project. Born in Boston in 1940, the several generations of his family had been in the construction business since coming from Italy. He himself had been apprenticed to his bricklayer father and recalls buying his first trowel in a store adjoining the Faneuil Hall Market. Growing up in the family home in Brighton with extended family in the North End, Fred was the first in his family to go to Boston Latin School on the way to a degree at M.I.T. as a civil engineer. However, he did not leave his roots behind and still lives, along with his extended family, in the house in which he grew up.

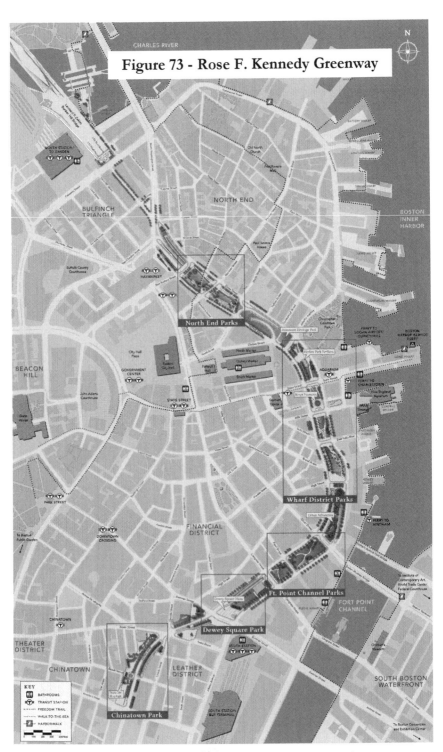

Figure 73 - Rose F. Kennedy Greenway

Even as an undergraduate at M.I.T, Salvucchi understood the significance of the design of highways that destroyed the fabric of neighborhoods. His own grandmother's house with her cherished tomato garden had been taken without adequate compensation in the wake of the building of the Massachusetts Turnpike. Even when working for the Boston Redevelopment Authority (BRA) in the early 1960s, he aided community activists opposing roads through their neighborhoods. Then as transportation advisor to Mayor Kevin White in the 1970s, he helped make the case for the expansion of public transit instead of highways. The design of the linear park that lies above the transit line of the abrogated Southwest Corridor of I-95 was another of his ideas. His experience working with anti-highway activists in East Boston gained their confidence while working at the "little City Hall" under Mayor Kevin White. That in turn became crucial in gaining their support when planning the third harbor tunnel to speed traffic to Logan Airport as part of the "Big Dig."

The decision by Governor Sargent to end highway construction of the Southwest Freeway led to the extension of the Red and Orange public transit lines. This was all preparatory to Salvucci's role as State Secretary of Transportation under Governor Dukakis starting in 1975. Having improved public transit, the next step was the removal of the elevated Central Artery in favor of the underground I-93 and the third tunnel that carried I-90 to its terminus at Logan Airport. He did so imbued with the moral as well as practical need to consider the needs of those affected derived from his family's values.

The completion of the "Big Dig" was a huge undertaking whose costs ballooned. Beset with problems in construction undoubtedly augmented by the traditional Boston corruption but also by Republican Party opposition, it was brought to completion only by massive infusion of federal money with bi-partisan support of the Republicans John Volpe and Representative Silvio Conte. Overriding the veto of President Ronald Reagan, it was helpful that the influential Ted Kennedy was senator from Massachusetts and Tip O'Neill, a son of Irish Cambridge, was strategically placed as Democratic Speaker of the House of Representatives. It is highly appropriate that the tunnel on I-93 carries the latter's name.

Figure 74 - Thomas Phillip ("Tip") O'Neill

Thomas Phillip ("Tip") O'Neill was born in 1912 in North Cambridge in an area known as "Old Dublin." His nickname came from a baseball player of his youth. His father, originally a bricklayer, rose in politics on the Cambridge City Council. The son, educated in Catholic schools, graduated from Boston College in 1936. He entered politics at age fifteen when campaigning for Al Smith in 1928. After a defeat while running for the Cambridge City Council on his first try, he never again was defeated while attending to his constituency following the dictum that "all politics are local."

O'Neill was elected to the Massachusetts House in 1936 as part of the Roosevelt landslide of that year. Elected as a "New Dealer," he remained one for the rest of his long career. Elected the first Democratic Speaker of the Massachusetts House in 1949, he went to the U.S. Congress in 1952 succeeding John F Kennedy in his safe Democratic district. O'Neill rose in the ranks under the tutelage of fellow Bostonian Majority Leader and later Speaker John McCormack until he himself was elected Speaker in 1977. An affable person, he remained cordial in his personal relations with the opposition during the Reagan presidency. While Speaker, he was the sole figure who nonetheless remained spokesperson for the liberal Democratic Party program. His personal characteristics made him an endearing figure even after his departure from his official position.

The several parks that have been created along the route of the "Big Dig" include one at the Wharf District commemorating the history of immigration to Boston; another at Chinatown commemorating the Chinese community, the country's fourth largest; and still another atop Dewey Square. With the Security State of the 21st century, the green spaces of Washington DC have been excessively bollardized while the green spaces of Boston's linear parks have opened up spaces for enjoyment for the first time in a hundred years.

The Chinese community first settled in the late 19th century in the South Cove area working in laundries. Mainly unmarried men, they had been driven from the Western mining camps where they had first been recruited to work on building the transcontinental railroad. Despite the Chinese Exclusion Act of 1882 that severely restricted family formation, families did begin to appear with the family-based restaurants serving Chinese cuisine as another means of livelihood. First limited to the one block Chinatown area on Beach Street near Stuart alongside the garment factories, restaurants proliferated in the decades after the First World War, increasingly upscale.

Family formation nevertheless occurred. Men who had been born in the United States who were thus American citizens were likely to go to China, marry there and conceive a family. They were then able to bring their children to the United States as American citizens. An example is the story of many was that of a man and wife who entered the United States in 1882 just prior to the implementation of the Chinese Exclusion Act. Working as a laundryman in Bridgewater Massachusetts in 1903, their son in turn opened a Chinese grocery store in Boston's Chinatown. He then went to China to marry and brought his son to Boston where he went to Boston Latin School graduating in 1927. The son went to university in China where he married before entering the insurance business in Boston. He in turn brought his young son out of China in 1938 who then also went to Boston Latin School, went to university in the United States and achieved an internationally recognized career as professor in city planning both in Hong Kong and Boston.

There was relaxation of the Chinese Exclusion Act in the light of the alliance with China after 1941 in the war against Japan. In their small number, the next English-speaking generation thus entered the professions along with other immigrant groups in the post-war era.

With the augmented immigration of political refugees from Taiwan and the relaxation of immigration restriction in the 1960s, Asian immigration has continued to enlarge the community. Despite the competing expansion of the Tufts Medical Center, a far more stable community has maintained itself as the cultural and social center in the old area as both residential and occupational integration has increased far beyond the boundaries of the old Chinatown. One conversant with Boston's political climate attributes the survival of Chinatown in their valuable site adjacent to downtown to the support the small Chinese community received from allies derived from the abolitionist strain among upper class Yankees.

6.7 Boston Politics and Thomas Menino

Thomas Menino was present at the opening of the new sewage plant and the new tunnel to East Boston, already Boston's first Italian-American mayor, and destined to be Boston's longest lasting, abdicating only in 2014. The mayor of Boston not only wielded the levers of power and of patronage; he was a symbol. The accession of the unabashedly Irish John Fitzgerald in 1908 marked the start of the long standing militantly Irish political hegemony. The election in his own right of Thomas Menino in 1993 marked an important departure of which he was well aware but not one that he broadcast widely. His route to longevity of power was to be mayor of a widely diverse city.

Figure 75 - Thomas Menino

Initially hesitant to enter political life, the first generation of Italian immigrants voted only for those from their own locale; the second generation voted for their fellow Italians. They managed to develop a unified voting bloc that combined the North End and East Boston along with the neighborhoods such as Hyde Park from which Menino arose. His grandfather Thomas left his native Italian village to settle in Hyde Park on the western edge of the city where there was a small Italian community; his extended family lived in the North End. His mother was American-born but fluent in Italian; his father worked as a foreman at the Westinghouse plant in Hyde Park.

Born in 1942, Menino grew up living in the apartment above his grandparents. He went to St Thomas Aquinas High School in Jamaica Plain and then for several semesters to Boston College before leaving to work for the Metropolitan Life Insurance Company. He did receive an Associate degree from Mt Ida Junior College; Harry Truman remains his idol as a fellow plain spoken non college trained politician. Recurrently elected to the City Council after the redistricting that occurred in 1981, as City Council President he was appointed mayor to the unexpired term of Raymond Flynn when the latter was appointed U.S. Ambassador to the Holy See in 1991. With a political base in the North End and East Boston as well as Hyde Park, Menino managed to be re-elected while continuing the development of the central city while also maintaining the quality of life in the neighborhoods.

Even more recently, a new wave of innovation has once again arisen around Kendall Square in Cambridge and Boston in the biotechnology sector where Harvard and MIT are prominent. In the 21st century, the central core city of Boston has once again had resurgence in people and ideas that few could have envisaged. In 2010, for the first time since the 1870s, the population rise in the core city has been greater than in the surrounding suburban belt. The words of the founder of the Lowell Institute at the time of its formation in 1836 still ring true that "the prosperity of New England, an otherwise barren and unproductive land, is based on the intelligence and information of its inhabitants," if perhaps no longer so clearly as he once had stated "on its moral qualities as heretofore."

THE END

BIBLIOGRAPHY

Bailyn, Bernard. *The New England Merchants in the Seventeenth Century.* Cambridge: Harvard University Press, 1955.

Baltzell,, E. Digby. *Puritan Boston and Quaker Philadelphia.* New York: Free Press, 1978.

Baxter, William T. *The House of Hancock.* Cambridge: Harvard University Press, 1945.

Bell, James B. *A War of Religion. Dissenters, Anglicans and the American Revolution.* Palgrave MacMillan: Basingstoke Hampshire UK, 2008.

Binford, Henry C. The First Suburbs. 1815-1860. Chicago: University of Chicago Press, 1985.

Carr, Howie. *The Brothers Bulger.* New York: Grand Central Publishing, 2006.

Cathcart, Dolita. "White Gloves, Black Rebels: the Decline of Elite Black National Political Leadership in Boston 1870-1929." Ph.D. Thesis Boston College Graduate School, 2004.

Cayton, Mary K. *Emerson's Emergence. Self and Society in the Transformation of New England, 1800-1845.* Chapel Hill: University of North Carolina Press, 1989.

Dalzell, Robert F. *Enterprising Elite.* Cambridge: Harvard University Press, 1987.

Daniels, John. *In Freedom's Birthplace. A Study of the Boston Negroes.* Boston: Houghton Mifflin Company, 1914.

Dauer, Manning J. *The Adams Federalists.* Baltimore: Johns Hopkins University Press, 1953.

Dolin, Eric J. *Political Waters.* Amherst: University of Massachusetts Press, 2004.

Donald, David H. *Charles Sumner.* New York: Da Capo Press, 1996.

Egnal, Marc. *A Mighty Empire. The Origins of the American Revolution.* Ithaca: Cornell University Press, 2010.

Ellis, Joseph. J. *Passionate Sage: The Character and Legacy of John Adams.* New York: W.W. Norton & Company, 1993.

Faust, C.H. "The Background of Unitarian Opposition to Transcendentalism." *Modern Philology* v35 (February 1938) p297-324.

Filler, Louis. *Crusade Against Slavery.* Algonac, Michigan: Reference Publishers, 1986.

Formisano, Ronald H. *Boston Against Busing.* Chapel Hill: University of North Carolina Press, 1991.

Gall, Allen. *Brandeis of Boston.* Cambridge: Harvard University Press, 1980.

Gans, Herbert J. *The Urban Villager.* New York: The Free Press, 1982.

Goodwin, Doris Kearns. *The Fitzgerald's and the Kennedys.* 1987

Gilchrist, David T. *The Growth of the Seaport Cities 1790-1825.* Charlottesville: University Press of Virginia, 1967.

Handlin, Oscar. *Boston's Immigrants.* Cambridge: Harvard University Press, 1959.

Higham, John. "Immigration Policy in Historical Perspective." *Law and Contemporary Problems.* v. 21 (Spring 1956) p 213-235.

Von Hoffman, Alexander. *Local Attachments. The Making of an American Urban Neighborhood, 1850-1920.* Baltimore: The Johns Hopkins University Press, 1994.

Howe, Daniel W. "The Decline of Calvinism: An Approach to its Study." *Comparative Studies in Society and History.* v14 (June 1972) p 306-327.

James, Henry. *Charles W Eliot.* Boston: Houghton Mifflin Company, 1930.

Jones, Keith. "American Nativism and Immigration: The Rise and Fall of the Immigration Restriction League 1894-1921." Master's Thesis Georgetown University, 2013.

Kantrowitz, Stephen. *More than Freedom.* New York: Penguin Books, 2012.

Karabel, Jerome. *The Chosen.* Boston: Houghton Mifflin, 2005.

Kermes, Stephanie. *Creating an American Identity. New England 1789-1825.* New York: Palgrave MacMillan, 2009.

Kirker, Harold and James Kirker. *Bullfinch's Boston 1787-1817.* New York: Oxford University Press, 1964.

Lodge, Henry Cabot. *Early Memories.* New York: Charles Scriber Sons, 1913.

Martin, Justin. *Genius of Place. The Life of Frederick Law Olmsted.* Cambridge: DaCapo Press, 2011.

Mills, Garrias. "Hawthorne and Puritanism." *New England Quarterly.* v 21 (March 1941) p 78-102.

Morgan, Edmund S. *The Puritan Dilemma. The Story of John Winthrop.* New York: Longman, 1999.

Nelson, William E Jr. *Black Atlantic Politics. Dilemmas of Political Empowerment in Boston and Liverpool.* Albany: State University of New York Press, 2000.

O'Connell, James C. *The Hub's Metropolis.* Cambridge: MIT Press, 2013.

O'Connor, Thomas H. *Building a New Boston. Politics and Urban Renewal 1950-1970.* Boston: Northeastern University Press, 1993.

_____*The Boston Irish. A Political History.* Boston: Northeastern University Press, 1995.

_____ *Civil War Boston*. Boston: Northeastern University Press, 1997

_____*Boston Catholics. A History of the Church and its People*. Boston: Northeastern University Press, 1998.

_____*The Hub. Boston Past and Present*. Boston: Northeastern University Press, 2001.

_____ *The Athens of America Boston 1825-1845*. Amherst: University of Massachusetts press, 2006.

Puleo, Stephen. *The Boston Italians*. Boston: The Beacon Press, 2007.

Puls, Mark. *Samuel Adams. Father of the American Revolution*. New York: Palgrave MacMillan, 2006.

Rawson, Michael. *Eden on the Charles*. Cambridge: Harvard University Press, 2010.

Renella, Mark. *The Boston Cosmopolitans*. New York: Palgrave MacMillan, 2008.

Sarna, Jonathan D. and Ellen Smith. *The Jews of Boston*. Boston: Combined Jewish Philanthropies, 1995.

Schneider, Mark R. *Boston Confronts Jim Crow*. Boston: Northeastern University Press. 1997

Schwartz, Harold. "Fugitive Slave Days in Boston." *New England Quarterly*. v27 (June 1964) p191-212.

Schwartz, Joseph. "Three Aspects of Hawthorne's Puritanism." *New England Quarterly*. v36 (June 1963) p 192-205.

Shand-Tucci, Douglass. *Built in Boston 1800-2000*. Amherst: University of Massachusetts Press, 1978

_____*The Art of Scandal: The Life and Times of Isabella Stewart Gardner*. New York: HarperCollins Publishers, 1997.

Smith, Carl. City Water, City Life. Chicago; University of Chicago Press. 2013.

Solomon, Barbara Miller. "The Intellectual Background of the Immigration Restriction Movement in New England." *New England Quarterly* v. 23 (March 1952) p47-59.

Strangis, Joel. *Lewis Hayden and the Struggle Against Slavery*. New Haven: Linnet Books, 1999.

Triber, Jayne. *A True Republican. The Life of Paul Revere*. Amherst: University of Massachusetts Press, 1998.

Trout, Charles H. *Boston: The Great Depression the New Deal*. New York: Oxford University Press, 1977.

Vale, Lawrence. *From the Puritans to the Projects*. Cambridge: Harvard University Press, 2000.

Ward, David. "The Industrial Revolution and the Emergence of Boston's Central Business District." *Economic Geography*. v.42 (April 1966) p 152-171.

Warner, Samuel Bass Jr. *Streetcar Suburbs*. Cambridge: Harvard University Press, 1978.

Warner, William B. "The Invention of a Revolutionary Machine. The Boston Committee of Correspondence." *The Eighteenth Century* v. 50 (Summer/Fall 2009) p 145-164.

Whitehill, Walter Muir. *Boston in the Age of John Fitzgerald Kennedy*. Norman, OK: University of Oklahoma Press, 1966.

_____*Boston. A Topographical History*. Cambridge: Harvard University Press, 1968

Wills, Garry. *Henry Adams and the Making of America*. Boston: Houghton Mifflin, 2005.

Wright, Conrad Edrick. *Massachusetts and the New Nation*. Boston: Northeastern University Press, 1992.

LIST OF FIGURES

INDEX

ABOUT THE AUTHOR

Mark N. Ozer As a professor of Neurology at Georgetown University Medical School, the author had a productive career in medicine. After retirement, he returned to his first love of history nurtured as an honors graduate of Harvard College. A resident of Washington since 1964, he has translated his interest in that city into a series of books: *Washington, DC: Politics and Place* (2009), *Washington DC: Streets and Statues* (2012) and *Washington Metroland* (2013), *Washington DC and the War of 1812: Like a Phoenix from the Ashes* (2014) and, most recently *Washington DC and the Civil War: The National Capital* (2015).

At the Osher Lifelong Learning Institute at The American University, he taught concerning the interaction of history and geography of many of the great cities of the world. Among American cities, in addition to his explorations of Washington as both a City and Capital, there has been *Baltimore: Persons and Places* (2013); and even more recently (in 2015), *Boston: Persons and Places*.

See www.markozerbooks.com for a full list including E-books

Made in the USA
Charleston, SC
05 March 2015